The Master of Contradictions

The Master of Contradictions

Thomas Mann and the
Making of *The Magic Mountain*

MORTEN HØI JENSEN

Yale
UNIVERSITY PRESS
NEW HAVEN & LONDON

Published with assistance from the Louis Stern Memorial Fund.

Copyright © 2025 by Yale University.
All rights reserved.
This book may not be reproduced, in whole or in part, including illustrations, in any form (beyond that copying permitted by Sections 107 and 108 of the U.S. Copyright Law and except by reviewers for the public press), without written permission from the publishers.

Yale University Press books may be purchased in quantity for educational, business, or promotional use. For information, please e-mail sales.press@yale.edu (U.S. office) or sales@yaleup.co.uk (U.K. office).

Set in Spectral type by IDS Infotech Ltd.
Printed in the United States of America.

Library of Congress Control Number: 2025932501
ISBN 978-0-300-23374-2 (hardcover)

A catalogue record for this book is available from the British Library.

Authorized Representative in the EU: Easy Access System Europe, Mustamäe tee 50, 10621 Tallinn, Estonia, gpsr.requests@easproject.com

10 9 8 7 6 5 4 3 2 1

For my brother Jacob, who pulled me out of the snow

Man is the master of contradictions, they occur through him, and so he is more noble than they. More noble than death, too noble for it—that is the freedom of his mind. More noble than life, too noble for it—that is the devotion of his heart. . . . Love stands opposed to death—it alone, and not reason, is stronger than death.

—Thomas Mann, *The Magic Mountain*

CONTENTS

PROLOGUE 1

CHAPTER 1. Arrival, 1912   10

CHAPTER 2. Sympathy with Death, 1914   32

CHAPTER 3. The Thunderbolt, 1914–1915   64

CHAPTER 4. A Good Soldier, 1916–1918   87

CHAPTER 5. Doubts and Considerations, 1919–1921   115

CHAPTER 6. Changes, 1922–1923   144

CHAPTER 7. Fullness of Harmony, 1923–1924   170

EPILOGUE   193

NOTES   195

ACKNOWLEDGMENTS   223

CREDITS   227

INDEX   229

PROLOGUE

Susan Sontag was not yet seventeen, but she'd already read *The Magic Mountain* twice, and now she was determined to go look up the famous author who, she knew, lived on San Remo Drive in Pacific Palisades, a neighborhood in Los Angeles by the foot of the Santa Monica Mountains. Of course she and her friend had called ahead and agreed on a date and time, but when they pulled up on the quiet, palm-screened street, they sat in the old Chevy for almost half an hour, "immobilized with awe," rehearsing what they were going to say.[1]

A few dozen feet beyond them, in an elongated two-story stucco-and-glass house couched behind a cluster of trees and bushes, was the god of their anxious pilgrimage, the Nobel Prize–winning German novelist Thomas Mann, author of *Buddenbrooks*, *Death in Venice*, *The Magic Mountain*, and *Doctor Faustus*. Now in his seventy-fifth year, Mann stood looking out from his large study on an avocado grove nestled beneath an implacable blue sky. He could smell the ocean—not the briny Baltic air of his native Lübeck, but the warm breeze blowing in from the Pacific, with its notes of orange and eucalyptus. Elizabeth Hardwick called it a "tragic jest of history" that Mann ended up in California, but it felt like paradise to him, even if the beach was littered with condoms, as he remarked one day to Mrs. Aldous Huxley.[2]

Walking up the winding driveway, the two teenagers approached the house to the sound of wind chimes and a dog's watchful bark. They were greeted at the door by a slight old woman with gray hair—Katia Mann, the lady of the house—and soon saw standing behind her the great writer himself, holding the barking family poodle, Niko, by his collar.

He looked "exactly like his photographs," Sontag later remarked: composed and distinguished, as if staring out from the frontispiece of one of his books. Dressed in a beige summer suit with a maroon tie and white shoes, Thomas Mann led his young guests into his large, book-lined study, where Katia served a delicate tray of cookies, cakes, and tea. As the ageing Mann lit up a cigarette, Sontag thought to herself that his mustache looked like "a little hat over his mouth."[3]

He spoke slowly, carefully, and inquired about their studies. But Sontag, beginning to feel that it was absurd of them to have come, was almost speechless. She was embarrassed, afraid of sounding foolish, and suddenly she realized she'd had too many cookies. She reached for another one without really meaning to. Soon, the conversation turned to contemporary fiction. Mann asked them if they'd read Hemingway, which they hadn't, before going on to speak of Proust and Joyce, Goethe and Nietzsche, the fate of Germany and the rise of Nazism.

But Sontag wanted to speak only of *The Magic Mountain*. When she first read it in H. T. Lowe-Porter's 1927 translation, almost two years earlier, she wrote in her journal that it was "the finest novel I have ever read."[4] For an entire month she felt she had lived inside the book. Reading it, she had to keep telling herself to slow down, to savor it, but in the end her excitement always got the better of her. When she finished it she simply started over again, reading one chapter aloud each night before going to sleep. And now here she was, sitting across from that novel's creator, a frail old man sipping tea and smoking cigarettes—a man who'd grown up in the previous century under imperial Prussian rule, who had lived through the First World War and the Weimar Republic only to be barred from his beloved Germany, and who was now improbably planted beneath a Southern Californian sun. She wanted to tell this man how much one of his novels meant to her, but she was afraid of sounding foolish.

"It sometimes happens," Thomas Mann suddenly ventured, as if sensing his young guest's pent-up admiration, "that I am asked which I consider to be my greatest novel."

Susan Sontag held her breath.

"I would say," he continued, "and have so replied in recent interviews—*The Magic Mountain*."[5]

* * *

There is something special about *The Magic Mountain*. It has an aura. In the jagged terrain of Thomas Mann's middle career, it is a lone summit, flanked on either side by the lesser elevations of occasional prose and political essays. It was, in fact, the only major work of fiction Mann published in middle age: he was thirty-seven when he started it, nearly fifty when he finished it, and almost sixty by the time he published his next big novel, the first of the four *Joseph* books. And though many readers may prefer the early, best-selling *Buddenbrooks* or the late masterpiece *Doctor Faustus*, no other book seems to embody the greatness and peculiarity of Thomas Mann so powerfully as *The Magic Mountain*.

The novel opens in the late summer of 1907 with the arrival of Hans Castorp—"life's problem child," as we will come to know him—at the International Sanatorium Berghof in Davos, Switzerland. An engineer about to embark on a career in shipbuilding, Hans Castorp intends to spend three weeks in the Swiss Alps visiting his soldier cousin Joachim Ziemssen, who is a tubercular patient at the Berghof and who early on cautions his visitor that "a man changes a lot of his ideas up here."[6]

Hans Castorp doesn't know it yet, but those three weeks will gradually, over the course of hundreds of pages, swell to seven years, and they will do more than simply change his ideas: they will confront him with sex and illness; with progress and reaction; with love and death. Many seasons that do not seem like seasons at all will pass, patients at the sanatorium will arrive vertically and depart horizontally, and down in the flatlands, unbeknownst to Hans Castorp, the world will move inexorably toward a terrible catastrophe. By the end of the novel, it is not only Hans Castorp but the world itself that has changed.

When I first read *The Magic Mountain,* in my early twenties, I found Hans Castorp's development throughout the novel to be analogous to the reader's own experience. Does she not feel that she, too, has changed over the course of those hundreds of pages, those seven long years? Upon turning the novel's final page, abandoning Hans Castorp to his uncertain but hardly promising fate, does she not feel within her that sense of exhilaration and exhaustion that always follows the conclusion of a long journey? Does not the world appear to be somehow *different*?

On its publication in 1924, in a two-volume edition of almost twelve hundred pages, *The Magic Mountain* firmly established Thomas Mann as the preeminent German novelist of his time. Between 1925 and 1930, it was one of the top five best-selling novels published in the Weimar Republic. The English translation by Helen Tracy Lowe-Porter, published in 1927, catapulted Mann to international literary fame. It was no wonder that, before the end of the decade, Mann was awarded the Nobel Prize in Literature, even if the Swedish Academy, in its citation, singled out *Buddenbrooks* as the principal justification for the award.

But the genesis of the novel was not a steady ascent to the heights of literary greatness. The story of the writing of *The Magic Mountain* is a tale of two Thomas Manns. Though he wrote the novel's first words in 1913, Mann set the manuscript aside two years later and did not return to it until the spring of 1919. He finally finished it in 1924. During the twelve years separating Thomas Mann's conception of *The Magic Mountain* and his completion of it, the world was radically altered in a way no one could have imagined possible. The novel's foreword announces that "the extraordinary pastness of our story results from its having taken place *before* a certain turning point, on the far side of a rift that has cut deeply through our lives and consciousness."[7]

That turning point was the First World War, an unprecedented calamity that claimed the lives of roughly twenty million soldiers and civilians, brought about the end of entire nations and long-standing empires, and saw the introduction of mechanized slaughter on a truly industrial scale—all of it in just a little over four years. Before the outbreak of the war, Thomas Mann had been a highly successful novelist whose fiction, especially *Buddenbrooks* and *Death in Venice*, was closely associated with a fin-de-siècle atmosphere of decadence and decline. During the war, however, he turned increasingly to writing in defense of German culture, particularly as political differences with his older brother Heinrich Mann, also a well-known novelist, intensified.

Heinrich was a pacifist and a progressive democrat, and in 1915 he wrote a famous essay about Émile Zola championing liberalism, democracy, and political engagement over the nationalistic militarism and "gloomy pessimism" of German culture.[8] Thomas Mann, perceiving the essay as a personal affront, responded three years later with *Reflections of a Nonpolitical Man*, a long and meandering essay in which he declared democracy "poisonous" to the German soul. Bristling with a million barbs aimed at Heinrich, *Reflections* was a conservative, at times even reactionary, defense of the deep well of German romanticism and pessimism against the level plane of sober reason and pedestrian democracy. The two brothers did not speak for several years.

And yet, by the early 1920s Mann emerged as one of the embattled Weimar Republic's most outspoken defenders. In 1922, he gave a famous address to a gathering of German students in which his aim, as he put it, was to win them over "to the side of the republic; to the side of what is called democracy, and what I call humanity."[9]

In other words, the forty-nine-year-old Thomas Mann who wrote *Finis Operis* underneath the last sentence of *The Magic Mountain* was not quite the same Thomas Mann who had first conceived of the novel more than a decade earlier. How did this change come about? Why did Thomas Mann, who had banged on the drum of German patriotism during the war, emerge less than a decade later as a literary spokesman for democracy and humanism? And did the writing of *The Magic Mountain* have something to do with it? Mann himself suggested as much. Of his newfound "infatuation" with humanism, he wrote in a letter to Arthur Schnitzler in 1922 that "it may be connected with the novel on which I have been working for all too long, a kind of *Bildungsroman* and Wilhelm Meisteriade in which a young man (before the war) is led by the experience of sickness and death to the idea of man and the state."[10] Hans Rudolf Vaget, the foremost expert on the composition of *The Magic Mountain*, has argued that "it is the painfulness of Mann's political learning process—fraught with ambivalence, as it had to have been—that lends *The Magic Mountain* its incomparable intellectual vibrancy."[11]

This vibrancy continues to enchant readers the world over. In the century since it was first published, *The Magic Mountain* has attained canonical status as one of the towering achievements of literary modernism, a novel as intellectually and aesthetically ambitious as James Joyce's *Ulysses,* Robert Musil's *The Man without Qualities,* and Marcel Proust's *In Search of Lost Time.* It has been translated into more than thirty languages and was adapted for the screen in 1982 by the German film director Hans W. Geißendörfer. Recent novels like Christian Kracht's *Imperium* (2012) and Olga Tokarczuk's *Empusium* (2022) bear the unmistakable signs of its influence, while the contemporary German novelist Jenny Erpenbeck, who as a teenager begged her father to let her borrow *The Magic Mountain,* has spoken eloquently of eventually reading it shortly before the country of her birth, the German Democratic Republic, ceased to exist. What struck her most, she said, was Mann's "uncompromisingly accurate representations of illness and in-between states and all the things that occupy us when we are in those states."[12]

* * *

This book doesn't presume to offer anything like a comprehensive analysis of *The Magic Mountain*. There's plenty I've left out, in part because, contrary to the novel's narrator, I do not necessarily find only thoroughness entertaining, but also for the more practical reason that I am not a scholar. I have tried to avoid what George Orwell called "the old mistake of wanting to read too much between the lines." In a review of Lewis Mumford's book on Melville, Orwell cautioned that "the criticism which sets out to interpret . . . is a dangerous method of approaching a work of art. Done with absolute thoroughness, it would cause the art itself to vanish."[13]

Perhaps too much has been made of the encyclopedic and intellectual aspects of *The Magic Mountain* and of Thomas Mann's writing in general—certainly at the expense of the playfulness of his fiction. In a letter to Hermann J. Weigand, author of the first English-language study written about *The Magic Mountain*, Mann played down his alleged intellectualism: "Perhaps I am too good at display, the 'show window,' at the manipulation of esoteric material. Perhaps I have always acquired knowledge solely for a purpose, for the moment, and in order to play with it."[14]

What this book tries to do instead is tell a story: the story of how Mann's novel came to be, the historical events that slowed and interrupted its progress, and the ensuing political development of its author in the years it was finally completed. Because so many of the tensions and conflicts of that time are resurgent today, I think the story of how Mann came to write *The Magic Mountain* when he did raises important questions that speak directly to our own time. Are politics and aesthetics separate spheres of human activity? Can the artist's irresponsible sympathy with death be reconciled with a responsible politics? How do we find meaning in a world that responds with hollow silence to questions about the very purpose of our existence? One hundred years after its publication, we are still, as the Polish poet Adam Zagajewski once put it, wrestling with the heroes of *The Magic Mountain*.[15]

This book is also the product of a long preoccupation with Mann's novel. I was twenty-three years old when I first read *The Magic Mountain* and thirty when I began writing this book—the same ages as Hans Castorp when he arrives at and departs from the International Sanatorium Berghof. Thomas Mann, who loved number symbolism, may have relished the irony that it took me seven years to finish, and that I am now the same age he was when he first conceived of the novel.

In order to figure out why Mann's novel is so important to me, I decided to begin at the source. In the winter of 2018, following in Hans Castorp's footsteps, I traveled by train from Hamburg to Davos, where I had arranged to stay for seven weeks (seven years seeming a bit of a stretch) at the Berghotel Schatzalp, the only real sanatorium mentioned by name in *The Magic Mountain*, which is a popular hotel and ski resort today. I wanted to breathe the same strange air as Mann's young hero, lose my way in the same snow, and walk along the same mountain paths—an easy enough thing to do in Davos, because there is a Thomas Mann Weg that stretches from the Waldhotel (the former sanatorium where Thomas Mann's wife, Katia, was a patient) through the forest up past the Schatzalp to Thomas Mann Platz. Along the way, the path is marked with plaques displaying well-known passages from *The Magic Mountain*.

Anyone who has read the novel will remember the lavishly detailed descriptions of life at the luxurious Berghof sanatorium, where patients take the mountain airs, eat huge meals, and idly pass the time in the horizontal position. As I was to discover for myself, much of the very real sanatorium-world of Davos is still intact, especially at Schatzalp. The room I stayed in—not, alas, room 34—had almost none of the amenities common to most hotels today; instead, it consisted of two old twin beds pushed together and a single armchair wedged into a corner. But when I opened the French doors I discovered a large balcony with a breathtaking view of the valley and the mountains, as well as an old, wooden lounge chair where I could wrap myself in a wool blanket, take my self-prescribed rest cure, and learn to live horizontally.

When I wasn't out on my balcony "playing king" (Hans Castorp's term for it), I could go down to the front desk and buy copies of *The Magic Mountain* in both German and English, or up to the small room beyond the bar and sit through one of the fortnightly screenings of Geißendörfer's film adaptation. Best of all, I could go to the cocktail bar adjoining the Jugendstil lobby, located in what used to be the X-ray examination room, and buy a Maria Mancini, Hans Castorp's beloved brand of cigar, which a waiter would then cut and light for me on the spot.

Most days I spent hiking up and down the magic mountain through waist-deep snow, or else sitting by the fireplace in the lobby with Mann's novels and diaries (and, occasionally, a Maria Mancini). Once or twice a week, groups of German-speaking tourists would drift through the lobby accompanied by a small, elderly guide—Klaus Bergamin, a local historian and *Magic Mountain* devotee—who spoke to them of the history of the hotel, the morbid details of tuberculosis treatment, and the fictional adventures of Hans Castorp and Joachim Ziemssen. One day, I overhead a waiter asking an American woman, whom I had noticed was also reading *The Magic Mountain*, what exactly the novel was about. Out of the corner of my eye, I saw her put the book down, tilt her head thoughtfully, and respond: "*Everything.*"

CHAPTER 1

Arrival, 1912

A journey is always an adventure, he thought, not knowing how far this particular journey would eventually take him—much further, at any rate, than the stamped destination on his ticket.

Munich's central station was abuzz with the commotion of travel: bent porters pulling handcarts heaped with trunks; whistling vendors hawking newspapers and refreshments; the deep din of the stationary locomotive that looked like an industrial sphinx. And everywhere a great hurrying crowd of hats, capes, canes, and kerchiefs—people coming, going, greeting, parting. It seemed like all of Europe was in a state of transit. But where were they coming from? And where were they going?

From his compartment, Thomas Mann looked out on all this bustle with faint trepidation. More than just a veteran of the rails, he was its survivor, too: six years previously he'd been on the overnight express to Dresden when it collided with a freight train. But apart from getting thrown against the walls of his compartment, Mann had suffered no injuries. Instead, he'd done what any other writer (those vampiric opportunists of life!) would have done: he turned the experience into a work of fiction, a short story straightforwardly titled "Railway Accident," in which the narrator, a writer, fears the loss of his manuscript in the wreckage.

The daylong trip on which Mann now embarked would fortunately pass without any such incident. Chuffing toward Switzerland, he crossed the emerald-tinted Lake Constance by steamer and, looking east, saw the Allgäu Alps looming mistily in the distance. In Zurich he boarded a train to Landquart, a small municipality in the canton of Graubünden on the eastern bank of the Rhine, and there began his journey's final ascent up to Davos in the Swiss Alps—an hour of near-constant climbing and weaving through forests, tunnels, ravines, and narrow mountain crevices. An engineering triumph when it first opened in 1890, this narrow-gauge railway line made Mann both dizzy and disoriented; with each new tunnel or horseshoe turn he lost his bearings, until finally he gave up figuring out which direction he was traveling in.

At last, after almost a full day of travel, the train rolled into the valley from the north, rounding Lake Davos before reaching the narrow strip of the village itself. The steeple of St. Johann Church looked to Mann like a defiant little tip of longing dwarfed by the snow-capped peaks encircling it. He wondered what it was like here during the winter months when—so he'd heard—the snow piled as high as six feet, and the corpses of deceased patients from the Schatzalp sanatorium had to be transported down the mountain by bobsled. Bobsled! He didn't know whether to shudder or laugh.

Disembarking the train, Mann removed his hat and took a deep breath of the celebrated alpine air, so unlike the salt and brine of his native Lübeck. He then made arrangements to have his luggage sent ahead to his lodgings while he proceeded on foot. He began singing quietly to himself:

> I came a stranger
> I depart a stranger.
> May was good to me
> With many a garland of flowers.[1]

Thomas Mann didn't know it, but the village where he'd just arrived owed part of its reputation to a London-based Dutch

ARRIVAL

banker, Willem Jan Holsboer. In 1867, Holsboer took his ailing young wife, Margaret Holsboer-Jones, to see Dr. Hermann Weber, an esteemed physician and one of the earliest advocates of open-air treatment for tuberculosis. When Weber suggested that Holsboer take his wife to Davos, he unwittingly set the alpine dwelling on its way to medical prominence.

The Holsboers arrived in Davos in May 1867 after a long and tiresome journey, the last leg of which had been an arduous seven-hour climb in horse carriage up from Landquart, an elevation of over three thousand feet. On Weber's advice, they sought out Alexander Spengler, a former jurist turned medical doctor. Originally from Mannheim, Spengler had been forced into exile for his involvement in the revolutionary upheavals of 1848. He fled to Switzerland where he abandoned law and decided to study medicine instead. After completing his studies in 1853, he accepted a position as district doctor in Davos, where he was struck by the apparent scarcity of tuberculosis cases. Even infected visitors seemed to recover once they had been sufficiently exposed to the alpine valley's climate, which Spengler speculated helped slow the putrefaction of the lungs. In 1862, convinced of the curative powers of the region, he published his findings in a supplement to the medical journal *Deutsche Klinik*.

The idea that tuberculosis patients would benefit from prolonged exposure to cold air in the dead of winter in a remote mountain valley, while at odds with prevailing medical wisdom, was not entirely new. A few years before Spengler, the German physician Hermann Brehmer had established the first sanatorium for pulmonary tuberculosis in Göbersdorf (now the Polish village of Sokołowsko) in Lower Silesia. Brehmer suspected—correctly, as it turned out—that the barometric pressure at higher altitudes is lower, making the air "thinner" and harder to breathe because there is less oxygen. Believing tuberculosis to be partly attributable to poor circulation, Brehmer proposed that life outdoors at a high altitude, combined with plenty of rest and a robust diet, would be the most favorable regimen for patients to follow.[2]

Despite Spengler's efforts, Margaret Holsboer-Jones did not survive. She died in October 1867 at the age of just twenty. This did not dissuade her grieving husband from becoming a convert to Spengler's cause, however. Not only did Holsboer remain in Davos, he went on to cofound the first *Curhaus*, or cure house, and even provided the capital for the construction of the narrow-gauge railway to Landquart, completely transforming Davos in the process. By the turn of the century the remote alpine valley's smattering of wooden chalets had become a cluster of art nouveau hotels and oblong modernist sanatoriums, many of them designed by esteemed architects like Max Ernst Haefeli and Otto Wilhelm Pfleghard. British, Russian, and French communities soon sprang up, dragging their attendant customs and products with them—Parisian boutiques, British newspapers, Russian vodka. Aristocrats and minor royalty soon followed, as did a torrent of winter sports enthusiasts and the odd literary celebrity, including Mark Twain, Arthur Conan Doyle, Robert Louis Stevenson, and John Addington Symonds.

The first sanatorium to enforce the strict daily routine so memorably described in *The Magic Mountain* was opened in 1899 by Dr. Karl Turban. (Many years later, Dr. Turban prophesied that Mann's "sensational novel, a dark distillation of a dark age, will soon be forgotten.")[3] Patients spent most of the day taking the *Liegekur*, or rest cure, wrapped in a thick camel-wool blanket on a balcony exposed to the cold air, and were required to measure their temperature at fixed intervals.

Because tuberculosis is a disease of time, the length of treatment was, from the sanitorium's perspective, profitably open-ended. "In slight cases 3 to 5 months will suffice," Dr. Turban wrote, adding: "Not infrequently the cure will extend to a year or more. Other things being equal, the chances of a lasting cure and of security against relapse are greater in proportion to the length of the treatment."[4] In other words: the longer you remained a paying customer, the likelier you were to be healthy.

Given the nature of tuberculosis, the patients in Davos were usually quite young. Having nothing to do all day but sit around and take their temperatures, they often took to engaging in activities most sanatoriums frowned upon or banned outright. One Englishman reported with horror that "some patients, especially hopeless cases, were tempted to plunge into a round of parties, drinking, gambling and worse!"—behavior contrary to the ethos of manly suffering doctors wanted to instill in their patients.[5] "Davos demands qualities the very opposite of the resigned sentimentalism in which too frequently the phthisical youth or maiden was encouraged," Alexander Spengler wrote. "Here is no place for weak and despairing resignation; here you are not pusillanimously helped to die, but are required to enter into a hard struggle for life."[6] In *The Magic Mountain*, Hofrat Behrens, the Berghof sanitorium director, similarly instructs patients not to "make a fuss" on their deathbed.[7]

But tuberculosis is a ruthless disease. An infection caused by the bacteria *Mycobacterium tuberculosis*, it is commonly transmitted by airborne droplets that are emitted when a person coughs or sneezes. Once inhaled, the bacteria lodges in the lung tissue where it can spend years multiplying and spreading to other parts of the body without making itself known to the infected host.[8] Equipped with an unusually thick and complex cell wall, *Mycobacterium tuberculosis* is a dogged, resilient killer.

Rather bizarrely, and in stark contrast to its gruesome nature, tuberculosis led a double life in the eighteenth and nineteenth centuries as an "edifying, refined disease," as Susan Sontag put it in *Illness as Metaphor*.[9] In cultural terms it was a "disease of born victims, of sensitive, passive people who are not quite life-loving enough to survive."[10] The many young writers' lives claimed by tuberculosis only added to its perversely romantic aura: victims included John Keats, Jens Peter Jacobsen, Anton Chekhov, Friedrich Schiller, the Brontë sisters, and Elizabeth Barrett Browning. The English poet Lord Byron once said he'd like to die of consumption, explaining: "All the ladies would say, 'Look at that poor Byron, how interesting he looks in dying!' "[11]

But the most interesting thing about tuberculosis was modern medicine's powerlessness to treat it. As industrialization helped enable its spread, it became endemic to Europe's urban populations, making a mockery of the material and technological advances of bourgeois civilization. Without a cure, sanatoriums remained the bedrock of tuberculosis treatment well into the twentieth century. With their half-hotel atmosphere and general proximity to mountains or thermal spas, some were even built to accommodate patients suffering from another quintessentially bourgeois disorder: neurasthenia.

Despite a pervasive cult of strength, manliness, and military virtue, fin-de-siècle Europe was beset by a post-Darwinian anxiety about health, hygiene, virility, and nerves. The increased speed of daily life in industrialized society created an epidemic of neurosis, or neurasthenia, sending waves of Europeans into the continent's many sanatoriums and health spas to convalesce or go to seed. Neither Thomas nor Heinrich Mann were strangers to these institutions. "I am a neurasthenic. That is my profession and my fate," Heinrich once wrote.[12] In his letters Mann frequently complained about the state of his nerves or of being overwrought or exhausted, and as a young man he spent time in Mitterbad in South Tyrol, the Weisser Hirsch sanatorium in Dresden, and the Bircher-Brenner private clinic in Zurich, among others. By the time he arrived in Davos he was already a veteran of Europe's extensive network of health spas and sanatoriums. In fact, he'd already written about them once before. In the early novella *Tristan* (1903), set in the fictional sanatorium Einfried, Mann stumbled on themes he would later develop in *The Magic Mountain*:

ARRIVAL

Occasionally a death occurs among the "serious cases," those who are confined to their beds and do not appear at meals or in the drawing-room; and no one is ever aware of it, not even the patient next door. In the silence of night the waxen guest is removed, and Einfried pursues the even tenor of its way: the massage, the electrical treatment, the injections, douches, medicinal baths, gymnastics, exudations and inhalations all continue, in premises equipped with every wonder of modern science.[13]

On Saturday, May 18, 1912, three days after his arrival, Thomas Mann saw his name printed in the *Davoser Blätter*'s (a newspaper for guests of the hotels and sanatoriums in Davos) *Fremdenliste,* or visitors' list, along with the names of hundreds of other recent arrivals to the Swiss alpine village. He was impressed by how cosmopolitan the clientele was: people had come here from Athens, Bilbao, Buenos Aires, Copenhagen, Constantinople, Leeds, Moscow, New York, Rio de Janeiro, and Valparaiso. In some cases, occupations were listed alongside the names: there were lawyers, directors, engineers, superintendents, building inspectors, here and there a baroness or an officer. Mann's own listing divulged no such information. It simply read: "Herr Thomas Mann, München."

He was here to visit his wife, Katia. She had been a patient at the Waldsanatorium since March; there was some trouble with her lungs, as she put it, severe enough for her doctor in Munich to suspect tuberculosis and recommend an extended period of convalescence in the Swiss Alps.[14] This diagnosis would later turn out to be wrong: in the 1960s, Christian Virchow, then a respiratory disease physician at the Hochgebirgsklinik in Davos (and an admirer of Mann) corresponded with and eventually visited Katia, who reportedly told him, "Your visiting me is appropriate, because without me *The Magic Mountain* would not have been written." Virchow obtained copies of Katia's chest radiographs and found no indication that she'd ever been infected with pulmonary tuberculosis. He suggested that she may simply have suffered from sinus problems that occasionally led to a build-up of mucus in her airways.[15]

Whatever the case, Katia was hardly in good health. She'd given birth to four children in five years, suffered two miscarriages, and had spent the month of September at a sanatorium in Sils-Maria. By February, she was making "slow, barely noticeable" progress, but not enough to be allowed to remain at home.[16] Following a brief stint at the Ebenhausen health resort near Munich, it was decided that she should go to Davos. On March 12, 1912, she left Munich with her mother, Hedwig Pringsheim.

Hedwig quickly developed a distaste for Davos. The atmosphere was too macabre, she thought. Everyone seemed to make light of their symptoms. In a letter to friend, she described a "busty" young patient from Cologne with a pneumothorax who made such ghastly whistling noises that a passing doctor suggested she join the orchestra. "At times one forgets altogether that one is in the house and valley of the doomed," Hedwig wrote.[17]

Thomas Mann, for his part, welcomed the prospect of some time away from home. For almost a year now he'd been at work on a novella that would prove to be both a departure from his most recent work and the culmination of everything he'd written so far. Inspired by a trip to Venice a year earlier, it would be "serious and pure in tone," Mann claimed, even though it portrayed an aging writer's erotic infatuation with a young boy.[18] As usual, the writing proved more difficult than expected and was slowed by concern for Katia's health, not to mention the demands of the couple's four young children. (It did help, however, that the family had a governess and a housemaid.) When Katia left for Davos, Thomas wrote to Heinrich that he was still struggling to come up with an ending. "Perhaps I'll have to wait for the change of air in Davos in mid-May to help me along. My vitality is extremely low right now."[19]

Visitors were not permitted to stay at the Waldsanatorium, so Mann lodged instead at the Villa am Stein, a small chalet that counted among its previous tenants Arthur Conan Doyle and Robert Louis Stevenson. What did Mann make of Davos? Surely it must have reminded him of Nietzsche's Zarathustra, who goes into the mountains and dwells there for ten years, marinating in solitude. During his own years of restless wandering, the German philologist would hike the Swiss Alps for as long as ten hours a day, passing through Rosenlauibad, Grindelwald, St. Moritz, Sils Maria, and Davos.[20] "I live as if the centuries were nothing," Nietzsche wrote to a friend, "and I pursue my thoughts without thinking of the date and of the newspapers."[21]

Of course, these surroundings also reminded Mann of his beloved composer Richard Wagner, especially his opera *Tannhäuser*, based on a German folk ballad in which the wandering poet-hero comes across an enchanted mountain, the Venusberg, where the Roman goddess of love resides. In the opera's first act, Tannhäuser has awakened as if from a dream, uncertain of how long he has lingered in the mountain's underworld:

> The time I dwelt here with thee
> By days I cannot measure—
> Seasons pass me how I scarcely know
> The radiant sun I see no longer.[22]

* * *

Time was important to Thomas Mann. He took a childish pleasure in the temporal symmetry of his biography: he was born in 1875, finished his first novel at twenty-five, married at thirty, and so on. "The order in which my life is related to the times in numbers stirs in me the pleasure I find in all order and coherence," he wrote.[23] His diaries pedantically, almost comically, record the exact time of phone calls, dinners, and train departures, and throughout his life he adhered to a rigid writing schedule, even in the difficult years of exile. It was a discipline "more typical of a bank clerk than an artist," the critic Marcel Reich-Ranicki once quipped.[24]

The discipline paid off. When Mann arrived in Davos in the spring of 1912 he was already, at the age of thirty-six, an author held in high esteem by his contemporaries and the broader German reading public. His first novel, the two-volume family saga *Buddenbrooks* (1901), an unusually mature and polished novel for an author in his mid-twenties, became a surprise bestseller, prompting the influential Berlin critic Samuel Lublinski to pronounce Mann "the most important novelist of the modern movement."[25] Subsequent novellas like *Tristan* and *Tonio Kröger,* both published in 1903, cemented the young Mann's literary reputation. By age thirty, his life had become a procession of readings and lecture tours. "You are probably scoffing at all the travelling," Mann wrote to Heinrich in January 1906. "But I can't help myself; I find the self-representation fun and each time the change of air pulls me out of the intellectual stagnation to which I am inclined."[26]

Even by the standards of a buttoned-up age, he was wound unusually tight. Behind the public-facing bourgeois facade there was a neurotic artist in constant fear of being pulled under by a romantic obsession with death, disease, and dissolution. In his youth, Mann had imbibed the pessimistic emotional atmosphere of the philosopher Arthur Schopenhauer, who in a famous passage in *The World as Will and Representation* (1818), compared the human predicament to that of a boatman sitting in his "frail boat in a stormy sea that is boundless in every direction."[27] Mann later described his youthful reading of the "symphonic music" of Schopenhauer's "denial of life" as a metaphysical intoxication that was closely related to a "late and violent outbreak of sexuality"—a recipe for romantic death-longing if ever there was one.[28]

Despite his discipline and industriousness, Mann was prone to artistic crises. "It is time to begin thinking about a masterpiece," he wrote to Heinrich, even though unfinished projects kept piling up instead. There were ideas for a historical prose epic about Frederik the Great, a Munich society novel titled *Maya*, the short story "A Miserable Man," and a long, Schillerian essay on "Intellect and Culture." All of them were left unfinished and abandoned. (Ingeniously, he attributed them to Gustav von Aschenbach, the ageing literary master of *Death in Venice*.) The work he did manage to complete failed to live up to the early promise of *Buddenbrooks* and *Tonio Kröger*. *Fiorenza*, Mann's lone attempt at playwriting, was panned by critics, while *Royal Highness*, his second novel, sold well but received mostly tepid reviews. Mann complained to Heinrich that he felt "bad and exhausted and used-up and dead and finished."[29] When he wrote, in a 1911 essay on Theodor Fontane, that the great Prussian novelist "felt himself aging at thirty-seven," he was not thinking of Fontane alone.[30]

In Lübeck, a compact little seaport of medieval church steeples and narrow cobblestone streets, Mann's father had been one of the town's most distinguished citizens. Senator Thomas Johann Heinrich Mann was the owner of J. S. Mann, Grain Merchants, Commission and Shipping Agents; a senator overseeing the city's tax office; a consul to the Netherlands; and a board member of the Lübeck-Buchen Railway Company. He was a handsome and discerning man with a taste for English suits and Russian cigarettes. In 1869 he married Júlia da Silva Bruhns, a dark-skinned and, by Baltic standards, very exotic beauty. Born in Rio de Janeiro, she was the daughter of a German plantation owner and his Portuguese-Creole wife. Together, the couple had five children: Heinrich, the oldest; followed by Thomas, Julia, Carla, and Viktor.

A hard-working and energetic man, the senator was also extremely prudent. In 1891, just fifty-one but in increasingly poor health, he made arrangements to liquidate the merchant business that had been in his family for three generations. He knew he'd already lost Heinrich to the literary vocation and that none of his other four children were suited for a career in commerce. He still hoped Thomas might one day find himself a "practical profession" but clearly entertained no illusions on that score. In the will he amended shortly before his untimely death on October 13, 1891, the senator encouraged his wife to ensure that all five children remain dependent on her. "Should she ever waver," he coolly remarked, "I commend her to read *King Lear*."[31] As one biographer has put it, "it was almost as if the senator wanted to liquidate the family as well as the business."[32]

In his early essay "Lübeck as Way of Life and Thought," Mann said his father endowed him with what he called "the serious conduct of life": the bourgeois ethical imperative to work diligently, marry responsibly, start a family, and carry out one's social obligations satisfactorily.[33] This inheritance was perhaps most pronounced in Mann's understanding of the role of the writer in the modern age. He had no use for the German Romantics' idea of writers as oracular poet-figures, gnarled with national folk wisdom. A modern man of letters, Mann believed, is "an artist of insight, separated from art in the naïve and trusting sense by self-consciousness, intellect, moralism, and a critical disposition."[34] In his pursuit of this role, Mann brought all the commercial acumen and bourgeois pragmatism of his forefathers, as the Mann scholar Tobias Boes has shown: he embarked on reading tours, made innovative use of author photographs, and carefully navigated Germany's network of literary and cultural organizations.

In contrast to her husband, Thomas Mann's mother was "distinctly Latin in type" and "extraordinarily musical," thus providing an intoxicating artistic corrective to the commercial sobriety of the Mann family home.[35] Still just forty years old when her husband died, Júlia Mann moved the family out of cold, wet, windy Lübeck to the Bavarian capital of Munich, settling near the Schwabing district, then home to a bustling bohemian arts scene that had also attracted Henrik Ibsen, Wassily Kandinsky, Paul

Heyse, and the symbolist poet Stefan George. In the new family home on Rambergstrasse, the atmosphere was more laid-back and social than it had been in Lübeck. Visiting painters, writers, and musicians often gathered to hear Júlia play the grand piano or sing Schubert, Schumann, or Brahms. "Everything had become lovelier and more cheerful," Viktor Mann recalled.[36]

But death continued to haunt the family. In 1910, Carla, the youngest daughter, committed suicide. The twenty-eight-year-old struggling actress had been engaged to a young industrialist from Alsace, Arthur Gibo, whose family objected to the union and threatened to cut him off if he went ahead with the marriage. When a former lover blackmailed Carla and then, after she'd submitted to him, cruelly sent an anonymous letter to the Gibo family anyway, the engagement was tearfully broken. On July 30, Carla traveled to her mother's house in Polling and there consumed enough potassium cyanide to "kill a company of soldiers."[37]

Feeling more betrayed than bereaved, Mann wrote to Heinrich that "I can't help feeling that [Carla] was wrong to separate herself from us. She had no feeling of solidarity when she did it, didn't have the feeling of our common destiny." He would use similar words when, in May of 1949, his eldest son, Klaus, killed himself in Cannes. "My inward sympathy is with the mother's heart and with Erika," he wrote in his diary. "He should not have done this to them. . . . The hurtful, ugly, cruel inconsideration and irresponsibility."[38]

Such reactions may strike us as cold but at least Mann knew whereof he spoke. As a young man, he suffered depressions severe enough to contemplate doing away with himself. On at least one occasion he had to assure Heinrich he wasn't seriously thinking of taking his life. "No, you can leave for Italy without the slightest worry that I shall commit any 'follies,' " he wrote in March 1901, but added: "Of course I cannot vouch for what may happen some day."[39] Mann was saved from these follies by his belief that, painful as life may turn out to be, one nevertheless had a duty toward it. To go on living is an ethical demand the world requires of us, even when the mere thought of going on seems less like a gift and more like a sentence. "There is no help for it," says the narrator of the early story "The Joker" (1897), "life has to be lived."[40]

And yet Mann secretly feared he did not have the strength that this life struggle required and that, like his father, he would die an early death. In *Buddenbrooks,* Thomas Buddenbrook worries that, at age thirty-seven, he is "losing his edge" and "wearing out much too quickly."[41] His steely self-discipline, his refined appearance and burgherly equilibrium, are exhausting him prematurely. At a crucial moment in the novel, he asks himself whether he is really a practical man, like his merchant forefathers, or a tender-hearted dreamer, like his musical son—before admitting that he is, of course, "a mixture of both": "He had his past record of achievements, but had that record not risen from an enthusiasm, an impetus, provided by his own powers of reflection? And if he was despondent now, if his energies seemed spent—though not, God grant, forever—was that not the logical consequence of this untenable condition, this unnatural and exhausting contradiction inside him?"[42]

* * *

Because he grew up in a world obsessed with health, illnesses abound in Mann's fictional worlds—not only in *The Magic Mountain,* an epic both of and about illness, but in *Death in Venice* (cholera), *Doctor Faustus* (syphilis), *Buddenbrooks* (typhoid fever, tuberculosis, pneumonia, Christian Buddenbrook's many ailments), and elsewhere. As we'll see, Mann spent considerable time observing medical procedures and operations while writing *The Magic Mountain,* while in his diaries he made a point of detailing even the slightest physical suffering, from muscle spasms and heart palpitations to the state of his bowels.

Mann's interest in illness, however, was not primarily medical but metaphorical. The philosopher Havi Carel argues that by "broadening the spectrum of embodied experience into the pathological domain," illness distances us from the routines and habits of normal, everyday life.[43] Being ill requires us to become preoccupied in unusual ways with our bodies, paying attention to things and details of which healthy people remain safely ignorant. For Mann, this distance served as a useful metaphor for the artist, who is like the sick person in being separated from the health and happiness of ordinary life. It was an insight he owed in part to Nietzsche, who in *On the Genealogy of Morals* writes that "an artist, no matter how consummate his art, is forever separated from the 'real,' from the actual."[44]

"Physical suffering seems to me an almost necessary concomitant of greatness," Mann wrote to his friend Kurt Martens, in 1906. "I distrust pleasure, I distrust happiness, which I regard as unproductive."[45] In *Buddenbrooks*, the titular merchant family's downfall is brought about in part because of the "contagion" of artistic sensibility. The family line dies out with Hanno Buddenbrook, the sickly, sensitive, and musical son of Thomas Buddenbrook. Hanno's grip on existence is tenuous from the very moment of his birth and he dies from typhoid fever at age fifteen. For the duration of his short life he is intense and gloomy, prone to fits of despondency, and he comes to regard the busy merchant life of his father with a kind of melancholy condescension: "He had once again felt how painful beauty truly is, how it plunged you into shame and yearning despair and at the same time gnawed away at your courage and fitness for daily life. He had felt it as a dreadful, gloomy mountain pressing down on him so heavily that once again he was forced to admit that something more than private grief must be weighing him down, that some burden must have oppressed his soul from the very beginning and would suffocate him one day."[46]

The "superiority of the artist's inferiority," in Adam Kirsch's words, was a prevailing fin-de-siècle belief, and Mann's earliest fiction is filled with characters of this type.[47] The titular hero of *Tonio Kröger*, who believes the artist must stand strangely remote and detached from the world, at the same time laments: "I tell you I am often sick to death of being a portrayer of humanity and having no share in human experience."[48] He compares himself to Hamlet, echoing Nietzsche's description of the Danish prince in *The Birth of Tragedy* as one of those who have "truly seen to the essence of things, they have understood, and action repels them; for their action can change nothing in the eternal essence of things." For Hamlet as for Tonio Kröger, "true understanding, insight into the terrible truth, outweighs every motive for action."[49]

By associating art and illness, Mann did not mean that an artist must in some sense be neurotic or ill in order to produce great work. He admired what the historian Friedrich Wilhelm Riemer described as Goethe's striving "to make from a dark product of nature a clear product of himself (that is, of reason) and to thus fulfill life's vocation and duty."[50] And he would no doubt have agreed with Lionel Trilling's claim, in his essay "Art and Neurosis," that "nothing is so characteristic of the artist as his power of shaping his work, of subjugating his raw material, however aberrant it be from what we call normality, to the consistency of nature."[51] The artist may be irresponsible in his sympathy with the demonic, the diseased, and the forbidden, but his irresponsibility attains social form by the shape-giving nature of art. The conflict, the separation, between art and life is momentarily healed by the sober, serious labor of the artist. Hence the austere and burgherly discipline that descended on Mann whenever he sat down at his desk. As Tonio Kröger exclaims: "As an artist I'm already enough of an adventurer in my inner life. So far as outward appearances are concerned one should dress decently, damn it, and behave like a respectable citizen."[52]

Mann fashioned his view of the artist partly in opposition to the example of his older brother, whose literary career started with a bang and ended with a whimper. Against his father's wishes, the rebellious Heinrich had left home at eighteen and found work as a bookseller's apprentice in Dresden and later as an unpaid assistant to Samuel Fischer's publishing house in Berlin, before embarking on a life of writerly nomadism, loafing around Europe without a fixed address for the better part of two decades. During that time, he churned out novels and stories at an astonishing pace, even though many of them met with poor sales and lukewarm reviews. Undeterred, Heinrich kept on writing as though possessed, in a style as sensuous and erotic as the Italian settings of so many of his novels.

Thomas Mann viewed his older brother's industriousness with horror. "Good God, you've finished something else already—and I'm not even finished with your last one," he wrote to him in 1907.[53] Any enviousness of Heinrich's productivity Thomas may have felt was canceled out by revulsion for the—in Mann's view—shoddiness of the final product. "Do you suppose I like his things?" Mann asked the novelist and newspaper columnist Ida Boy-Ed. "We almost came to blows over his last book. Yet the feeling that his artistic personality arouses in me is a far cry from contempt. It is more like hatred."[54]

The book they nearly came to blows over was *The Hunt for Love* (1903), a six-hundred-page Munich society novel that, incredibly, took Heinrich just six months to write. When he read it, Thomas dispatched a long and unusually vehement letter to his brother objecting to the novel's "strained jokes, these vulgar, shrill, hectic, unnatural calumnies of the truth and humanity, these disgraceful grimaces and somersaults, these desperate attacks on the reader's interest!" He accused Heinrich of lacking discipline, of betraying his literary gifts for the sake of cheap sensationalism, and even suggested the novel's title ought to have been: *The Hunt for Sensation*.[55] In the privacy of his notebook, under the heading "Anti-Heinrich," he continued his outburst: "I consider it immoral to avoid the discomforts of indolence by writing one bad book after another."[56]

Heinrich's response hasn't survived, but it isn't difficult to imagine the injury it caused—especially since, by this time, *Buddenbrooks* was already in its eighteenth printing, a detail Thomas rather cruelly alluded to in his letter. The rift between the two brothers became serious enough for their mother to get involved. "You are *both* god-gifted, dear Heinrich," she pleaded in a letter to her oldest son. "How can 1½ years have changed everything just because your last books didn't satisfy throughout? It has *nothing to do* with your fraternal problems!"[57]

And yet, what is a brother if not a kind of alternate version of one's self, an embodiment of potentials and possibilities, a reminder of roads not taken? In *Buddenbrooks*, Thomas is impatient with and frequently hostile to his dissolute and aimless older brother, Christian, whose lack of discretion and constant preoccupation with himself is a source of embarrassment to Thomas—"the important thing is control and balance," as Thomas tells their sister, Antonie.[58] The two brothers' strained relationship eventually comes to a head when the usually placid Christian confronts Thomas, accusing him of lacking sympathy, love, and humility. "I've had it up to here with all your tact and discretion and balance, with your poise and dignity—I'm sick to death of it," he erupts. Thomas responds: "I have become what I am . . . because I did not want to become like you. If I have inwardly shrunk away from you, it was because I had to protect myself from you, because your nature and character are a danger to me. I am speaking the truth."[59]

Mann's portrayal of the Buddenbrook brothers was not primarily a reflection of his relationship with Heinrich, however.

"All literary characters are emanations of the author's self," Mann wrote, and so it is with Thomas and Christian Buddenbrook.[60] They are *both* Thomas Mann, or versions of him. Thomas fears in Christian what he fears in himself: the neuroses, the indolence, the mania. He decides to marry in part because he is afraid of becoming a bachelor like his brother. "That sort of life smacks of loneliness and indolence, and I have my own ambitions, as you well know," Thomas Buddenbrook tells his sister; "a man first wins the world's trust as master of his own house, as a family man."[61]

Curiously, Thomas Mann explained his decision to marry Katia Pringsheim, the daughter of a wealthy Jewish family, in similar terms. In a letter to Heinrich shortly after their engagement, Thomas assured his brother that getting married was something he had submitted to "out of a kind of feeling of duty, a kind of morality, an inborn imperative, which, since it constitutes a move *away* from the desk, I've long feared as a form of slovenliness, but which I've in fact learned with time to recognize as something moral." He went on: "Once again, the point is to maintain a humane strictness about oneself, and often enough the whole of bliss eventuates in a clenched jaw."[62]

Marrying out of a concern for one's social position was common enough at the time, but even so Mann's reasoning contained a subtext whose meaning was hardly lost on Heinrich. He was keenly aware of his younger brother's "sexual inversion," as Mann himself referred to it: his attraction to men. When Thomas was fourteen and very smitten with his classmate Armin Martens, Heinrich wrote to a friend that all his brother really needed was enough money for a prostitute: "A real sleeping cure with a passionate, not yet overly experienced girl will cure him."[63] A few years later, in 1906, when *Simplicissimus* published Heinrich's "Abdication," the fictional story of a homosexual relationship between two boys at a boarding school, Thomas wrote at once to congratulate him, calling it "the most revealing and extraordinary piece you've written." In fact, he liked the story so much that he felt as if he'd written it himself. "In a word: I do not take part in it; I *am* part of it," he rhapsodized to his older brother. Heinrich had made a point of dedicating the story to Thomas.

Because homosexuality was widely viewed as a kind of bourgeois apostasy, it became associated in Mann's mind with art and death, and therefore as something opposed to the health his literary ambitions demanded. Inhabiting the role of a family patriarch, on the other hand, allowed him "to hide in the bourgeois without actually becoming bourgeois," as he later put it.[64]

Some of Mann's biographers have taken this reasoning a little too much at face value, as though no other explanation for his decision to marry to Katia were possible. The biographer Ronald Hayman, for instance, argues that Mann was "building a dam to divert the course of his sexual energy, sacrificing his natural inclinations on the altar of his public image." No doubt Mann's sexual inclinations played a part in his decision to marry, but it isn't—it *can't* be—the only reason. It's cheap to view Mann's long career merely as the product of sexual repression, just as it is ungenerous to characterize fifty years of marriage as little more than a concession to literary ambition. Rather more callously, Hayman goes on to claim that Mann liked and admired Katia but "wasn't in love with her."[65] How could he possibly know?

Worst of all, such sweeping claims remove Katia from the equation. Though she lived a life largely in service of her husband, she was no mere appendage. "Part tomboy and part scholar," she was given private tutoring lessons and eventually passed her Abitur, the required entrance exam for university.[66] In 1903 she became the first female student to enroll at the University of Munich, where she studied mathematics and experimental physics with Wilhelm Röntgen, the Nobel Prize–winning inventor of the X-ray machine that plays such a memorable role in *The Magic Mountain*.

Despite her obvious intelligence and impressive ancestry (she was the granddaughter of Hedwig Dohm, an influential feminist writer), Katia's studies effectively ended with her marriage. "Maybe I would have completed my studies and taken my degree," she once mused, with typical modesty. "However, I had studied for only four or six semesters when I got married; soon after that the first baby arrived, and the second one right away, and very soon the third and fourth. That was the end of my studies."[67] In a 1961 letter to her twin brother, six years after Thomas Mann's death, she put it rather more poignantly: "I have never in my life been able to do what I would have liked to do."[68]

* * *

Here was Katia now, wrapped in her camel-wool blanket, assuming the horizontal position on her south-facing balcony. Perched on a hillside some 350 feet above Davos, the Waldsanatorium offered sweeping views of the valley and the mountains beyond it. And with its stylish art nouveau interiors designed by Walther Koch and Arthur Wiederanders, it offered the highest standards in comfort and hygiene, as well as the latest advances in medical technology.

Despite the strict timetable for Katia's treatment, Thomas Mann visited his wife as often as he could. He sat with her on the balcony, listening to the impressions she'd formed of the other patients. There was the dim and vulgar Frau Plür, whom Katia couldn't stand; a charming Russian lady with an infuriating habit of letting doors slam behind her; a grieving Spanish widow who saw both her sons succumb to their illness and who took to wandering restlessly about the sanitorium garden, speaking what little French she knew: "*Vous savez, tous les deux,*" she kept repeating to herself.[69]

But as the days wore on, Mann found he was struggling to adjust to the thin mountain air. "I am only painfully becoming used to this altitude of five thousand feet," he wrote to a friend, adding that the climate was making him feverish and that for some reason his cigars tasted like papier-mâché. Eventually he came down with a bronchial cold and reluctantly let himself be examined by Dr. Friedrich Jessen. After thumping Mann on his chest, Dr. Jessen told him he had a moist spot on his lung and recommended that he extend his stay in Davos. Mann reported this back to his family doctor in Munich, who responded frankly: "I know you very well. You would be the first one to be examined in Davos who did not have some spot or other. Return to Munich immediately. You have no business in Davos."[70]

When he did return to Munich—on June 12, 1912—Mann quickly paid his in-laws a visit and informed them that Katia would likely remain in Davos until the fall. Hedwig Pringsheim was not surprised. Those institutions hold on to their patients with an iron grip, she scoffed. After visiting Katia again later that summer, she was blunter in her verdict. "Just between you and me," she wrote to Maximilian Harden, "I think Davos is all bogus."[71]

But the Swiss alpine village and its community had made an impression on Thomas Mann. In the weeks and months after his visit, he became conscious of a glimmering, the faintest whisper, of an idea for a new novella: the story of a simple-minded young man who goes to Davos and finds himself caught between "bourgeois decorum and macabre adventure." In contrast to the Venetian novella, this one would be light and humorous—a satirical companion to its gloomier cousin. All Mann had to do was draw on the characters and anecdotes Katia kept supplying him with in her letters. He hadn't yet figured out how the story was going to end, but that would come to him. He did have a title, though: he would call it *The Enchanted Mountain*.

CHAPTER 2

Sympathy with Death, 1914

Thomas Mann had a habit of reading from his books even as he was still writing them—mostly to family and friends but on occasion to the general public also. In his diaries audience reactions were recorded in detail: "When I left the platform for an intermission there was no applause," he once wrote with chagrin. "I returned, read the examination scene, and again at the end of it there was not a trace of applause."[1] Being a studied veteran of the lecture circuit, however, Mann knew how to draw a curtain about his listeners. Of a later reading he noted with pride: "The ovations virtually frenetic, shattering. Throngs of people wanting autographs afterward, paying homage."[2]

Almost two years after his trip to Davos, Mann decided he'd written enough of his new work-in-progress to hazard a public reading. On Friday, January 30, 1914, at the newly opened Galerie Caspari, located across the street from Café Luitpold, the storied Munich café where Henrik Ibsen used to hold court over foam-capped tankards of Löwenbräu, Mann read from his Davos novella in public for the first time. Clad as usual in a custom-tailored suit with a starched collared shirt and necktie, Mann had been invited to give a reading as part of a series of lectures hosted by Wilhelm Herzog, the soon-to-be editor of *Das Forum*. Adorning the walls of the Caspari that evening was a new exhibit by the German Expressionist Ludwig von Hofmann—a minor artist, but one whose idyllic paintings of naked youths bathing, dancing, or horse-riding were then in vogue. Mann "fell madly in love" with one painting in particular, *The Spring,* which would shortly find its way onto a wall in his study—and, more obliquely, into the manuscript from which he now read.[3]

What did the audience that evening make of Mann's latest work? What were they expecting? Looking up now at the podium, their heads tilted in thoughtful sympathy, they listened to the tale of a young man who travels from Hamburg to Davos, where he is met by his cousin, a tubercular patient at something called the International Sanatorium Berghof. They heard how the young man and his cousin enjoyed a dinner so rich that one or two empty stomachs in the audience no doubt rumbled with envy. And yet how strange this story was! There were digressions about time and death, the dissection of psyches and the decomposition of lungs. There were references to corpses on bobsleds and a description of a building with so many balconies it "looked as pockmarked and porous as a sponge."[4] What on earth had Thomas Mann come up with now?

The following day's report in the *Münchner Neueste Nachrichten,* describing the excerpt as "a thought-provoking story with an ironic mood," didn't give much away, not even the title, which Mann surely made a point of mentioning.[5] A month before the reading, an announcement in *Die neue Rundschau* had erroneously referred to the novella as *The Sorcerer's Apprentice,* a mistake on the part of Oskar Bie, the *Rundschau's* editor. "The title," Mann now wrote to a friend, "is *The Magic Mountain.*"[6]

* * *

The novel begins late in the summer of 1907 with the arrival in Davos of Hans Castorp, a twenty-three-year-old engineering student who, having been orphaned at a young age, grew up in the care of his grandfather and his uncle, and who looks set to embark on a career with the shipbuilding firm Tunder and Wilms in Hamburg. He is blond and blue-eyed, impeccably well-dressed, and seems to everyone back home "an honest, unadulterated product of the local soil, superbly at home in it."[7]

But all is not as it seems with our young hero. Reading on, we gradually learn that, back in Hamburg, the family doctor suspects Hans Castorp of being anemic and has prescribed him a daily glass of robust porter—believed to help build his blood, but which Hans Castorp enjoys for its soothing, dozing effects. We also learn that although he is a decent tennis player and oarsman, he prefers sitting on a terrace of the boathouse with a drink in hand, "listening to music and watching the boats as they drifted among the swans."[8]

More significantly, we learn that work, that most supreme of bourgeois virtues, doesn't really agree with Hans Castorp. In fact, it strains his nerves and tires him out. He prefers it when time passes "easily, unencumbered by the leaden weight of toil."[9] When he first meets Ludovico Settembrini, a fellow patient and Italian humanist, he says with remarkable candor: "I only really feel healthy when I am doing nothing at all."[10]

What are we to make of all this? One the one hand, Hans Castorp is presented to us as an ordinary, healthy young man, firmly grounded in the norms and values of his burgherly environment. Yet the more we read on the more misleading this early impression begins to seem; and the more misleading it seems, the more our initial impression of Hans Castorp begins to crumble.

The philosopher Alexander Nehamas, in his reading of the novel's early chapters, alerts us to an incident that occurs on the morning of Hans Castorp's first day at the Berghof. Standing on the balcony of his room, taking in the mountain vistas that surround him, Hans Castorp suddenly overhears a Russian couple in a neighboring room having sex. He responds rather prudishly: "Well, they're married, for heaven's sake, that's as it should be at least. But in broad daylight, that is a bit much. And I'm almost certain that they disturbed the peace last night, too. After all, they

SYMPATHY WITH DEATH

are ill, that's why they're here, or one of them is at least, and a little self-control wouldn't be out of place."[11]

As Nehamas shrewdly points out, Hans Castorp's comment that at least one of the Russians must be sick "casts his own presence at the sanatorium in an ambiguous light. Since he, too, is there, why should he be different from them?"[12] Nehamas reminds us that Hans Castorp has come to Davos not simply to visit his cousin but to recuperate a little himself. At the end of the second chapter it is mentioned, almost in passing, that his family doctor actually insisted on a change of air. Hans Castorp returned from his final exams looking a little pale, a change in constitution that is put down to the long period of concentrated work he has just completed. And since his cousin happens to be at a sanatorium in Davos, why not take this opportunity to pay him a visit and reap the benefits of the region's celebrated air?

But if Hans Castorp is not as healthy as he imagines himself to be, is he then sick? And if he is not actually sick, then what, if anything, is wrong with him?

Notice that Hans Castorp is only ever referred to by his full name—a habit that is "somehow necessary, as if to fortify his insufficiently firm grip on the will to exist," as Stephen D. Dowden puts it.[13] Something about Hans Castorp is undefined. When asked by the director of the Berghof why he chose to become an engineer, he claims he did so purely by chance, and that he could just as well have become a doctor or a clergyman.[14] Similarly, when local citizens of Hamburg wonder if Hans Castorp will one day take part in the city's political life, given his good family name, they cannot decide if he would stand as a conservative, like his grandfather, or as a progressive, given that he has entered the field of commerce and technology. "That was quite possible—but so was the opposite."[15]

The scholar Børge Kristiansen has argued that Hans Castorp's insufficiently firm grip on existence, this preference for doing nothing, must be understood as a symptom of the "twilight of meaning" that characterized European thought at the dawn of the twentieth century—what Mann's friend Hermann Broch, in his novel *The Sleepwalkers* (1930-32), called the "disintegration of all values": the idea that man had been driven out of his "former estate" into "the horror of the infinite."[16] Hans Castorp, in Kristiansen's reading, bears the burden of the nihilism of his time.[17] In *The Will to Power,* Nietzsche defines nihilism as the absence of an answer to the question: "why?"—and the nihilistic disposition as a "yearning for nothingness."[18] Crucially, he understood that one can be a nihilist and not know it—indeed, that one definition of nihilism is to go on living a life that corresponds with the belief that *life is nothing,* as the philosopher Nolen Gertz has shown.[19]

The Magic Mountain's narrator tells us from the beginning that Hans Castorp "had not planned to take this trip particularly seriously, to become deeply involved in it," yet the sight of his paperbound book *Ocean Steamships* lying neglected on the seat beside him as his train first approaches Davos suggests otherwise. Hans Castorp is not aware of it, but he arrives at the Berghof having *already* begun to lose interest in his profession, and by extension the solid bourgeois world in which he was raised. The reason for his lack of interest is buried in a long narrative digression in the subchapter "At the Tienappels":

> All sorts of personal goals, purposes, hopes, prospects may float before the eyes of a given individual, from which he may then glean the impulse for exerting himself for great deeds; if the impersonal world around him, however, if the times themselves, despite all their hustle and bustle, provide him with neither hopes nor prospects, if they secretly supply him with evidence that things are in fact hopeless ... if the times respond with hollow silence to every conscious or subconscious question, however it may be posed, about the ultimate, unequivocal meaning of all exertions and deeds

... then it is almost inevitable, particularly if the person involved is a more honest sort, that the situation will have a crippling effect, which, following moral and spiritual paths, may even spread to that individual's physical and organic life.[20]

The narrator here suggests that Hans Castorp is "sick" because the time in which he lives cannot provide him with meaning; that he has, in effect, continued to pursue an essentially meaningless life—a life in which the question "why" is answered with an invalidating silence. The suggestion is repeated about a third of the way through the novel: "Hans Castorp would not have stayed with the people up here even this long beyond his originally planned date of departure, if only some sort of satisfactory answer about the meaning and purpose of life had been supplied to his prosaic soul from out of the depths of time." Since no such answer is forthcoming, and since he only really feels healthy when he is doing nothing at all, Hans Castorp might as well stay at the Berghof, where there is no time as such, and do nothing. And yet to do nothing at all, in the strictest, most literal sense possible, is to be dead.

* * *

When he left Davos in June 1912, Mann had envisioned *The Magic Mountain* as a comic companion to *Death in Venice,* one in which Gustav von Aschenbach's Dionysian conflict, as T. J. Reed writes, is "echoed in the comic conflict of bourgeois respectability and macabre adventures."[21] Mann's notebook from the early months of *The Magic Mountain*'s composition—he didn't write the first words until September 1913—include references to rib resections, time and spatial movement, the writings of Petrarch, Carducci, and Leopardi, and even the minor character Frau Stöhr's twenty-eight different recipes for fish sauce. By the end of 1913, he estimated he had written almost a quarter of what he was still calling a novella, though by early January he told a friend that he was already behind schedule.²²

There were external reasons for this. On January 5, 1914, the Mann family moved into a stately, three-story villa on Poschingerstrasse, a broad, poplar-lined avenue in Munich's Herzog Park neighborhood, near the banks of the Isar River, which Mann said he could hear roaring like the sea.²³ But the move was complicated by the absence of Katia, whose poor health had once again required her to go take the cure, this time in Arosa, Switzerland, where she would remain until the middle of May. It was her fourth such trip in just two and a half years. "I'm very disturbed that my wife could not be here for the move," Mann wrote to his friend Ernst Bertram. "She has been in Arosa for two days. It was suggested that she spend several months in the Alps. It is hard."²⁴

Then there was the more general matter of his literary career, over which Mann continued to despair almost constantly. To be sure, there was plenty of outward success: *Royal Highness*, despite its lukewarm critical reception, sold twenty-five thousand copies in its first year; *Death in Venice*, published in February 1913, had sold eighteen thousand copies by the end of the year.²⁵ *Buddenbrooks*, meanwhile—long since a runaway literary and commercial success—was nearing sales of a hundred thousand copies.²⁶ And yet Mann worried his time might be up: "I probably should never have been allowed to become a writer. *Buddenbrooks* was a novel of the bourgeoisie and means nothing to the twentieth century," he wrote to Heinrich. "*Tonio Kröger* was merely larmoyante, *Royal Highness* vain, *Death in Venice* only half-cultivated and false. There you have my latest realizations, consolation for the little hour of one's death."²⁷

Ironically, as if to confirm Mann's anxieties, in *The Blue Review* in 1913 appeared one of the first English-language notices of his work, a review of *Death in Venice* by the young English novelist D. H. Lawrence, Mann's junior by a decade. Lawrence, who would marry the German Baroness Frieda von Richthofen in 1914, was then living in a Bavarian town just outside of Munich. Though he acknowledged Mann as the most famous of contemporary German novelists, ruddy, full-blooded Lawrence was left cold by *Death in Venice*, describing its author as "over middle age," "physically ailing," and as "full of disgusts and loathing of himself as Flaubert was." And as might be expected of the author who would one day write *Lady Chatterley's Lover*, Lawrence bristled at Mann's aesthetic reserve: "Physical life is a disordered corruption, against which he can fight with only one weapon, his fine aesthetic sense, his feeling for beauty, for perfection, for a certain fitness which soothes him, and gives him an inner pleasure, however corrupt the stuff of life may be." Lawrence ended his review by declaring that "Thomas Mann is old—and we are young."[28] Mann, actually, was only thirty-eight.

If he'd read Lawrence's review, Mann might have nodded gravely with assent. He was deeply ambivalent about the painstaking self-discipline his writing demanded, and thoroughly anxious about the quality of the writing it produced. In *Death in Venice*, Gustav von Aschenbach, his brow furrowed by decades of daily exertion at his desk, takes little pleasure in the national honor his literary accomplishments have brought him. "It seemed to him that his work lacked that element of sparkling and joyful improvisation, that quality which surpasses any intellectual substance in its power to delight the receptive world," he reflects. Wearied by the toil and struggle of his writing, he fears the "moral indifference" inherent in art, the contradiction of its being, on the one hand, a highly moral product of bourgeois discipline, and yet an immoral and even anti-moral preoccupation with death, vice, and passion on the other.[29]

But the somber composure—that tight-fisted self-control—was necessary and had to be maintained at all cost. It was the ticket price for being a modern man of letters, as Mann understood it. Of

Goethe he later wrote: "At bottom, he knew no rest." In his famous essay-portrait, Mann depicts the author of *Faust* and *Wilhelm Meister*, not as the poet-genius enshrined in German cultural tradition, but rather as a self-conscious modern writer not unlike himself: "Caution and slowness, a maternal patience in production, are inseparable from his genius. As a creative artist he is more a slow than an impetuous and improvising nature."[30]

Mann also attributes to Goethe what he calls an "ironic nihilism ... that profound naturalistic inhuman lack of conviction which is characteristic of the artist." He quotes the slightly eerie impression Goethe made on Charlotte von Schiller, the wife of Friedrich Schiller, who recalled: "He talked ... in nothing but sentences that had a contradiction in every one, one could interpret as one liked, but one had a painful feeling that the master was saying to himself that he cared not a jot for any of them."[31] In a much later essay, Mann approvingly quotes Chekhov's nagging suspicion: "Am I not fooling the reader ... since I cannot answer the most important questions?"[32]

Mann kept returning to this question of the purpose of his writing, all that nervous, inflexible, and above all terribly lonely labor. What was the point of it? What was its social value? Was it just a trick, a kind of joke, something not to be taken seriously? Mann would always remember the Swedish novelist Selma Lagerlöf's response when, during a reception, she was asked about her novel *Gösta Berling's Saga* (1891) and its worldwide popularity: "Dear me, yes ... that all came about, but you must not imagine that I ever gave it much weight while I was doing it. I wrote it for my little nieces and nephews. It was just an entertainment like any other. The whole thing was a kind of joke."[33]

Unlike his younger brother, Heinrich Mann had no trouble at all explaining what the social value of his fiction was. Ever since his 1905 novel *Professor Unrat* (literally "Professor Rubbish," best known for its 1930 film adaptation as *The Blue Angel*, starring

Marlene Dietrich), he had been embarked on a lonely struggle to embrace liberal and democratic ideas for Germany. "I want to create heroes, real heroes, generous, gay and loving humanity in contrast to the hostile race of today, given completely to reaction," he wrote in a letter to Ludwig Ewers.[34] His 1909 novel *The Little Town*, the story of an opera troupe's arrival in a small Italian town on the brink of social and political upheaval, incurred the opposition of even his own publisher.[35] Preposterously, Insel Verlag insisted that Heinrich remove the word *democracy* from his introduction so as not to contaminate the public's faith in the nation.[36] Not that anyone was paying much attention: *The Little Town* was a commercial disaster, selling fewer than a thousand copies in its first six months of publication.

In 1911, Heinrich published his essay "Spirit and Action," his most direct assault yet on the apolitical complacency of his fellow writers. "The times demand," he intoned, "that they become agitators, unite the people against power [and abandon their] cult of the self."[37] Then, in the summer of 1912, *Simplicissimus* published the first serial installations of Heinrich's most ambitiously political novel yet, *Der Untertan* (alternately translated in English as *Man of Straw* and *The Loyal Subject*), a brilliant satire dripping with contempt for the militarism and anti-Semitism of German society. His portrayal of the budding authoritarian Diederich Hessling is really a kind of anti-bildungsroman, or a bildungsroman in reverse: whereas the genre traditionally tracks a character's progress toward individuality and self-realization, *Der Untertan* shows us Hessling's loss of individuality to the mass mentality of the army, the state, and the nation. Early in the novel, as the kaiser rides through Berlin on horseback, Hessling is intoxicated by the power embodied in the figure before him: "We are an atom of that Power, a diminutive molecule of something it has given out. Each one of us is as nothing, but massed in ranks as Neo-Teutons, soldiers, bureaucrats, priests and scientists, as economic organizations and unions of power, we taper up like a pyramid to the point at the top where Power itself stands, graven and dazzling."[38]

Thomas Mann, initially surprised by Heinrich's turn toward liberalism, soon took to referring to his older brother as "a passionate democrat of the newest stamp."[39] In 1910, Thomas declined to sign an appeal for electoral reform in the *Berliner Tageblatt*, remarking in a letter to Kurt Martens that the writers who did sign it, Heinrich included, "would write their names on practically anything that's put in front of them." He added: "Insofar as I can see my future work, it certainly will have nothing whatever to do with democracy."[40]

Prior to 1914, German politics were virtually absent in Mann's work. In this he was quite typical of his time. Feigning indifference toward politics was almost a mark of distinction for German writers—for whom the cultural sphere was far superior to the banal concerns of the polis, as the sociologist Wolf Lepenies has argued.[41] But this did not prevent Mann's writing from being, almost despite itself, alert to the sense of crisis so palpable at the time. In a review of *Death in Venice*, published in the March 1913 issue of the literary periodical *März*, Heinrich Mann made a point of emphasizing the political subtext of his brother's novella, comparing it to the social novels of Émile Zola that had revealed the corruption and predicted the collapse of the Second French Empire. Reality often imitates art, Heinrich claimed, and the inner logic of *Death in Venice*, as he saw it, clearly willed the downfall of Germany's Wilhelmine empire.

Heinrich was on to something. In its opening paragraph, *Death in Venice* alludes to a threat shadowing the peace of Europe, a possible reference to one of the diplomatic crises that preceded the First World War, like the Agadir Crisis in the summer of 1911, when a quarrel between Germany and France over Morocco escalated to such a degree that a war seemed all but certain.[42] And with its portrayal of the breakdown of discipline, the dissolution of conventional morality, the surrender of the "exemplary and definitive" Gustav von Aschenbach to the Dionysian abyss—how could it not be viewed, in retrospect, as an unwitting prophesy of Europe's gradual and then sudden descent into that festival of death in the summer of 1914?[43]

But Thomas Mann felt more and more unmoored intellectually and politically. In November 1913 he had sent a despairing letter to Heinrich complaining of feeling "weighed down by the misery of the times, of the fatherland, without anyone having the strength to lend it form." He envied his brother having found "a proper intellectual and political standpoint." He was consumed instead, he wrote, by "a growing sympathy with death, which is deeply inborn: my entire interest has always been captured by decay, and that is probably what prevents me from developing an interest in progress."[44]

* * *

On the morning of his first day at the Berghof, Hans Castorp joins Joachim Ziemssen and the other patients for early breakfast in the dining hall. (Readers of the novel will soon become acquainted with the concept of early and late breakfasts.) Seated at one of the seven dining tables, where pots of jam and honey, bowls of rice and porridge, dishes of meat and eggs are lavishly spread out before him, Hans Castorp is soon startled by the slamming of a door leading into the hall—a banging, clattering noise our young hero cannot stand. "Damn it," he mutters to himself, "What kind of sloppiness is that?" Before he is able to identify the culprit, however, he has been distracted by the conversation of one of his tablemates.[45]

Hans Castorp doesn't know it yet, but this moment marks his first encounter with Clavdia Chauchat, the alluring Russian temptress who, more than anyone, will consume his attention, especially in the first half of the novel. And it is precisely her sloppiness—

her slinking gait, her bad posture, her blatant disregard for bourgeois norms—that will seduce Hans Castorp and arouse his innate sympathy with death, his predilection for disease and dissolution.

During that same breakfast—and in marked contrast to the other patients—Hans Castorp makes a point of wearing his hat, since he is "all too definite in his own civilized habits to change them lightly and adopt strange new ones for a mere three weeks." Or so the narrator tells us. But we already know this isn't true; as we've seen, Hans Castorp is anything *but* too definite in his civilized habits. The tenuousness of his attachment to the bourgeois world "down below" is clear from the novel's earliest pages. What's more, despite repeatedly proclaiming his difficulty acclimatizing to the Berghof, Hans Castorp is actually settling in quite nicely, something the coquettish narrator puts down to the "docility of youth, with its ability to adapt to the ideas and customs of almost any environment in which it may find itself."[46]

The attentive reader will notice that, bit by bit, Hans Castorp unwittingly begins adopting the vocabulary of the staff and patients he encounters, as well as their behavior and body language. When he first arrives, for example, he is perplexed by his cousin's manner of speaking, which is accompanied by "a nonchalant, but somehow vehement shrug."[47] And yet the very next day Hans Castorp himself gives a shrug "in perfect imitation of the shrug he had first seen Joachim give the evening before."[48] Among the residents of the Berghof, a shrug is a gesture that symbolizes indifference to the conventions of bourgeois society. When Hans Castorp at one point brings up the recent death of the charming young patient Leila Gerngross, Director Behrens, too, responds with a shrug.[49]

During the course of those first three weeks, it becomes increasingly clear that Hans Castorp will not be returning to the flatlands once his visit is over. He is not aware of this himself, which is one of the novel's chief sources of dramatic irony. But the longer he lingers up there in the mountains, the stranger and more perverse life in the flatlands below begins to seem to him. On what he still imagines to be one of his last nights in Davos, he realizes that taking the rest cure on his balcony is "by any criterion the most agreeable state of affairs that [he] could remember ever having tried out."[50] And as he lies out there, wrapped in his camel-wool blanket, *Ocean Steamships* forever unread beside him, we recall the narrator's remark, earlier in the novel, that Hans Castorp cherishes his leisure time, work being a strain on his nerves, something that tires him out. "I only feel really healthy when I am doing nothing at all," as he says.[51]

Then, just as Hans Castorp is about to prepare for his return to Hamburg, he catches a cold. He is examined by Director Behrens, who thumps him on his chest and suspects a moist spot on his lung. "I don't know if you were already febrile down in the plains," he tells Hans Castorp, "but in any case you had a fever on your very first day here, and not because of any catarrh—that, at least, is my opinion."[52] He adds that, paradoxically, the air in Davos is good both for fighting off illness *and* for cultivating it. The air creates a revolution in the body that causes latent illnesses to erupt.

Hans Castorp thus receives medical confirmation of what the reader has, by now, long suspected: he did not catch a cold on his arrival; he arrived in Davos *already sick*. But the latent illness that erupts is not tuberculosis; it is his sympathy with death. We know that the loss of his parents and grandfather at a young age not only affected Hans Castorp's mind and senses—"his senses in particular"—but also revealed to him bourgeois society's habit of glossing over the "almost indecent" physicality of death, a habit Hans Castorp passionately objects to.[53] Thus he claims to be in his element when dealing with people who have recently lost a loved one; considers a coffin "an absolutely lovely piece of furniture"; and believes there is "something edifying" about funerals.[54] At one point, a few months into his as yet undetermined stay as a patient, Hans Castorp makes a habit of visiting the serious and moribund cases, even going so far as to inspect the recently deceased—in defiance of the Berghof's practice of concealment. "When it comes to death," he tells his cousin, "when one speaks to the dead or about them, Latin comes into its own. It's the official language in such cases, which only points up how special death is."[55]

The character who most clearly recognizes this sympathy in Hans Castorp is Ludovico Settembrini, the Italian humanist and pedagogue whose rhetorical prowess and linguistic felicity make an instant impression on Hans Castorp. Less charitably, the Italian also reminds him of an organ grinder, the kind of street musician who would appear in Hamburg during the Christmas season, holding out his hat for coins—a teasing juxtaposition. By dressing the Italian humanist in threadbare clothing, Mann implies a connection between Settembrini's wardrobe and his ideas. For this eloquent organ grinder is a staunch advocate of reason and enlightenment, ideas he believes "will liberate the human race entirely and lead it on paths of progress and civilization toward an ever brighter, milder, and purer light." Settembrini is the grandson of a Carbonaro, a Mazzini-like member of a secret political society advocating liberal and patriotic ideas, and the son of a lawyer who agitated tirelessly for a unified Italian republic. He himself is a freelance writer and man of letters, activities that link him to the same noble struggle of his father and grandfather, since literature, he claims, is "nothing other than the union of humanism and politics." In short, he is the incarnation of what Thomas Mann will soon refer to, disparagingly, as a *Zivilisationsliterat,* or civilization's literary man.

Though himself a patient at the Berghof, Settembrini frequently disparages the institution and its staff, comparing it to the underworld and Director Behrens and his assistant Dr. Krokowski to Rhadamanthus and Minos—in Greek mythology, they are judges of the dead in the underworld. With his critical, ironizing attitude, the Italian humanist is quick to perceive that Hans Castorp is being adversely affected by the unusual environment of the Berghof. As early as the second time they meet, he encourages the young visitor to pack his bags and return to Hamburg that very night.

Settembrini is kindly disposed to Hans Castorp from the start, not least because as a man of reason he approves of the young engineer's choice of vocation, regarding him as "the representative of a whole world of labor and practical genius."[56] But he recognizes, too, that Hans Castorp doesn't have a firm enough grip on existence. In one of their early exchanges, while admonishing Hans Castorp for suggesting there is something worth admiring about illness, Settembrini accuses him of "playing the intellectual dilletante, temporarily experimenting with possible points of view." This adaptability of Hans Castorp's, his receptiveness and openness to ideas, is something Settembrini looks down on as a lack of resolve. When Hans Castorp counters that in general he tries not to be too quick to form opinions, Settembrini reprimands him: "That's pure sluggishness! ... Form opinions! That's why nature gave you eyes and reason."[57]

Settembrini also chastises Hans Castorp for his love of music, an art the Italian humanist describes as having "something semi-articulate about it, something dubious, irresponsible, indifferent." Like a narcotic, music inflames our emotions, dulls our sense of reason, and is therefore to be regarded as "politically suspect," since it leads us astray from the path of progress and health.[58] Settembrini's comments echo Nietzsche's famous criticism that Wagner's music was "sick." In *The Case of Wagner*, Nietzsche described the composer as a "seducer on a large scale" who "flatters every nihilistic ... instinct and disguises it in music."[59] Much earlier, in *The Birth of Tragedy*, he called German music "a narcotic of the worst kind, doubly dangerous to a people beloved of intoxication, which hails lack of clarity as a virtue."[60]

Once Hans Castorp catches a cold and is sentenced to three weeks of bedrest, Settembrini, concerned by the young engineer's condition, fearing his alienation from life in the flatlands below, visits him in his room—symbolically, he brightens the room by turning on the ceiling lamp as he enters. Aware that Hans Castorp's early contacts with death have given rise to his sympathy with it, Settembrini cautions him that death should not be set up in opposition to life, but rather honored as "the cradle of life, the womb of renewal." When separated from life, he explains, death is a "very depraved force, whose wicked attractions are very strong and without doubt can cause the most abominable confusion of the human mind." Touchingly, Settembrini then asks Hans Castorp if he will allow him to lend a hand in his exercises and experiments, if he will permit him to "play a corrective role" in his intellectual formation—an offer Hans Castorp gratefully accepts.[61]

But his effusive acceptance is ironic, because Hans Castorp was only half-listening. In fact, when Settembrini first enters his room, he blushes, preoccupied as he was with thoughts of Clavdia Chauchat, which is to say thoughts of illness, love, and death.

* * *

Hans Castorp is not the only figure in Mann's fictional world inclined to a sympathy with death. In a famous chapter in *Buddenbrooks*, Thomas Buddenbrook is deeply moved by his reading of Arthur Schopenhauer's *The World as Will and Representation*, particularly by a chapter in the second book, "On Death and Its Relation to the Indestructability of Our Inner Nature," in which Schopenhauer writes that death "often appears as a good thing, as something desired, as a friend."[62] What was death? Thomas asks himself. "It was the return home from long, unspeakably painful wanderings, the correction of a great error, the loosening of tormenting chains, the removal of barriers—it set a horrible accident to rights again."⁶³ In *Death in Venice*, Gustav von Aschenbach renounces every kind of "sympathy for the abyss," yet in his destructive passion for the young Tadzio finally succumbs to his "forbidden longing [for the] unarticulated and immeasurable, for eternity, for nothingness." How can a writer be fit to be an educator, he asks in the novella's final pages, "when one has been born with an incorrigible and natural tendency towards the abyss?"⁶⁴

What does it mean to have sympathy with death? In a notebook entry from 1914, Thomas Mann described it as seeing morality "not in reason and discipline, but in surrendering to what is harmful, so that one feels it moral to degenerate"—a remark Clavdia Chauchat will repeat almost verbatim in a fateful conversation with Hans Castorp.⁶⁵ Elsewhere, Mann calls it the "formula and basic definition of all romanticism."⁶⁶

It has been demonstrated that, while he was writing *The Magic Mountain*, Thomas Mann carefully studied *The Romantic School in Germany*, the second volume of the Danish critic Georg Brandes's *Main Currents of Nineteenth Century Literature* (1872–90).⁶⁷ In chapters 12 and 13, Brandes writes about the German poet and philosopher Novalis (1772–1801), whom he envisions as a guide to the "hidden depths" of the German soul. Mann made copious notes in the margins of his copy of *The Romantic School*, frequently writing "Zbg" (*Der Zauberberg* is the German title of *The Magic Mountain*) next to passages such as this: "To [Novalis], illness is the highest, the only true life: '*Leben ist eine Krankheit des Geistes.*' Life is a disease of the spirit."⁶⁸

No German poet embodied Romanticism's "sympathy with death" more eloquently than Novalis did. His despair at the death of his young fiancée, Sophie von Kühn, in 1797 is described by Brandes as a "longing for death ... and desire for annihilation."⁶⁹ Three years after her death Novalis published his famous *Hymns to Night*, a series of six prose poems that were quite literally the product of the subterranean world: in 1798, Novalis enrolled in the Frieberg

Mining Academy, having previously worked as an official in the saltworks in Weissenfels. Deep in the nocturnal world of the mines, he claimed to have experienced a "joyful elevation above the world."[70]

In his pioneering study of *The Magic Mountain*, Hermann J. Weigand was the first to emphasize Novalis's importance for Mann's conception of the novel. "Ever since the days of Novalis it had been common to find disease interesting and to regard it as a vehicle for spiritual growth," he writes.[71] Weigand, too, emphasizes the centrality of the Romantic movement's interest in disease, particularly in Germany, where it was part of a more general opposition to the nineteenth century's prevailing rationalism. The more he adapts to and even embraces life at the Berghof, Weigand writes, the more Hans Castorp "puts himself beyond the pale of the bourgeois law of mental-moral behavior [and] cuts loose from all that is tried, sanctioned, and familiar."[72]

Cut loose is right: separated from the bourgeois world down in the flatlands, where time is measured according to calendars and clocks, life at the Berghof is lived at a leisurely, glacial pace—while also always threatening to be cut short by tuberculosis. When Hans Castorp first arrives, he is surprised to hear that Joachim will likely stay at the Berghof sanatorium for at least another six months. "Six months? You've already been here for almost that long! We don't have that much time in life!" he exclaims. But Joachim explains that units of time—a day, three weeks, six months—are notions from the flatlands. "You wouldn't believe how fast and loose they play with people's time around here," he says.[73] A little later, as the two cousins partake of one of the novel's many sumptuous meals (asparagus soup, stuffed tomatoes, a roast with vegetables, a bottle of wine, dessert and cheeses), Joachim says that at the Berghof time "doesn't really pass at all, there is no time as such"—thus raising the eerie possibility that the Berghof is indeed, as Settembrini suggests, a kind of underworld.[74]

The narrative of *The Magic Mountain* is divided into seven chapters and spans seven years, but as the philosopher Paul Ricoeur observes, the relation between the length of time narrated by each chapter and the time taken to narrate it, is not proportional.[75] More than half the novel is taken up with the first year that Hans Castorp spends in Davos, the second anniversary of his arrival is not reached until about two-thirds of the way through, and so on. In other words, within the novel's content-time, the years pass with increasing speed. But do they always seem to? Doesn't the reader's sense of time weaken or become suspended?

In a later subchapter, "A Stroll on the Shore," the narrator explains that, while it is not possible to narrate time as such, it is possible to make time the subject of narrative. Indeed, Thomas Mann famously described *The Magic Mountain* as a *Zeitroman,* or time novel. As an example, the reader is reminded of the diaries of opium eaters, whose "temporal scope" during their brief, drug-induced ecstasy expands to years, to decades, even to eternity. Then, as if to challenge us, the narrator wonders whether the reader can recall when certain comments made by Joachim took place, only to reveal that even Hans Castorp himself cannot remember. In fact, Hans Castorp cannot recall at any given moment his own age.[76] Like the opium eaters, and like the dead, he has lost track of time.

* * *

Back in Munich, the time had come for a so-called *Herrenessen,* a gentleman's dinner party. On February 18, 1914, Thomas Mann welcomed his first guests in the new villa on Poschingerstrasse 1. The company that evening including Bruno Frank, a poet, playwright, and neighbor; Alfred Pringsheim, professor of mathematics and Mann's father-in-law; Maximilian Brantl, a lawyer and family friend; and, most significantly, Ernst Bertram, an unsalaried lecturer in German literature at the University of Bonn.

Mann had first met Bertram a year previously, though they began corresponding in 1910, when Bertram read a paper on Thomas Mann's work to the Literary Historical Society that Mann said brought tears to his eyes.[77] In the difficult and lonely years that lay ahead, Bertram became one of Mann's most intimate friends—an intellectual sparring partner and confidant—and, in 1918, godfather to Elisabeth Mann, the family's youngest daughter.

Perhaps Bertram held forth that evening about his planned study of Nietzsche, a study that would eventually appear four years later as *Nietzsche: Attempt at a Mythology*. In the book's second chapter, "Knight, Death, and Devil," which Mann later said he read with great emotion, Bertram celebrates what he regards as Nietzsche's courage "not to avoid what is terrifying—death—or what is questionable—the devil—but rather to seek it out, to affirm it, to *will* it."[78] The chapter's title is a reference to a famous engraving by Albrecht Dürer of the same name, an engraving Nietzsche himself mentions in *The Birth of Tragedy* as a symbol of Schopenhauerian pessimism, and which Thomas Mann said always put him in mind of Nietzsche. "Here we have," Mann writes in a short essay on Dürer, "another essential element of the German and Dürer character-world, intimately bound up with the 'Männlichkeit und Ständigkeit,' the knightliness between the Devil and Death; passion, odour of the tomb, sympathy with suffering."[79]

Like Hans Castorp, Thomas Mann was intimately acquainted with death. "I saw my father die, I know that I will die, and that thought is the most personal to me; it is behind everything that I think and write," he once said.[80] His fiction is filled with some of the most sensitive and moving deaths in literature, from Johann Buddenbrook to Joachim Ziemssen to Nepomuk Schneidewein. It's a current in Mann's writing that pushes against the bourgeois ethos. In his essay "The Storyteller," Walter Benjamin claims the primary goal of bourgeois society is to remove death from public life: "Today, people live in rooms untouched by death. They are newcomers to eternity, and when the end approaches, they are stowed away in sanatoriums or hospitals by their heirs."[81] As a novelist, Mann felt it his duty to describe the whole truth about existence. From the previous century's writers—Tolstoy, Turgenev, Flaubert, Fontane, Ibsen, Jacobsen—he had inherited what he called a "truthful, blunt, and unfeeling submission to the real and the factual."[82]

Mann's inclination toward a sympathy with death was never more obvious than when he listened to music. His daughter Monika regarded music as her father's only weakness. "When Papa is listening to music," she later wrote, "he arouses in me the idea that he is more musical than most musicians taken together but that, had he chosen it or been chosen by it, he would have fallen into an abyss." And what about music would have tipped Mann into the abyss? Monika perceptively continues: "It's inarticulateness would have corrupted him and delivered him to the devil. He is too fully and wholly the man of the word—of the prosaic, the intrinsic, the ascetic—so that music for him is necessarily somehow linked with sin."[83]

Whatever else was discussed during the dinner party on February 18, we can be sure there was music involved. Mann and Bertram occasionally played chamber music together until Mann gave up the violin (he hated being a dilettante and didn't have time to practice, Katia recalled).[84] On the other hand, he always had time for the piano: Klaus remembers his father withdrawing into the drawing room before dinner to play the large Bechstein by the bay windows. Sitting there alone, with dusk lowering its curtains, Mann would play the same rhythm over and over again, "always the same desperate tenderness; always that swelling, weeping, jubilating song."[85] It was always the so-called "Tristan" chord from Wagner's *Tristan and Isolde* (1865), an opera inspired by the writings of—who else?—Arthur Schopenhauer.

*　*　*

The subtle process by which Hans Castorp slowly surrenders to his sympathy for death is one of *The Magic Mountain*'s most remarkable stylistic achievements. Speaking to a group of Princeton students in the late 1930s, Thomas Mann explained that only by reading *The Magic Mountain* twice can the reader "penetrate and enjoy its musical association of ideas."[86] He is referring here to the novel's use of the leitmotif—a technique Mann appropriated from Richard Wagner. The critic Alex Ross defines leitmotifs as "identifying sonic tags" that, in Wagner's music, gesture both forward and backward in time, and serve to "indicate what characters are thinking or sensing—or even what they are unable to perceive."[87]

As an example of this, consider the phrase *horizontal life*, or "living horizontally," which is repeated countless times throughout *The Magic Mountain*, first by Joachim Ziemssen, who is repeating a joke of Ludovico Settembrini's: "Settembrini says we live horizontally—we're the horizontals."[88] Settembrini, of course, is using the metaphor mockingly, since it implies resignation, a refusal or inability to live a normal, healthy, upright life. A few hundred pages later, the phrase is repeated when Hans Castorp, Joachim Ziemssen, and Karen Karstedt, one of the Berghof's hopelessly ill patients, are strolling through the local cemetery. There, they see all the crosses and headstones of the sanatorium's former patients: "unsettled folk who had found their way here from all over the world and had returned now for good and all to the horizontal position."[89] As James Wood has commented: "The metaphor moves back and forth between its meanings, hovering somewhere between life and death, somewhere between art and sickness, somewhere between criticism and surrender, and somehow containing with itself both sets of opposed meanings. And each time the phrase appears, it has a true human pathos and power, not a theoretical one. Here the very form of [*The Magic Mountain*] is itself the master of contradictions."[90] In a novel whose entire community is built on daily rituals and repetitions, these leitmotifs cast a web of repeated words and phrases whose meanings change subtly with each repetition. And these repetitions help us understand what the novel's characters, as Alex Ross puts it, are thinking, sensing, or unable to perceive, such as Hans Castorp's growing sympathy with death.

When he first arrives, this sympathy is still latent, and he himself is not really aware of it, though he recognizes death as something that polite bourgeois society suppresses and avoids—much like sex, a subject with which Hans Castorp is much less familiar (for now). With extraordinary delicacy, Mann shows us how these two preoccupations—death and sex—are gradually linked in our young hero's mind. As Hans Castorp's grandfather is lying-in-state, for example, his old servant Fiete's face is described as being darkened by "a shadow of respectability."[91] Later, when Hans Castorp hears the Russian couple having sex in the adjoining room, his face is described, like Fiete's, as having "darkened" with "a shadow of respectability."[92] In fact, at the very moment he becomes aware of the Russian couple Hans Castorp is gazing down from his balcony with "thoughtful sympathy" at a Mexican patient dressed in all black who is mourning the deaths of her sons, both of whom had been patients at the Berghof.

Tellingly, the phrase is repeated again in the famous scene in which Hans Castorp goes in for his X-ray. In the little room in the basement adjoining the lab is Clavdia Chauchat, likewise waiting to be examined by Director Behrens and Dr. Krokowski. Staring at her, observing her legs, hips, arms, and breasts, Hans Castorp becomes lost in thought, then suddenly recalls that she, too, is there to be X-rayed, and that Director Behrens will soon be looking inside her body. At that thought, Hans Castorp "turned his head to one side, and his face darkened with the shadow of respectability."[93]

Death and sex are most clearly imbricated in the figure of Clavdia Chauchat herself. This enchanting Russian patient, whose never-to-be-seen French husband is a civil servant working in Dagestan, is the siren whose song so bewitches Hans Castorp that he throws caution and reason to the wind and—unbeknownst to himself—decides to stay in the sanatorium. Though he doesn't actually speak to her until the "Walpurgis Night" chapter (some three-hundred-odd pages into the novel), it is she who occupies his thoughts and fantasies, and who unconsciously convinces him to stay—to become, in effect, ill.

One of the reasons for Hans Castorp's attraction to Clavdia Chauchat is that she physically resembles a former classmate of his, Pribislav Hippe, who at age thirteen suggestively lets Hans Castorp borrow a pencil from him. Hippe, too, has "bluish-grey" and "slightly slanted" eyes, a "husky, opaque, slightly gruff voice," and "prominent, strong, distinctive cheekbones" that prompt his fellow classmates to nickname him "the Kirghiz," the same Asiatic tribe whose features Hans Castorp identifies in Clavdia Chauchat.[94] Despite being from Mecklenburg in the north of Germany, Hippe becomes associated in Hans Castorp's mind with the East and, by extension, with the opposition to the Western bourgeois world that Chauchat, too, represents.

Hippe, or the memory of him, will surface unbidden whenever Hans Castorp sees or thinks of Clavdia Chauchat, to the extent that the young boy and the tubercular woman become almost indistinguishable in his mind. Chauchat's appearance, in fact, is often described as either boyish or verging on the androgynous. Observing her physical features as they await their X-rays, Hans Castorp notices that she is "not at all broad in the hips," just as earlier on he thought her "not at all suited for motherhood."[95] This, of course, casts a shadow on the question of Hans Castorp's sexuality, something Settembrini alludes to when, comparing him to a young nun, he explains that he didn't mean to "cast any aspersions on your masculinity."[96]

Settembrini doesn't need to: Hans Castorp has done it for us already. The point is driven home when, on Walpurgis Night, he finally finds the courage to speak to Clavdia Chauchat. And what are the first words he addresses to her? *"Do you have a pencil, perhaps?"* And as he utters these words, he imagines he is "standing in the brick schoolyard" where he once asked Pribislav Hippe the very same question.[97]

At this point in the novel, the philosophical battle lines between time and eternity, health and illness, reason and dissolution, have been drawn, and Hans Castorp, for now, has picked his side. He tipsily thanks Settembrini for trying—in vain—to play a corrective role in his education at the Berghof, saying, "You're not just anybody, a face with a name, you're a representative of something, Herr Settembrini, a representative here and now and at my side—that's what you are," thereby acknowledging him as the voice of humanistic reason, and his role in the novel as a representative of a specific worldview.[98] Yet despite his genuine affection for the Italian, Hans Castorp goes to Clavdia Chauchat—goes East, so to speak. And as he does, he hears Settembrini calling out behind him: "*Eh! Ingegnere! Aspetti! Che cosa fa! Ingegnere! Un po' di ragione, sa! Ma è matto questo ragazzo!*"[99] ("Hey, engineer! Wait! What are you doing! Engineer! A little bit of reason, please! But he is crazy, this young man!")[100]

What ensues is one of the most famous exchanges in the novel: the first conversation between Hans Castorp and Clavdia Chauchat, most of it in spoken in French—a conversation, what's more, for which Hans Castorp has spent many months readying himself. Since his passage from visitor to patient, from healthy to ill, he has been consumed with the study of life and death, primarily from a physiological perspective. He drags his cousin to pay a visit to Behrens at his residence in the northwest wing of the Berghof, where Hans Castorp rambles on about illness and death. "If someone is interested in life," Hans Castorp inquires of the director, "it's death he's particularly interested in. Isn't that so?"[101] Following this visit, Hans Castorp begins his studies of life and death by ordering one volume after another on anatomy, physiology, and biology from the local bookdealer—tellingly, he finds that *Ocean Steamships* "no longer had anything to say to him."[102] Shortly after this he begins his visits to both the recently deceased and the so-called *moribundi*, the most serious cases at the Berghof. As he does so Hans Castorp seems to us, the readers, greatly changed from the civilian who arrived in Davos just a few months prior. Standing at the bedside of a recently departed patient, for instance, he holds forth to his cousin about the Latin one uses when one speaks about the dead:

> It is sacred Latin, the dialect of monks, a chant from the Middle Ages, so to speak, a kind of muted, subterranean monotone. Settembrini would not be pleased with it, it's nothing for humanists and republicans and pedagogues of that ilk. It comes from a different intellectual direction—from the other one. It seems to me you have to be clear about these two intellectual directions, or dispositions, as they might more accurately be called—the religious and the freethinking. They both have their good points, but what I particularly have against the freethinking one—the Settembrinian one, I mean—is that it assumes that only it truly represents human dignity. That is an exaggeration. In its own way, the other contains a great deal of human dignity, too, and contributes to moral conduct and decorum and noble formality, certainly more than "freethinking" does—and always with an eye to human weakness and frailty.[103]

In just a little over six months, Hans Castorp has come a long way intellectually—far enough that he can now articulate his doubts

SYMPATHY WITH DEATH

and reservations about Settembrini's liberal worldview in a language of his own. We recall how unfamiliar the Italian humanist's manner of speaking at first seemed to Hans Castorp; recall his disbelief at Settembrini's assessment of music as having "something only semi-articulate about it, something dubious, irresponsible, indifferent"; recall that Hans Castorp previously thought of progress as "something like the improvement of hoists and cranes during the nineteenth century," rather than as a political and social ideal; and finally, how opposition begins to stir in his soul, how he tests Settembrini's views and prepares himself to be influenced by them, only to find it "all the more permissible afterward to let his thoughts and dreams run free in another direction, in the *opposite* direction."[104]

And standing there, in the direction opposite reason, the world republic, and beautiful literature, is Clavdia Chauchat with her Kirghiz eyes, high cheekbones, and chewed-up fingernails. On Walpurgis Night she tells her "little bourgeois," as she calls Hans Castorp, that she loves her freedom and independence above all else, that it is her illness that allows her liberty from the conventions of bourgeois morality. "It seems to us," she tells Hans Castorp with Nietzschean aplomb, "that one ought not to search for morality in virtue, which is to say in reason, in discipline, in good behavior, in respectability—but in just the opposite, I would say: in sin, in abandoning oneself to danger, to whatever can harm us, destroy us."[105]

Hans Castorp, meanwhile, confesses his love for her, tells her that he knew her from before, long ago, when he was just a schoolboy and needed to borrow a pencil, and that the moist spot Behrens found in his lungs is "the lingering traces of my age-old love for you, proof that I was sick even back then." Then, in a long, mock-lyrical passage, he rhapsodizes: "The body, love, death, are simply one and the same. Because the body is sickness and depravity, it is what produces death, yes, both of them, love and death, are carnal, and that is the source of their terror and great magic! But death, you see, is on the one hand something so disreputable, so impudent that it makes us blush with shame; and on the other it is a most solemn and majestic force—something much more lofty than a life spent laughing, earning money, and stuffing one's belly—much more venerable than progress chattering away the ages"[106]—whereupon Clavdia Chauchat thanks him and takes her leave, before adding: "Don't forget to return my pencil."[107]

* * *

On May 12, 1914, Katia Mann finally returned from Arosa, which meant family life on Poschingerstrasse could begin at last—no doubt a great relief to Thomas Mann, who always felt lost without his wife at his side. "Theoretically he is the head [of the family], practically he is the child," Monika later recalled.[108] Simple household matters, such as the children losing their gloves or having to see the dentist, were left for Katia to handle. Klaus Mann quipped that their father would be surprised to learn that his children even had gloves or teeth.[109] Mann himself was fond of the story of Johann Sebastian Bach's domestic cluelessness. When the great composer was approached about the details of his late wife's funeral arrangements, Bach said through a curtain of tears: "Ask my wife!"

Poschingerstrasse was the family's home for almost two decades. The nerve-center, naturally, was Thomas Mann's study: a dark, moderate-sized room with a constant aroma of ink, tobacco, leather, and eau de cologne. The writing desk was kept meticulously neat, while books and papers were piled high in teeming heaps on the chairs, the chaise-longue, and the round oak table. The door was closed from nine in the morning until noon, the hours when Mann was writing, and then again in the afternoon, when he napped or chipped away at his voluminous correspondence. "During all these hours we had to be quiet," Klaus and Erika recalled, "and there were terrible moments when he would come to the door of his study, demanding 'Qui-et, there!' in a voice in which vexation struggled with the incapacity to believe we had forgotten again."[110]

In the daytime Mann, like God in heaven, was everywhere present but nowhere visible. Yet the oft-repeated claim that he was an indifferent or cruel parent seems inaccurate. "There is nothing frightful about Father," Klaus recalled. "He is gentle and good . . . at once touchy and lenient."[111] Barred in the daytime, the children were admitted into the study in the evenings, when the Magician, as they nicknamed their father, read to them from *Arabian Nights*, *Grimm's Fairytales*, or a volume of stories by Tolstoy.[112] He did so slowly, in a sonorous voice, all the while tapping the ash from his cigarette into a Turkish brass cup. These were cherished moments. So too were holidays and family gatherings, occasions on which Mann behaved like "a little schoolboy," carefully arranging the wax figures under the tree at Christmas and adorning the family dog with a ribbon.[113]

When he wasn't at home writing, Mann kept up with the cultural life in Munich. During the winter and spring of 1914, he attended a lecture by the Viennese feuilletonist Karl Kraus and a performance of Shakespeare's *The Tempest* at the Munich Art Theatre, as well as a banquet honoring the playwright Frank Wedekind on his fiftieth birthday.

Though it was hardly Paris or London, and least of all Berlin, Munich had enjoyed a reputation as a cultural metropolis since before the turn of the century, when writers like Henrik Ibsen and the Nobel Prize–winning Paul Heyse called it home. "To be in Munich and not see Ibsen is like being in Rome and not seeing the Pope," the novelist Arne Garborg once quipped.[114] In the Schwabing district, places like Café Stefanie, nicknamed Café Megalomania, was always filled with aspiring young painters and sculptors, many of whom had come to Munich to enjoy the city's unique blend of Bavarian gaiety and bohemian idleness. "Few places are so democratic," an American traveler informed readers of *The Century* magazine. "In the great beer halls where Munich spends many of its leisure moments, one man is exactly as good as another."[115]

This democratic good cheer did not extend to all of Munich's citizens, however. The relative tolerance enjoyed by the city's mostly assimilated Jewish population was increasingly under threat by populist fears of the so-called *Ostjuden,* Jewish refugees from the East, many of whom had fled Russian pogroms. Munich's first anti-Jewish organization, the Deutsch-Sozialer Verein, was founded in 1891.[116] One of the organization's more vocal members warned against being "sucked dry by the international Jewish stock-exchange pump" and "driven into the arms of a Social Democracy by a cartel of usurious Jewish cattle dealers, heartless clearance-sale jobbers, and aggressive pushcart peddlers."[117] Thomas Mann would later draw on the specter of German anti-Semitism in *The Magic Mountain* for the minor character Wiedemann, a businessman and anti-Semite who appears toward the end of the novel. A subscriber to a fictional anti-Semitic newspaper called *The Aryan Light,* his "erroneous belief" is described as "a restless paranoia that drove him to pluck out any uncleanness that lay hidden or disguised in his vicinity, to hold it up to public disgrace."[118]

The rise of anti-Semitism was compounded by the rise of the German nationalist movement. According to the historian Fritz Stern, "It was in the 1890s that cultural pessimism and antimodernity became the twin resentments of the disaffected, conservative elements of imperial Germany." One of the best-known nationalist organizations was the Pan-German League, whose manifesto advocated for the "preservation and expansion of the German spirit" and the awakening of "the racial and cultural kinship of all sections of the German people."[119] The Munich branch of the league, one of the largest in the country, was led by the publisher Julius Friedrich Lehmann, who explained that the league "seeks, as much as possible, to exclude [Jewish] influence from our political and cultural life."[120]

No one knew it at the time, but within just a few years these two intertwined ideological movements, anti-Semitism and pan-Germanism, would find their most significant supporter in the guise of a twenty-four-year-old aspiring artist who had arrived in Munich in May 1913. This young man found lodgings on Schleissheimer Strasse, settling in a small, spartan room with a view of the Löwenbräukeller, one of the beer halls he would frequent when he wasn't at home reading or out somewhere painting. On the registration form he was required to fill out, the newcomer signed himself: "Adolf Hitler, architectural painter from Vienna."[121]

CHAPTER 3

The Thunderbolt, 1914–1915

On the morning of June 28, 1914, shortly after surviving an amateurishly executed bombing, the Austrian Archduke Franz Ferdinand and his wife, Sophie Chotek, were shot to death in Sarajevo by a twenty-year-old Bosnian Serb, Gavrilo Princip. At the time, few people imagined that this half-bungled assassination would have the cataclysmic consequences it did. In some places public reaction to the archduke's death was muted, even indifferent. In Joseph Roth's novel *The Radetzky March*, rumor of the assassination reaches a remote garrison town on the Russian border, where a group of dissipated Austro-Hungarian soldiers drunkenly deliberate whether or not to call off their party. "We don't care about rumors! I shit on rumors! If it's true, we'll learn soon enough anyway!" one officer exclaims.[1] Roth's close friend Stefan Zweig, who was summering in Baden bei Wien at the time, later recalled that the initial shock and excitement of the crowds gathering in the main squares was quick to die down. "Two hours later signs of genuine mourning were no longer to be seen," he wrote. "The throngs laughed and chattered and as evening advanced music was resumed at public resorts."[2] Even in Vienna, the amusements in the Prater Park remained open to the public.

That summer, Thomas Mann and his family had as usual retired to their country villa in Bad Tölz, a small but popular spa town some twenty-odd miles south of Munich. Built in 1908, the villa had a spacious garden for the children to play in and was located near Klammer Pond, where they learned to swim. Klaus

Mann called it "the beloved idyll of so many summers," and there was nothing to suggest 1914 would be any different.³ The weather was warm and picnic-perfect; all throughout town carefree vacationers drank cool beer in the balmy sun, crowding the cobbled Markstrasse from the Stadttor down to the banks of the Isar River.

But by early July, it was clear that some sort of crisis was brewing in the aftermath of the archduke's assassination. Military leaders in Austria began clamoring for a preventive war against Serbia, while the Hungarian prime minister cautioned against disturbing the peace. Kaiser Wilhelm II's response was characteristically baffling: he encouraged a de-escalation while also offering Germany's unconditional support of the dual monarchy—the famous "blank check"—before swiftly departing for a vacation on his royal yacht in the Norwegian fjords.

On the surface, it was not clear to anyone whether this was yet another Balkan crisis or something more ominous. No doubt many people felt like Robert Musil's Ulrich, who, in *The Man without Qualities,* wonders to himself, "Was there a war actually going on in the Balkans? Some sort of intervention was undoubtedly going on, but whether it was war was hard to tell. So much was astir in the world."⁴ Even an obsessive newspaper reader like Thomas Mann betrayed no urgent concern about the fate of the continent. He went about his business as usual, briefly interrupting his summer retreat for a trip to Freiburg in mid-July to read from the manuscript of *The Magic Mountain.* Writing to his mother, he assured her that war would be avoided: "They will go to the brink and then somehow reach an agreement."⁵ This was not an unreasonable assumption. After all, in the last decade, brinkmanship had averted one crisis after another—who was to say that this time things would be any different?⁶

But as July drew to a close, the political situation escalated dramatically. One day, as the older Mann children were about to perform a play in the garden with their cousins, they were briskly interrupted by their governess. "You'd better forget about it," she told them. "War has been declared on Germany and our Austrian ally."[7] The Mann family quickly packed up the house and hastened back to Munich, where Viktor Mann and Katia's brother Heinz Pringsheim had both been called up for duty and would shortly be departing for the front.

Within a month of the archduke's assassination, a series of diplomatic blunders and acts of political incompetence had ushered Europe into its first military conflict in over forty years. The continent's tenuous alliances proved no match for decades of military armament, colonial rivalry, and mutual distrust. All attempts at de-escalation failed miserably. By early August, the Central Powers of Germany and Austria-Hungary were at war with the Allied Powers of Britain, France, Russia, and Serbia. In time, the total number of belligerents would total thirty-eight.

Serenus Zeitblom, the narrator of Mann's novel *Doctor Faustus* (1947), recalls that "the first blazing days of 1914 found me changing from one overcrowded train to another in teeming railroad stations—their platforms filled with rows of abandoned baggage." Describing the public response to the outbreak of war, he claims "there is no denying that in our Germany its primary effect was elation and historical exuberance, the rapture of beginning anew and tossing everything aside, liberation from a global stagnation that could take us no farther, enthusiasm for the future, an appeal to duty and manliness—in short, a heroic festival."[8]

Though historians like Jeffrey Verhey have since questioned the extent of the German public's enthusiasm for war, it was clearly a time in which emotions ran high.[9] As soon as news of the mobilization order spread, hundreds of thousands of people gathered in the country's largest squares and joined in the general confusion, fear, and excitement. Massive crowds marched and cheered through the streets, waving their flags and singing the "Deutschlandlied" and "Die Wacht am Rhein." Others panicked and withdrew all their money from banks, or began hoarding food, forcing shopkeepers to close their stores for fear of looting. Others still responded with indifference—like Franz Kafka, who in his diary on August 2 casually wrote: "Germany has declared war on Russia. Swimming in the afternoon."[10]

In some cases, the excitement erupted into violence. When the house band at Café Fahrig on Munich's Karlplatz was instructed to stop playing patriotic songs, a group of drunken patrons decided to smash up the place.[11] A few days later, while walking across the very same square, the playwright Ernst Toller witnessed a mob harass and beat up two women for speaking French: "They protested that they were Germans, but it did not avail them in the least," he wrote.[12] A little farther up the street, on Odeonsplatz, thousands of war enthusiasts gathered to cheer the declaration of war on Russia on August 1. Among them was Adolf Hitler. He is visible in a famous photograph of the crowd, standing open-mouthed and gazing in the direction of the Feldherrnhalle. The outbreak of war had roused him from his lonely, impoverished existence to a life swelling with purpose. "To me those hours seemed like a release from the painful feelings of my youth," he would later write in *Mein Kampf.* "Even today I am not ashamed to say that, overpowered by stormy enthusiasm, I fell down on my knees and thanked heaven from my overflowing heart."[13] He volunteered for military service at once. By late October, he was on his way to the Western Front to fight in the First Battle of Ypres.[14]

The writer Ernst Jünger, Hitler's senior by four years, likewise volunteered for service immediately. For him, too, the outbreak of war felt like a release, an unbuttoning of the starchy world of Wilhelmine Germany. In the opening pages of *Storm of Steel* (1920), his unparalleled narrative of his wartime experience, Jünger recounts the euphoria he and other young men felt in the early days of the conflict as they volunteered to join the army:

We had come from lecture halls, school desks and factory workbenches, and over the brief weeks of training, we had bonded together into one large and enthusiastic group. Grown up in an age of security, we shared a yearning for danger, for the experience of the extraordinary. We were enraptured by war. We had set out in a rain of flowers, in a drunken atmosphere of blood and roses. Surely the war had to supply us with what we wanted; the great, the overwhelming, the hallowed experience. We thought of it as manly, as action, a merry dueling party on flowered, blood-bedewed meadows. "No finer death in all the world than . . ." Anything to participate, not to have to stay at home![15]

What explains this euphoria, this sudden "yearning for danger"? Europe had been at peace since 1871, the longest such period in its history, and despite a multitude of conflicts in overseas colonies and growing unrest in the Balkans, few people seriously expected anything to change. "People no more believed in the possibility of barbaric relapses, such as wars between the nations of Europe, than they believed in ghosts and witches," Stefan Zweig wrote of his parents' generation in *The World of Yesterday*; "our fathers were doggedly convinced of the infallibly binding power of tolerance and reconciliation. They honestly thought that divergences between nations and religious faiths would gradually flow into a sense of common humanity, so that peace and security, the greatest of goods, would come to all mankind."[16]

Given all that we know today about the First World War—the mustard gas and machine guns, the waterlogged, rat-infested trenches, the millions of anonymous deaths by shells falling from the sky—it is difficult to understand why anyone would welcome a calamity of such magnitude. But as the historian Jörn Leonhard has shown, no one in the summer of 1914 had any real sense of the possible dimensions of the war, not even those military leaders now hastening to wage it—despite the brutal testing of new military technologies on the native populations of colonies in Asia and Africa.[17] There was a widespread assumption that the war wouldn't last beyond Christmas, and that, despite the many advances in weapons technology, traditional infantry offensives would prove decisive. (Many armies didn't even introduce camouflaged uniforms until heavy losses early on had made it plain that soldiers decked out in colorful tunics made easy targets.)[18] There was simply *no* historical frame of reference for the anonymous, mechanized slaughter of millions that would make the war so melodramatically disproportionate to its presumed ends, in Paul Fussell's caustic words.[19]

In order to understand the excitement of young men like Adolf Hitler and Ernst Jünger, or the countless other writers and intellectuals who cheered the war, we have to try to forget what we know about the war and its outcome and look back instead over the years preceding it, that period of extraordinary and unprecedented social, technological, and cultural transformation. "Modernity did not rise virgin-born from the trenches of the Somme," the historian Philipp Blom writes. "Well before 1914, it had already taken a firm hold on the minds and lives of Europe. The War acted not as a creator, but as a catalyst, forcing old structures to collapse more quickly and new identities to assert themselves more readily."[20]

In Germany, the transformation from an agrarian society to an industrial empire had not been without its drawbacks. Many German writers and thinkers feared the kind of society that would arise from modernity and its (in their minds) attendant scientific-rational paradigm. Apocalyptic thinking was widespread. "The whole of our European culture," Nietzsche wrote in his notebooks, "has long been in an agony of suspense, increasing with each passing decade, as if in anticipation of disaster, like a torrent, restlessly, violently rushing *to its end,* refusing to reflect, afraid to reflect."[21] In influential books like Max Nordau's *Degeneration*

(1892), opposition to modernity mixed with a post-Darwinian anxiety about health and race to form a particularly noxious atmosphere of declinism and doom. Others quite simply found life in an age of peace and positivism to be existentially boring. The expressionist poet Georg Heym spoke for many when, in 1911, he wrote in his diary, "my God—I am suffocating with my unused enthusiasm in this banal time.... I hope at the very least for a war. But even that does not happen."[22]

When it came, the war served as a solution to the profound ambivalence with which so many writers and intellectuals regarded Germany's unification and modernization. Here, they felt, was the moral and spiritual unity 1871 had lacked; here was a chance to halt Germany's inexorable drift toward the banal and soulless materialism of Western Europe. "German thought and German feeling," the economist Werner Sombart wrote, "express themselves in the unanimous rejection of everything that even distantly approximates English or western European thought."[23] In accordance with this line of thinking, the war was recognized as *eine innere Notwendigkeit*, an inner necessity, one that promised deliverance from the menace of modernity.[24]

The war also injected German writers with an intoxicating sense of purpose, the longed-for recognition that they, too, were vital to the survival of the nation. Before the war's outbreak, according to Roy Pascal, most German writers "stood remote from and hostile to the practical objectives and actions of national and imperialistic politicians."[25] In August 1914, all of that changed virtually overnight. If, before the war, culture was of only marginal concern to the clanging machinery of the German state apparatus, it was now hoped that a new society in which state and culture finally became one would emerge from the rubble. Some writers therefore volunteered for the army, while others at once set about writing militaristic propaganda defending the German Empire. On October 4, 1914, ninety-three "representatives of German science and art," including Richard Dehmel, Wilhelm Röntgen, Max Planck, Ludwig Fulda, and Gerhart Hauptmann, all signed a letter addressed "To the Civilized World," protesting the "lies and calumnies" of Germany's enemies and vowing to "carry on this war to the end as a civilized nation, to whom the legacy of a Goethe, a Beethoven, and a Kant is just as sacred as its own hearths and homes."[26]

The political unity that had eluded Germany until its unification in 1871 was compensated for by the belief that Germans were united by a shared culture, that Germany was above all a *Kulturnation*, or nation of culture—that culture was, in fact, "a noble substitute for politics."[27] For the writers, artists, scientists, and intellectuals who signed the manifesto, any attack on Germany was therefore also an attack on its most sacred cultural achievements. Alarmingly, German militarism was even seen as inseparable from those achievements: "Without German militarism German culture would already have disappeared from the soil of the earth," the manifesto read.[28] It was surely statements like this that eventually led the German-Jewish writer and industrialist Walther Rathenau to suggest eradicating the word *Kultur* from the German vocabulary.

Thomas Mann was not among the signatories of the "Manifesto of the 93," as "To the Civilized World" became known. Given that he was not (yet) a Nobel laureate and didn't have any institutional affiliation or academic titles, it is unlikely that he was approached. Nevertheless, as we'll soon see, he was in broad agreement with its general sentiment.

* * *

One day in the spring of 1908, almost a year into his new existence as a patient at the Berghof, Hans Castorp is walking along the street in Davos Dorf with his soldier cousin when the subject of war is suddenly broached. Hans Castorp expresses his hope that a war will be avoided—only to be swiftly rebuffed by Joachim Ziemssen, who tells him, "War is necessary. Without war the world would soon go to rot, as Moltke said."[29]

The two cousins soon come across Settembrini, who in the weeks since Walpurgis Night has left the Berghof and taken lodgings in town above a tailor's shop, where a Galician Jew turned Jesuit scholar by the name of Leo Naphta also lives. He is there on the street with Settembrini, striking in his "caustic" ugliness and by the coarseness of his voice, which sounds like "a piece of cracked porcelain when you rap it with a knuckle."[30] Reluctantly, because he fears yet another adverse influence on Hans Castorp, Settembrini introduces the parties to one another, at which point the conversation soon returns to the topic of war. Hans Castorp admits that he understands nothing of politics and hasn't looked at a newspaper since arriving at the Berghof—an admission Settembrini at once chastises him for. The Italian humanist, of course, is well informed on current events and sincerely believes the world is headed in the right direction: "The general European atmosphere was imbued with ideas of peace and plans for disarmament. Democratic ideals were on the march. He claimed to have confidential information that the Young Turks had just completed preparations for their revolutionary uprising. Turkey as a constitutional nation-state—what a triumph for humanity!" Naphta vehemently disagrees. The political developments Settembrini praises are merely "the last, feeble twitches of what little instinct for self-preservation a doomed international system still has. The catastrophe will, indeed must, follow—is coming toward us from all directions."[31]

In historical terms Naphta is right of course. Catastrophe did follow: the First World War is a source of dramatic irony in *The Magic Mountain* because we know it is coming but the characters do not. It is like some distantly approaching army that can be heard but not seen. And yet, strictly speaking, Settembrini is not wrong either: at the time this exchange takes place there were plenty of reasons for thinking that a European war would be averted. Depending on where one looked, there was even cause for optimism. The publication in 1889 of Bertha von Suttner's novel *Lay Down Your Arms!* helped to inspire popular interest in the burgeoning peace movement. In 1905 the Anglo-German Friendship Committee was established in response to the naval arms race between Britain and Germany. The Hague Conventions of 1899 and 1907, alluded to by Settembrini, marked a shift in thinking about international law and the use of courts of arbitration to settle disputes among nations. And surely the fact that Europe's royal families were all related and their nations economically intertwined (Britain and Germany were each other's biggest trading partners in the years before the war) meant that military conflict was never a serious possibility. "There will be no war in the future," the Russian financier Ivan Bloch flatly declared in 1899, "for it has become impossible, now that it is clear that war means suicide."[32]

It's easy to scoff at such remarks, knowing as we do that continental suicide was exactly what lay in store for the European powers, but as the historian Christopher Clark cautions us this is a problem of perspective that leaves little room for contingency, choice, or agency.[33] Nothing was predetermined. As late as July 1914 the possibility of averting an all-out war still—narrowly—existed. As late as early August, a member of Germany's general staff remarked in his diary: "If anyone had told me [in July] that the world would be ablaze a month later, I would have only looked at him with pity. For, after the various events of the last years, the Morocco-Algeciras crisis, the annexation crisis of Bosnia-Herzegovina, one had slowly but surely lost the belief in the war."[34]

Mann is also making a subtle joke here. Settembrini has reprimanded Hans Castorp for not reading newspapers once before. In the earlier subchapter "Encyclopedia," he asks the young engineer if he has heard of the earthquake in Lisbon. Hans Castorp mistakenly assumes Settembrini is referring to some recent event that has slipped his notice, but the Italian means, of course, the 1755 earthquake that devastated the Portuguese capital, killing tens of thousands of people. News of the catastrophe spread quickly and was widely discussed by Enlightenment thinkers across Europe, challenging the foundations of their philosophical optimism. Settembrini explains that Voltaire rebelled against the earthquake, protesting "in the name of the mind and reason against this scandalous offense of nature."[35]

At the novel's end, when the "thunderbolt" of war strikes Europe (a knowing reference to Nietzsche, who in a letter to Erwin Rohde described the Franco-Prussian War as "a terrible thunderclap"),[36] Hans Castorp is likened to an "entranced sleeper ... sheepishly rubbing his eyes, like a man who, despite many an admonition, has failed to read the daily papers."[37] But the very man who admonished Hans Castorp to read the newspapers did not believe war was coming either: Settembrini's liberal rationalism is shaken to its core, just as the optimism of Enlightenment philosophers was by the Lisbon earthquake. And surely Mann is mocking himself too: what was he before the war if not a dutiful, newspaper-reading bourgeois who believed, until the final moment, that war would be averted?

To most of the frivolous and distracted patients of the International Sanitorium Berghof—"creatures of the moment," the narrator writes, "incapable of thinking that things may change again, craving constant variety"—events in the "flatlands" are of almost no concern. "Things are only serious down Below," Joachim Ziemssen at one point says. Indeed, part of *The Magic Mountain*'s greatness lies in precisely this portrayal of a society unaware of its impending collapse and destruction. As Golo Mann would later describe the mood of those years:

Never had a great European war seemed more probable than in the years before 1914. People knew this; every citizen could know it and yet nobody really believed it. Their reason could have told people that war was close at hand; their powers of imagination failed to make it a living threat. This was because they had long lived in peace and had become used to it, to a solid, international order of things, to banknotes that could be exchanged anywhere for gold, to travel without passport. Was all this to suddenly stop and make way for an unknown nightmare? The living know they will die but they do not believe it because they have become used to life and only know life. Such, more or less, must have been the mood before 1914.[38]

Thomas Mann first commented on the impending war in a letter to Heinrich on July 30, 1914. Telephone lines to Munich had been temporarily blocked for military purposes and there were rumors of a mobilization order. "I have to say I feel shaken and confounded by the terrible weight of reality," he wrote. "I was optimistic and skeptical until today—one's temperament is too reasonable for the monstrous to be regarded as possible. And I still incline to the belief that it will be pushed only to a certain point. But who knows what insanity can seize Europe once it has been pulled into the fray!"[39]

The next day it was official. On the night of July 31, drummers marched through the streets of Munich sounding the alarm for mobilization. In the next few weeks, 3,000,000 soldiers and 850,000 horses would be transported on railroads across Germany to front lines in the east and the west. Between August 2 and 18, a military train crossed the Hohenzollern Bridge over the Rhine every ten minutes. The very technology that in the nineteenth century had become a symbol of civilizational progress was now used to reverse that progress—a hideous irony Leo Naphta might have relished.

Thomas Mann's attitude toward the war soon changed profoundly. Was it being back in Munich and seeing the cheering crowds, the marching troops, the singing, the flags, the enthusiasm? Whatever the case, when he next wrote to Heinrich on August 7, he and Katia having in the meantime returned to Tölz, Thomas Mann sounded like a religious convert:

> I still feel as if I'm dreaming—and yet I suppose I should be ashamed that I didn't think it possible and didn't see that the catastrophe was bound to come. What a visitation! What will Europe look like, inwardly and outwardly, when it is over? I personally have to prepare for a total change in our material circumstances. It is fairly certain that if the war lasts long, I shall be what is called "ruined." So be it! What would that signify compared with the upheavals, especially the large-scale psychic upheavals, which war must necessarily bring? Shouldn't we be grateful for the totally unexpected chance to experience such mighty things? My chief feeling is a tremendous curiosity—and, I admit, the deepest sympathy for the execrated, indecipherable, fateful Germany.[40]

We can only imagine Heinrich Mann's response to this letter. Poor Heinrich who, to his undying credit, remained steadfast and unwavering in his opposition to the war and Germany's conduct in it. During the July Crisis, he had completed the manuscript of *Der Untertan*, which had begun serialization in *Zeit im Bild* in the spring. On August 13, however, he received word that serialization would cease immediately. The novel's satirical portrayal of a nation in thrall to militarism, nationalism, and commercialism was viewed as anti-German at a time that demanded national unity. "At this moment a great public organ cannot criticize German conditions in the form of a satire," the editors of *Zeit im Bild* wrote to Heinrich. "We might face the most severe censorship problems were we to publish anything of the least political intent, particularly regarding the person of the Kaiser."⁴¹ As a result, *Der Untertan* would not appear in book form until 1918, after the war was over.⁴²

The timing of *Zeit im Bild*'s decision could not have been worse. After more than a decade without a fixed address, Heinrich had recently returned to Munich with his fiancée, the Prague-born actress Maria "Mimi" Kanova, settling on Leopoldstrasse on the other side of the Englischer Garten. At the age of forty-three, the calm and constancy of domestic life finally beckoned: the couple were married in the midst of all the upheaval on August 12. Heinrich had asked Thomas to be a witness at the wedding, but the mobilization of troops made the train ride from Tölz to Munich virtually impossible. In the end, neither brother ever attended the other's wedding.

Adding to the tension between them was the issue of the two thousand marks Thomas had loaned Heinrich a few years earlier, a sum he told his older brother not to worry about paying back.⁴³ Yet in a letter of September 13, 1914, Thomas asked if Heinrich might be able to return the money after all, given the financial constraints the war would undoubtedly bring. Heinrich replied that he would be able to repay him half the amount, not more. His own financial situation was hardly ideal, especially now that *Der Untertan* would not be published in book form. "My work will be just as little suited after the war as now," he wrote, a little bitterly. But Thomas wouldn't hear of such defeatism. "I don't share your pessimism about your work and its future in Germany," he responded. "Rather, I think you are being most unfair to German culture. Your fame has been climbing steadily these past ten years. Can you really think that as a result of this great, fundamentally decent, and in fact stirring peoples' war, Germany would be so set back in her cultivation or ethos that she could permanently reject your gifts?"⁴⁴

One imagines Heinrich reading this letter with a steadying hand on his brow, shaking his head and rolling his eyes. A decent war? A stirring *peoples'* war? Did Thomas have the slightest idea what was happening? The war was quickly metastasizing in ways no one would have thought possible just a few weeks earlier. The use of modern artillery weapons, which did not require a target to be within direct line of sight, made a mockery of the virtues of patriotism and courage the authorities were drilling into their troops. The war made killing and being killed totally anonymous. The number of casualties speak volumes: by the end of September, after less than two months of war, 26,000 German troops were dead, 46,000 were missing, and more than 130,000 had been wounded.[45] Within the first five months, German losses would number more than a million.[46]

As part of the Schlieffen Plan to encircle the French army, the Germans ruthlessly swept through neutral Belgium in August and September, leveling whole towns and killing thousands of civilians. The occupation of Leuven, a small town sixteen miles east of Brussels, provoked widespread international outrage when the German army, fearing Belgian resistance and the arrival of British troops, simply laid waste to the town. The university library and its 230,000 books were deliberately burned to the ground; hundreds of civilians were dragged from their homes and summarily shot; the town's remaining population of roughly fifteen hundred people were deported to internment camps. German soldiers systematically looted the abandoned homes and set fire to the remains—actions that would echo throughout Europe and feed Anglo-French caricatures of Germans as war-mongering barbarians.[47]

As news of the calamitous early weeks of war spread, Heinrich Mann grew increasingly despondent. His youngest brother, Viktor, remembered him during those early August days as unusually, even desperately sad. "He who usually carried his head so straight now had it half-bowed and was always looking at the ground."[48] One evening in late September, Heinrich went to Torggelstube, a wine bar in the center of Munich frequented by the city's literati. It was located next door to the Hofbräuhaus where, just six years later, Hitler would announce the National Socialist Program. Erich Mühsam reported that while all the other patrons drunkenly celebrated Germany's decisive victory over the Russian Second Army at the Battle of Tannenberg in East Prussia, Heinrich threw up his arms in protest: "What's the use of victories? Winning and losing are just concepts. How can a country win if it is hated by the rest of the world?"[49] In Bad Tölz, stationed in his small study with its pastoral view of meadows, valleys, and spruce trees, Thomas Mann asked himself the same question, with the difference that he viewed hatred of Germany as proof of its distinction, its radical conservative opposition to democracy. "It is not easy being German," he wrote, "not as cozy, say, as being English, let alone as distinctive and jolly as being French."[50]

In order to make sense of his feelings, Mann temporarily set aside the manuscript of *The Magic Mountain* and began writing an essay that would plant him knee-deep in the intellectual trenches of the war. (Though he had served as a volunteer in the Royal Bavarian Infantry in 1900, Mann was declared unfit for service due to his weak stomach and bad nerves.) Writing to Richard Dehmel, who despite being in his early fifties was already serving at the front in Flanders, Mann confessed to feeling "heartily ashamed" for not being able to volunteer for service. "It was this shame that gave rise to my little essay in the *Rundschau*—that made me feel the need to put my mind, at least, directly in the service of the German cause," he explained.[51]

Finished around September 12 and published in November, "Thoughts in Wartime" was unlike anything Mann had ever written, setting the tone for all of his subsequent wartime writings. It was indignant, wounded, prideful, bellicose. The author of *Tonio Kröger*, who once so eloquently despaired of "having no share in human experience," who believed that all strong emotions lack taste, who stood so strangely remote and aloof from society's concerns—this same author now plunged headfirst into a collective experience of intense emotional fervor.⁵²

Looking back on the blighted world rapidly receding behind him, Mann bid good riddance to its banality and mediocrity, its "peace and frivolous manners." "Wasn't it swarming with vermin of the spirit like maggots?" he asked. "Didn't it seethe and stink of civilization's decay? ... How could the artist—the soldier in the artist—not have thanked God for the collapse of this peaceful world he was fed up with, just fed up?"⁵³

Like so many other writers, Mann bought into the myth of European decadence and decline, a myth the outbreak of war appeared to validate. Surely here was proof that European civilization had at last exhausted itself—proof, as Mann put it, of "the need for a European catastrophe" to prepare the way for purification and regeneration.⁵⁴ A German victory was almost beside the point: what mattered was the struggle itself, its moral and spiritual necessity, this frightening ordeal that would "elevate" the German people, make them "prouder, stronger, freer, happier."⁵⁵

This was Mann at his most elastically and culturally Nietzschean. Despite the German philosopher's horror of war and hatred of Prussian nationalism, a "bellicose form of Nietzscheanism" became fashionable in Germany in the years leading up to the First World War. Nietzsche's notebooks, published posthumously by his *völkish* sister as *The Will to Power* (1901), were raided for rhetorical outbursts that, skillfully manipulated and in some cases even fabricated, could be used to sanction violence and brutality. Perversely, 150,000 pocket-sized copies of *Thus Spake Zarathustra* were printed for German soldiers to carry with them into the trenches.⁵⁶

Mann's "Thoughts in War" also invoked the old antagonism between German *Kultur* and Western *Zivilisation*, describing the Germans as a "distinctly unrevolutionary" and "inward-looking" people; a people more suited to "depth and irrationality" than to reason and civilization; more interested in metaphysics and music than in parliamentary politics. This line of thinking is what Walter Lepenies has called the "specific German ideology": by playing off "romanticism against the Enlightenment, the Middle Ages against the modern world, culture against civilization, and *Gemeinsschaft* against *Gesellschaft*," it expresses a belief that Germany's destiny is a special one, a *Sonderweg*, necessarily different from and even opposed to the path of the Western European democracies.[57] And like the signatories of the "Manifesto of the 93," Thomas Mann affirms the militant nature of the German soul, its inherent contempt for the pacifist ideals of civilization and democracy. He quotes Schiller's *The Bride of Messina*:

> For man withers in peace
> Idle repose is the grave of courage
> Law is a friend to the weak,
> It wishes to level all,
> And would happily flatten the world.
> But war conjures up strength,
> Elevating everything to the extraordinary,
> Giving courage even to the coward.[58]

"Thoughts in Wartime" was completed just as the First Battle of the Marne ended, a battle that resulted in a German retreat on the Western Front and the ensuing mental breakdown of General Helmuth von Moltke, whom the Kaiser swiftly replaced with Erich von Falkenhayn. For anyone still entertaining the delusion that the war would be over by Christmas, this was the decisive wake-up call, a scenario secretly feared by all but planned for by none. Slowly but surely, the war of movement congealed into a war of attrition, or what Falkenhayn called *Stellungskrieg*: positional warfare.[59] Though both sides would continue to pursue the illusion of an offensive breakthrough until at least 1916, trench warfare gradually replaced traditional offensive maneuvers as armies now stared each other down through the coiled lacework of barbed wire, across huge swathes of muddy, shell-hollowed fields above which the sky thickened with the smell of gunpowder and the stench of rotting flesh. It was here on the Western Front that the war's appalling meaninglessness became most apparent. We need only consider the fact that the first and the last British soldiers to be killed in action—sixteen-year-old John Parr and forty-year-old George Ellison—were both shot near Mons, Belgium. As Jörn Leonhard observes, "Fifty-two months of war separated their deaths, but they had defended more or less the same piece of territory."[60]

* * *

One day in the fall of 1914, probably after the publication of Mann's article, there was an argument in Heinrich's apartment in Leopoldstrasse. Agnes Speyer-Ulmann, sister-in-law of the novelist Jakob Wassermann, remembers the two Mann brothers engaging in "the most animated political argument about the war." Heinrich, of course, defended France and predicted the defeat and fall of the German Empire, at which point Thomas reportedly stormed out and slammed the door behind him. From that day on, Speyer-Ulmann wrote, "they no longer spoke to each other. Did not greet each other in the street."[61]

Heinrich Mann was not the only German writer outraged by his brother's canting patriotism. Though many greeted "Thoughts in Wartime" enthusiastically—Count Harry Kessler, traveling with his regiment to join Austro-Hungarian troops at the Carpathian Front, called it "on target and deep"—there was no shortage of disbelief and indignation among Germany's literati.[62] Wilhelm Herzog probably spoke for many a bemused writer when, in the December 1914 issue of *Das Forum*, he indignantly asked: "What reason does a writer like Thomas Mann have to express thoughts in wartime that during peacetime at least he always suppressed?"[63]

What reason indeed? What had gotten into him? What explains the suddenness, the intensity of his patriotism? Generations of Mann scholars have pondered and puzzled over this question. To Erich Heller it is a "stumbling block for the author himself as well as for his critics."[64] Hermann Kurzke calls it "the question of all questions," one of "the great riddles a biography must solve."[65] Mann himself, in a letter to Paul Amann, explained the outburst of "Thoughts in Wartime" as "an action sprung from rage, sprung from the simplistic, if you will, but urgent need to come to the intellectual rescue of my reviled nation."[66]

On the one hand, Mann's belligerence was hardly unique: he was swept up in a collective experience that, for a time at least, carried away plenty of other renowned individuals, including Rainer Maria Rilke, Gottfried Benn, Hermann Hesse, Robert Musil, Max Weber, Walther Rathenau, Georg Simmel, and Max Scheler. Even the gentle pacificist Stefan Zweig was not immune: "I must confess that there was something fine, inspiring, even seductive in that first mass outburst of feeling," he later wrote. "It was difficult to resist it. And in spite of hatred and abhorrence of war, I would not like to be without the memory of those first days."[67]

On the other hand, the war provided Mann with the solution to his intellectual drift. The gulf separating the artist from society, the underlying theme of virtually all of his prewar writing, was paved over in an instant: the outsider came in from the cold, hot and frenzied with purpose. As Hermann Kurzke has argued, the war even offered an intoxicating synthesis of Mann's contradictory nature: the Apollonian world of his father was fused with the Dionysian world of his mother.[68]

The war also fed Mann's literary vanity, his desire to be looked upon as Germany's foremost representative writer. In *Death in*

Venice, Gustav von Aschenbach considers himself a soldier and warrior in the "compulsive service of art," which is "a war, an exhausting struggle."[69] A few years later, Mann self-aggrandizingly claimed the events of the war were "foreshadowed in me and through me," pointing to *Death in Venice* as "something final, the late work of an epoch, on which uncertain lights of a new era are falling."[70] And in a case of life imitating art, Mann would spend the late fall of 1914 writing a long prowar essay about Frederick the Great, the Prussian king about whom Aschenbach wrote a historical novel that "epitomized an ethos of manly suffering."[71]

For all that the war occupied Mann, his wartime writings rarely give the impression that he knew a great deal about its gruesome reality. The daily horrors of soldiers' lives on the front later documented in novels like Henri Barbusse's *Under Fire* (1916) or Erich Maria Remarque's *All Quiet on the Western Front* (1929) seem very remote from the overheated rhetoric of "Thoughts in Wartime." Heinrich Mann hit the mark when, walking around Munich one day with Erich Mühsam, he bitterly said to him: "My brother enjoys [the war] like he does everything: aesthetically."[72]

* * *

Despite their relative domestic comfort, the Mann household endured an authentically frightening few months in the early summer of 1915, less than a year into the war. In May and June, the whole family, Thomas Mann excepted, was stricken with appendicitis. Everyone was successfully operated on save for nine-year-old Klaus, who was soon suffering from peritonitis, abscesses, and intestinal paralysis to boot. He had to undergo five grueling operations, one of which actually required the removal of his intestines from his abdominal cavity.[73] His condition was so alarming that doctors doubted he would survive. Relatives outside Munich prepared to attend his funeral.[74] "As long as I was allowed to see him (at present I may not) my impressions were such that I hardly believe in a happy outcome," Thomas Mann informed his publisher, Samuel Fischer. "Let's hope I am mistaken. It would hit me very hard, but what would become of my wife I cannot bear to imagine."[75]

Shortly after Klaus's recovery, the family's beloved black border collie, the "harmless, feeble-minded" Motz, had to be put down.[76] Suffering from a disfiguring skin disease, his back covered with boils, the dog was dispatched by the local gunsmith with a shot to the spine and one to the head. He was buried near a tree at the edge of the garden in Tölz, his grave marked by large stone placed there by the children.

With so many distractions and interferences, Mann found the discipline that novel writing demanded difficult to sustain. Despite having returned to the manuscript of *The Magic Mountain* in early January, Mann's progress soon stalled. How much had he written? Because the original 1,201 manuscript pages have been lost and are presumed to have been destroyed in the Allied bombings of Munich during the Second World War, we can't know with absolute certainty how far the novel had progressed. Hans Rudolf Vaget, in his account of the novel's genesis, estimates that Mann had written up to and perhaps even beyond the "Hippe" subchapter, or roughly one-quarter of the final manuscript.[77] In other words, the novel had already long outgrown its original conception. From a letter to Paul Amann in early August, we know that Mann now viewed *The Magic Mountain* as a novel that, somehow, would be about the ongoing war. "For conclusion, for resolution I see no other possibility but the outbreak of the war," he explained, before adding, a little grandiloquently, "As a storyteller one cannot ignore this reality, and I believe I have some right to it, since the premonition of it has been in all my conceptions." At the same time, Mann doubted whether it would be possible to go on merely "telling tales." What he'd written so far about the war struck him as woefully inadequate, and he admitted to Amann that he was tempted to embark on a "thoroughgoing, sober discussion, a coming to terms on a personal and self-analytic basis with the burning problems of the day."[78]

Which is exactly what he did. Sometime during the fall of 1915, *The Magic Mountain* joined another incomplete manuscript, *Confessions of Felix Krull*, in the purgatory of the abandoned, where it would languish for a further four years. He turned his attention instead to what would become *Reflections of a Nonpolitical Man*—a thoroughgoing discussion, to be sure, though it would turn out to be anything but sober.

But there was a final piece missing—a last, crucial ingredient that would make all the difference, infusing *Reflections of a Nonpolitical Man* with mouth-scorching heat and face-puckering bitterness. In July 1915, Wilhelm Herzog's *Das Forum* ran a short essay titled "Preface to an Essay on Zola," before the journal was shut down by the Bavarian Ministry of War for publishing "unpatriotic aestheticism and Europeanism."[79] Though the essay's author read from the text on June 18, 1915, at a salon hosted by *Das Forum* in Munich's Hotel Continental, it was proving difficult to find a home for what was apparently just a biographical essay on the French novelist. Finally, in the November issue of the Leipzig-based monthly *Die Weissen Blätter* (which a month previously had published a story titled "The Metamorphosis" by the young Prague-based writer Franz Kafka), the completed essay, titled simply "Zola," was published at last. It opened with a thinly disguised taunt: "Writers who affect a self-assured and 'representative' demeanor during their twenties will generally see their talents wither by mid-career."[80]

The essay's author was Heinrich Mann.

CHAPTER 4

A Good Soldier, 1916–1918

New Year's Eve, 1915. At the Manns' house on Poschingerstrasse in Munich, the holiday season was festive, if not as lavish as in years prior. There were candles, music, champagne, perhaps even punch and *pfannkuchen,* a Thomas Mann New Year's favorite. And there were guests, of course: Alfred Pringsheim, Bruno Frank, Ernst Bertram, Maximilian Brantl.[1] Probably others. The conversation, naturally, centered on the war, then about to enter its bloodiest year: 1916 would see both sides resign themselves to a war of attrition on the Western Front, culminating in the wasteful horrors of the Somme and Verdun, battles that, together, would account for the loss of roughly 1.5 million men, as well as the environmental devastation of acres of land, where human and animal remains and millions of unexploded ordinances continue to contaminate the soil to this day.[2]

As was his custom, Thomas Mann read to his guests from the metastasizing manuscript of the *Reflections,* of which he'd now written the first two chapters. In a recent letter to Paul Amann, he had described the project as "a kind of essay, or no, they are almost private scribblings, which attempt to create a fusion—a strange and rash experiment—between contemporary events and a revision of my personal point of view."[3] Without going into specifics, he admitted that the book was becoming something of a burden to him. In his conversations with Ernst Bertram, he was more forthcoming: "My brother," he told him, is "not really tolerable at the moment."[4]

That evening, after the guests had left and before he installed the new calendar pages ("always a significant ritual for me"), Mann dispatched a short letter to Brantl.[5] "I forgot to ask you a favor today," he wrote. "I know you have the issue of *Die Weissen Blätter* which contains my brother's Zola essay. Would you lend it to me for a while?"[6]

* * *

Unlike his younger brother, Heinrich Mann had not rushed to lecture the German reading public about the war. He elected to suffer in private instead, or else by seeking out the company of a few like-minded friends and fellow writers—Wilhelm Herzog or Erich Mühsam, for instance. His health, ever precarious, was giving him trouble yet again. He'd spent part of the previous summer taking the cure in a sanatorium in Bad Kissingen, sixty-odd miles east of Frankfurt. With disgust, he wrote to his wife that the German-speaking guests had agreed to fine one another for using Italian, French, or English words, and that on the spa grounds a "well-dressed Jewish gentleman" had read out a newspaper report about twenty-one thousand Russian casualties to a salvo of enthusiastic cheers. "Such is the way the spa-guests spend their time," he sighed.[7]

Despite living less than a mile from one another, the two brothers had not spoken since the early weeks of the war. Their mother tried in vain to mediate between them, even though she sided with Thomas on the matter of the war. "My dear, good Heinrich," she pleaded, "don't speak out against your fatherland because it now defends itself with all its might;—it only wanted to demonstrate its loyalty to its own allies and was forced into this struggle which will cost its life—or so the enemy would like."[8]

But how could he not speak out? How could he go on remaining silent when the whole country had turned into a madhouse? When so many German writers, including his own brother, were lining up to serve as the kaiser's useful idiots?

No, Heinrich felt he'd been silent long enough. He resolved to finally write the essay he'd been planning about Émile Zola, the French writer whose Rougon-Macquart novel cycle, with its unflinching portrayal of the greed and corruption of the Second French Empire, he regarded as one of the highest achievements of literature and democracy. Here was the kind of writer Heinrich wanted to emulate: one who knew how to translate his literary insights into action, who understood that the writer's first duty is to justice and truth, consequences be damned.

And so, over the span of more than seventy pages, Heinrich Mann rhapsodized about the Frenchman's long and distinguished career, his courageous dissent during the Dreyfus affair, his theory of the novel as a vehicle for social and political improvement. By carrying within himself the "rhythmic waves of modern democracy," Heinrich wrote, Zola embodied the very antithesis of the political quietism and complacency that plagued Wilhelmine Germany's literary culture.

This was protest disguised as biography. When Heinrich Mann wrote of Zola's *The Earth* (1887) that it was "a novel of the time," a portrait of how "the worst of all conceivable regimes, capitalist militarism, is driving its people toward catastrophe, toward war or revolution," no one doubted the essay's subtext. In all but name, "Zola" was Heinrich Mann's *J'accuse...!*—an impassioned defense of democracy, justice, and the ideal of truth against the "tyranny of patriotic numskulls."[9]

The essay made an instant splash. "If France can be proud of Zola," Frank Wedekind wrote to Heinrich Mann, "then in my opinion we can be even prouder that this work has been written by a German in such times as these." The publisher Kurt Wolff agreed and went even further by obtaining the rights to all of Heinrich Mann's novels and stories, which he reissued in a ten-volume collected edition. "For the assumption of this responsibility, the signing of the contract with you, is for me the greatest undertaking I have ever entered," he wrote to Mann.[10] The November issue of *Die Weisse Blätter* quickly sold out. A few months later the magazine's editor, René Schickele, ran afoul of the German censors and had to flee to Switzerland and continue publication there instead.

When Thomas Mann first laid eyes on "Zola" it hit him like a thunderbolt. "Poor Tom has obviously been very upset by the Zola essay," Ernst Bertram wrote to his lover, Ernst Glöckner, on January 29, "and in his new work he attacks his brother (whom he does not name) so violently and relentlessly that we felt a little as if we were caught between the two of them."[11] Seismographically sensitive to even the hint of criticism, Mann soon convinced himself that Heinrich's essay was directed solely and squarely at him. "I have read it and am myself surprised that it is directed almost more against me than against Germany," he wrote to Bertram on January 15.[12] Heinrich's later attempt to explain that the essay was directed at "a legion" of writers supporting the war would be in vain.[13] "Zola" burst the dam of what Thomas Mann until then had considered an intellectual reckoning, allowing a torrent of fraternal hostility to flood the manuscript.

* * *

As the war entered the new year, the grim reality of a protracted military conflict on the continent was beginning to set in among Europe's civilian populations, Germany's in particular. The British blockade of the North Sea and the Channel meant that Germany was denied all its overseas imports—including, crucially, agricultural imports—creating a severe food shortage that, according to some estimates, would contribute to the deaths of seven hundred thousand people before the end of the war.[14]

Because of the blockade, as well as the enormous demands of the military, ordinary Germans were forced to consume all manner of ersatz food products: ersatz milk, sausage, coffee, eggs—even ersatz beer. During the so-called turnip winter of 1916-17, when potatoes became virtually unobtainable, the authorities recommended replacing them with turnips—or Prussian pineapples, as they came to be called.[15] Malnutrition and starvation were widespread. "People collapsed, fell sick, grew desperate," Ernst Toller recalled.[16] In Erich Maria Remarque's best-selling novel *All Quiet on the Western Front* (1929), the situation among the general population during the war is so terrible that Paul, the main character, brings his family the meager rations he is served at the front.

The Mann household, though better off than most, was not spared these privations. Klaus Mann remembered that for the children the war primarily meant there was never enough to eat. The once sumptuous Sunday dinners at their grandparents' family home on Arcisstrasse now typically consisted of "an emaciated bird—a dubious sort of heron with a disturbingly fishy flavor."[17] When the shortages and rationing grew worse, the children were sent on expeditions into the city or its suburbs, lining up on frigid winter mornings for a quarter-pound of margarine or a half-dozen eggs. Katia, too, would ride around Munich on her bicycle for several hours a day looking for provisions. Golo Mann recalled that "our previously pampered mother developed into something of a heroine, with two difficult tasks: protecting and feeding her highstrung and hardworking spouse as best she could, while making sure that the others, the four children and the three 'girls'—the cook, the chambermaid, and the maid—did not suffer too much deprivation."[18] At mealtimes, Katia always took the smallest portion of whatever food was served, prompting her husband to demand that everyone share something from their plate with her.

Thomas Mann later called the war years the most difficult of his life. Certainly, to his family, he was a more dyspeptic husband and father than ever before. Sunk in the gloom of his study, always donning a gray tunic suit jacket, he seemed a bitter, estranged, and distant figure. Klaus Mann recalled his father's impatient response whenever someone asked him what he was working on. " 'It's just a book,' he says, with a strangely unfocused look in his eyes. 'No, not a novel. Just a book. It has to do with the war.' "[19] It was an impression shared by Golo: "We had once loved our father as tenderly as our mother, but that changed during the war. I can remember all too well certain scenes at mealtimes, outbreaks of rage and brutality that were directed at my brother Klaus but brought tears to my own eyes."[20]

The labor of the *Reflections* was a joyless ordeal. "The whole intellectual reckoning-up of which I wrote you (the labor of several months) now bores me frightfully," he wrote to Paul Amann in March 1916, "and only out of a sense of order and bourgeois disinclination to 'let anything go to waste' will I probably pull together what I have written and attempt to make something usable out of it."[21] The strain of writing burdened him physically: that spring he succumbed to the flu and, shortly after, a skin inflammation that left him incapacitated for several weeks. It was the kind of suffering that was practically written into the text's most barbed locutions. "The cruel strain of those days," Klaus Mann wrote, "the bleak seriousness of the author's life, his lack of political training, even the inadequate food and chilly temperature in his studio during the winter months—all these elements worked together to create the peculiar climate, the perplexing mixture of violence and melancholy, that prevails in the *Reflections*."[22]

Reflections of a Nonpolitical Man is the strangest and most puzzling book Thomas Mann ever wrote. Stretching to more than six hundred pages, it combines aesthetics and autobiography; politics and philosophy; criticism and confession. Its tone is by turns anguished, rambling, shrill, and hyperbolic—not exactly qualities the coolly ironic author of *Buddenbrooks* and *Death in Venice* was known for. In the prologue, Mann called it a book he felt himself "drafted" to write, one that kept him from his "true calling and occupation" and whose "feuilletonistic tone" ill-suited him. Preposterously, he likened the writing of it to completing "two years of military service of the mind," at one point even referring to himself as a "war casualty."[23]

Begun in earnest in September 1915, completed sometime in March 1918, *Reflections* is the document of a tortured, obsessive, and intellectually unsettled mind. It is a polemic, but it is a polemic sunk by the personal and intellectual cargo of its author. "I want to say everything—that is the purpose of this book," Mann writes—on page 427 in the original German edition.[24] *Reflections* is as digressive as a drunk telling a story; every now and then Mann stops and admonishes himself to "get to the point," to "begin again," or to simply "continue!"[25] In the prologue, he maintains that *Reflections* is the work of an artist but not a work of art; it is an effusion, a diary, a notebook, an inventory. He won't even call it a book: "This searching, struggling, and probing toward the essence, toward the causes of an anguish, this dialectical fencing all the way into the fog *against* such causes—the result was naturally no book."[26] In a letter to the writer Adele Gerhard, Mann claimed he intended *Reflections* to be read as "a novel."[27]

What is it then? On one level, *Reflections* is a reactionary manifesto brimful with all the tropes of German nationalism: it extols the morally ennobling virtues of war; berates the English, the American, and the French; rhapsodizes about the "truly holy sound" of the word *Volk;* and approvingly quotes nationalist authors like Paul de Lagarde and Heinrich von Treitschke. More significantly, it regards Germany as a "special case" among European nations, one to which reason, enlightenment, and democracy are spiritually foreign.[28] "German higher culture thoroughly resists being politicized," Mann writes.[29] The subordination of life to the social and political threatens what is unique about Germany, a more inwardly spiritual and nonpolitical country than its neighbors to the west. For Mann, this was the real issue of the war: he seriously believed the Triple Entente posed a spiritual and existential threat to the inner character of the German people. "Whoever would aspire to transform Germany into a middle-class democracy in the Western-Roman sense and spirit," Mann warns, "would wish to take away from her all that is best and complex, to take away the problematic character that really makes up her nationality; he would make her dull, shallow, stupid, and un-German, and he would therefore be an antinationalist who insisted that Germany become a nation in a foreign sense and spirit."[30]

Mann infused the conventional distinction between *Kultur* and *Zivilisation* with Nietzsche's distinction between the Apollonian and the Dionysian: "Civilization," the philosopher Rüdiger Safranski writes, is "Apollonian, life-preserving, optimistic, alleviating, rational, and cultivated. It restrains the dark drives, civilizes them. It is livable surface. The Dionysian is deep, elemental, instinctual, wild, even evil."[31] The victory of the Western, Apollonian view of life, as Mann saw it, would mean the suppression of the Dionysian and primordial depths of our nature from which the greatest art springs forth.

Since *Reflections* is a book by Thomas Mann, however, it bristles with the inconsistencies and contradictions of an artistic mind. "A trace of the actor, the lawyer, of play, artistry, detachment, of lack of conviction and of that poetic sophistry that allows the one speaking at the moment to be correct, and who in this case was I, myself—this trace is undoubtedly to be found everywhere," Mann teases in the prologue.[32] With his characteristically ironic temperament, Mann again and again reveals himself to be a highly questionable convert to Germany's cause. And it is precisely these nuances and reversals, this dialectical dance of Mann's mind, that makes *Reflections*, despite itself, a strangely moving book. While ostensibly taking up intellectual arms on behalf of the German soul, *Reflections* is also the confession of a mysterious authorial malaise and thus constantly speaks against itself. Again and again, Mann questions his own patriotic credentials. "I doubt whether a person like me is "suited" for patriotism," he admits, and later claims not be "a very genuine German" because of his "Latin, South American blood."[33] Unlike other conservative-nationalist authors, he emphasizes the significance of the Jewish contribution to the development of the German Empire. He even insists that literature and conservatism are fundamentally antithetical. Literature, he writes in the prologue, "is democratic and civilizing from the ground up; even more correctly: it is *the same* as democracy and civilization."[34] Could it then be, he wonders, that he was actually furthering Germany's drift toward democratic progress by virtue of being a writer? Several hundred pages into the book, he offers a kind of answer: "Conservative? Naturally I am not."[35]

But perhaps the most salient quality of the *Reflections* is its wounded intimacy. Mann explained to Ernst Bertram that his need to view things in intimate terms led him to see the fate of Germany "symbolized and personified in my brother and myself."[36] Heinrich is never addressed by name, appearing instead under the guise of *Der Zivilisationsliterat*, or "civilization's literary man," an epithet repeated 172 times throughout the book. It is a distinction Heinrich shares with the French novelist Romain Rolland, whose own wartime book, *Above the Battle* (1915), accused Thomas Mann of "criminal glorification of violence."[37]

"Civilization's literary man" signifies the type of writer who conceives of literature as a tool in the struggle for democracy and progress. Mann thought democratic civilization would achieve "absolute domination" in the political as well as the cultural sphere; that art would become subordinate to political imperatives.[38] "The political artist is the one who is *most hungry for effect*," Mann writes, emphasizing the reference to Heinrich Mann's *The Hunt for Love*, "but he covers up this hunger for effect with the doctrine that art must have consequences, and specifically, political ones."[39]

Mann described his own relationship to politics as a nonrelationship and the political sphere as something technical, better left to experts. The most important aspects of the human sphere, he argued, existed "beside, above, and beyond the state." But by maintaining that what is human is fundamentally alien to politics Mann was merely inverting the argument. It would have been truer to say that human beings are not *only* social beings, that we have metaphysical as well as political needs. The critic Eskil Elling describes *Reflections* as, at times, resembling "a caricature of reactionary aestheticism, the rambling of someone who, despite wanting to be the "master of opposites," was incapable of accepting that we can inhabit opposite perspectives at various times, democracy in the public square and irony in the study, without needing a grand meta-narrative to reconcile them."[40]

Worst of all, for a book occasioned by the outbreak of the First World War, *Reflections* is woefully silent on the concrete realities of war and the immeasurable suffering it inflicted on tens of millions of people. "Death does not become more terrible when we see it multiplied ten thousand times before our eyes," is among the most repugnant statements in the book.[41] Mann's defense of German culture's "sympathy with death" against civilization's life-preserving imperatives, at a time when a generation of young men were being slaughtered on an industrial scale, is morally repugnant. If ever Heinrich was right to accuse his brother of being "incapable of coming seriously to grips with the reality of another human being's life," then here was the proof.[42]

In one of his wartime notebooks, Thomas Mann claimed the origin for the *Reflections* was "largely artistic: to avoid intellectual overburdening of *The Magic Mountain* and to make the work of art 'lighter.' "[43] It was a kind of intellectual exorcism, as Katia Mann would later explain: "in the course of writing it, Thomas Mann gradually freed himself from the ideas which had held sway over him.... He wrote *Reflections* in all sincerity and, in doing so, ended by getting over what he had advocated in the book."[44]

The character of Ludovico Settembrini grew out of the specter of "civilization's literary man." Throughout *The Magic Mountain*, he espouses the international brotherhood of humanity but in the case of Austria proves himself to be less pacificist than he believes.[45] We see Settembrini's relation to civilization's literary man also in his suspicion of music: "the musical attitude seems to the literary moral sense at the very least to be undependable, at the very least, suspicious," Mann observed.[46] Settembrini even proudly informs Hans Castorp and Joachim Ziemssen that he has been asked to contribute a literary essay to a work called *The Sociology of Suffering*, whose explicit purpose was to eradicate human suffering. The invitation comes from the International League for the Organization of Progress. "Working from Darwin's theory of evolution," Settembrini explains, "[the League] advances the philosophical viewpoint that humankind's innermost natural purpose is its own self-protection."[47]

This is Mann at his most overtly sarcastic. In his diary, he called it "a comic bit of rationalism."[48] We can practically read Nietzsche's aristocratic contempt for Settembrini's utilitarianism between the lines. What modern, progressive Europeans really want, the philosopher grumbles in *Beyond Good and Evil*, "is the universal green pasture happiness of the herd, with security, safety, comfort and an easier life for all."[49]

It becomes possible, then, to read *The Magic Mountain* as a novel partly about the limits and failures of the more positivistic strain of nineteenth-century liberalism—a triumphalist worldview that failed to recognize or halt Europe's drift toward nationalism, reaction, and the industrial carnage of the First World War. Settembrini, the novel's representative of this worldview, shares its myriad flaws, believing, for instance, that self-perfection is the ultimate goal of humankind. And like so many nineteenth-century liberal utopians, he celebrates technology as "the most dependable means by which to bring nations closer together, furthering their knowledge of one another, paving the way for people-to-people exchanges, destroying prejudices, and leading at last to the universal brotherhood of nations."[50]

As Hans Castorp intuits and Naphta's ripostes reveal, Settembrini is not always the paragon of reason and virtue he makes himself out to be. His attitude toward the part of the world he routinely describes as "Asiatic" and "barbaric" is plainly racist, as is his concern with "the problem of the health of our race."[51] He also shares in the (at the time) widespread Italian animosity toward the Austro-Hungarian Empire, viewed by liberals as a bastion of Catholic reaction and conservatism, not to mention a territorial rival of Italy's in the Adriatic. "One must deal a fatal blow to Austria and crush her, first to avenge past wrongs and second to open the way for the rule of justice and happiness on earth," Settembrini says early in the novel.[52]

More than just a vessel for a philosophical point of view, however, Settembrini is, or becomes, one of *The Magic Mountain*'s most endearing characters. One cannot help but smile a little—half with affection, half with pity—whenever he enters the stage. It's one of the novel's great distinctions that its central characters are never merely reducible to the philosophical worldview they represent; Settembrini, even when Mann is at his most sarcastic, is always first and foremost Settembrini, as if Mann were gradually convinced by his fictional creation as a dynamic individual rather than a static representation.

This was a development that would come later, however. For the writer of *Reflections*, civilization's literary men were first and foremost existential adversaries who cheered the armies of the Western allies and even wished for a democratic invasion of Germany. Crucially, Mann saw that even those who profess love for humanity are not always fearful of shedding blood.

A GOOD SOLDIER

* * *

By the time Thomas Mann finished *Reflections of a Nonpolitical Man*, on March 16, 1918, the First World War was well into its fifth calendar year and the German High Command were feeling cautiously optimistic. The Treaty of Brest-Litovsk, signed on March 3, ended Russia's participation in the war, freeing up dozens of German divisions along the Eastern Front for a surprise spring offensive in the west. America's entry into the war did not yet pose an immediate threat; the 175,000 troops that landed in Europe in January required special training and as yet had no combat experience.[53] The French and Italians troops were weak and the British needed time to recover from heavy losses incurred in the fall. "The army in the west is waiting for the possibility to become active," General Ludendorff informed the kaiser and Reich chancellor Prince Max von Baden. "It will be difficult, but it will end in victory." When Max von Baden asked what would happen if the offensive should fail, Ludendorff said: "Then Germany will simply go under."[54]

In the early morning hours of March 21, over a million German shells pummeled the British front lines for hours on end.[55] Lieutenant Ernst Jünger, whose infantry battalion took part in the surprise assault, recalled the "gigantic roaring" of the German guns that made the earth shake uncontrollably underneath him. From his dugout, he saw a "colossal wall of flame over the English lines, gradually obscuring itself behind crimson, surging clouds." He decided that "even the greatest of the battles we had experienced seemed like a tea party by comparison."[56]

There were renewed offenses, too, in the great fraternal war still raging in Munich. In December 1917, Thomas Mann received a letter from Heinrich headed "Attempt at a Reconciliation," in which his older brother reassured him that the Zola essay was "not aimed against you but against a legion" of German writers who, like him, had decided to support the war. He insisted that he'd never written anything out of a sense of "brotherly hate," assuring Thomas that "you needn't think of me as an enemy."[57]

They hadn't spoken in over three years. Even so much as the sight of a letter bearing Heinrich's handwriting was enough to assault Mann's nerves.[58] When they both happened to attend the same public lecture, they just ignored each other. Rumor of the brotherly feud had by now become an established fact of German intellectual life, which suited Thomas fine. "Let the tragedy of our brotherhood unfold," he wrote in his response to Heinrich on January 3, 1918. Thomas was still hung up on the "truly French spitefulness" of that "hackwork" of a Zola essay, whose second sentence alone was "monstrously excessive." As for the attempt at a reconciliation? "Every line of your letter was dictated by moral smugness and self-righteousness. Don't expect me to fall sobbing upon your breast."[59]

Júlia Mann was shattered by Thomas's rejection of Heinrich's rapprochement. "You and I will have to be satisfied that what you did was the last unmistakably good act," she wrote to Heinrich on January 7. "From now on I beg you—*in your writings as well*—to let the matter rest, and not to utter a *hint* of criticism which, in the hands of evil people, would only lead to sensationalism over the rift between two great brothers."[60]

Perhaps his mother's letter persuaded Heinrich not to send the response he'd already written to Thomas. Besides, faced with such bitterness and contempt, what was the point? "I think I will leave your book unread," Heinrich wrote in the unsent letter, "not out of disrespect, but because I desire a polemical connection to you less than the other, the natural one." It was a moving, wounded plea. The final sentence read: "The time is coming, I only hope, in which you will learn to see people, not shadows, and, then, that you will see me."[61]

But Thomas continued his shadowboxing. He soon set out for a tour of occupied Belgium and Northern Germany that began with a poorly received reading from *The Magic Mountain* at the Krupp Hall in Essen. The material Mann read was all plotless psychology delivered by an "ineffably superior aristocrat," the *Essener Volkszeitung* wrote the next day, observing that by the end of the reading "the hall was already very empty."[62]

Mann did better in Brussels, where on January 9 German soldiers staged a performance of *Fiorenza* at the Théâtre Royal du Parc. The next morning, Mann breakfasted with General Hurt, the military governor of Brussels, and his officers—"all dapper and affable people, and one and all, for what service I know not, decorated with the Iron Cross First Class." One of the officers addressed Mann as "Herr-Comrade-in-Arms," a distinction the guest of honor found entirely appropriate: "the vicissitudes of war hit me as hard as they did these people," he remarked.[63] Brussels was the closest Mann ever got to seeing anything resembling the reality of the war.

On March 2, he was finally able to write to Paul Amann that "the monstrosity [*Reflections*] is concluded: twelve chapters, politics, morality, art, philosophy, autobiography, an indescribable ragout, a thing without genre, quite without precedent."[64] He spent most of the spring correcting the proofs of the book, a task in which he was assisted by the dependable Ernst Bertram, whose Nietzsche study had recently been completed and who would soon become godfather to Mann's fifth child and youngest daughter, Elisabeth, born on April 24. Mann was instantly smitten with her and began writing a poem, *The Song of the Child: An Idyll*, in her honor. He didn't understand why, but he "loved her from the first day more than the other four taken together," as he put it to a friend.[65]

Having sold their vacation home in Bad Tölz the previous year, the Mann family spent the summer of 1918 on Lake Tegernsee in the Bavarian Alps, where they rented a large villa belonging to the son of the Tyrolian painter Franz Defregger. Mann spent his time there reading the work of the Austrian writer Adalbert Stifter, hiking the nearby Hirschberg mountain, or playing ninepins with Bruno Frank. There were boat rides on the lake and days spent frolicking on the beach, which reminded Mann of the Lido in Venice. But the increasingly dire news from army bulletins sent ripples of unease through the summer idyll. On the day the family left Munich for Lake Tegernsee, Mann had admitted to Paul Amann that "in spite of all I feel a certain awe of what the future will be like, and am beginning to ask myself whether for my kind of person, and the after all loose and unorganized things that my kind of person has to offer, there will be any room in it at all."[66]

* * *

As the summer of 1918 drew to a close, there was no longer any doubting that Germany would lose the war. It was not question of if but rather of when, and of how. The initial gains of Ludendorff's spring offensive notwithstanding, the influx of American troops (as many as 250,000 every month) decisively tipped the war in the Allies' favor.[67] By mid-July, German forces along the Western Front "were in continual retreat."[68] Strategic blunders, heavy losses, and the spread of the Spanish flu all took their toll. The Battle of Amiens on August 8, the beginning of the so-called Hundred Days Offensive, was described by Ludendorff as a "black day" for the German army. Before long, reports of disciplinary problems, including instances of desertion and self-mutilation, started reaching the German High Command. "What's the point of sacrificing ourselves?" asked a soldier in a letter home. "Maybe for the fatherland and its holiest possessions? No, they all buried patriotism a long time ago."[69]

Despite facing all but certain defeat, many Germans continued to believe in a coming victory—in part because the German High Command were less than forthcoming about how bad things really stood. In Berlin, people appeared to take the "failures in the west in stride," Count Harry Kessler noted in his diary on August 11. "This evening the brothels in the Friedrichstrasse were packed. Life continues to bubble as usual. Soldiers and whores, the crowd with champagne and music amid clouds of cigarette smoke."[70]

Returning from Lake Tegernsee on September 9, Thomas Mann soon buried himself in the manuscript of Ernst Bertram's *Nietzsche: Attempt at a Mythology*, soon to be published. "Feel the *Nietzsche* to be a good, *moving* book, and the author a friend in the most comforting and virtually highest sense of the word," he wrote in his diary on September 14. He recognized its connection not only to his *Reflections* but to his future works, particularly "the romanticism of death plus affirmation of life in *The Magic Mountain*."[71] He finished reading the manuscript four days later and felt "as proud of this work as if I had written it myself."[72]

On its publication, *Nietzsche: Attempt at a Mythology* became something of a hit, with twenty-one thousand copies in print by 1929, and was awarded the inaugural prize of the Nietzsche Society in 1919.[73] It was admired by Herman Hesse, the philosopher Karl Jaspers, and the poet Gottfried Benn. According to the scholar and translator Walter Kaufmann, with the exception of Elisabeth Förster-Nietzsche's popular biographies no other book on Nietzsche could match its influence at the time.[74]

It is not hard to see why Mann admired it. A psychological portrait built up around a series of reflections on various recurring themes in Nietzsche's life and writing—his relationship to Goethe, Protestantism, Wagner, music—Bertram's book is written in associative and lyrical prose, placing Nietzsche in dialogue with Luther, Hegel, Hölderlin, and Goethe, among others, all of whom Bertram quotes from liberally, so that the book becomes a kind of running commentary on, and a musical accompaniment to, Nietzsche's thinking. What's more, Bertram's portrayal of what he calls Nietzsche's anti-German fanaticism as a "love-hate, a hatred stemming from the most profound feeling of kinship, from the guilty conscience of an inner identity," must have appealed to Mann, wrestling as he was with what it meant to be German.[75]

Although much more subtle than other attempts to refashion Nietzsche as a patriotic conservative, *Nietzsche: Attempt at a Mythology* nevertheless points forward to the "frankly irrationalist epistemology which was to become a hallmark of the Weimar radical right," as Steven E. Aschheim has shown.[76] One of Bertram's central insights in the book—that Nietzsche was a man who embodied the many contradictions of his time, a "storm-laden cloud born of an antagonistic polarity"—is consistently misapplied to show that Nietzsche's hammer blows against Christianity or Germany were really just misdirected hammer blows against himself.[77] In Bertram's view, Nietzsche is never more obviously Christian than in *The Anti-Christ*, never more Lutheran than when he yearns for the Hellenistic south, never more German than when he claims to be a "good European." It may be true to say of Nietzsche, as Bertram does, that his writing partly arose out of a struggle with himself, but it is nonsense to take this insight to mean that Nietzsche meant the opposite of what he said.

Katia was less enamored of Bertram's book than her husband. Mann became irritated with her one morning during breakfast when she "took a skeptical attitude toward Bertram and the 'importance' of his book."[78] A few days later he made a note of her "often harshly expressed skepticism" toward the war.[79] In fact, she had long since lost whatever confidence she had in Germany. When they quarreled about this, Thomas was "no match" for Katia's "alert, legalistically logical intelligence," Golo Mann claimed. No matter how much she loved him, she was "much too strong and naïve a personality to want, or be able to, humor him."[80]

As the most calamitous war in human history hastened toward its end, Mann's daily life slowly began to assume its usual routines. He went for his walks with the family dog, Bauschan, observed the young soldiers running their drills in the park, attended the theater, and prepared for the publication of *Reflections*. "What part will the book play?" he wondered. "For it is possible that it will play a part. But it is also possible that its unreadability will prevent it from becoming noticed. Will the conservative press seize upon it?"[81]

Before long, historical events once again caught Mann—and the general German population—completely unaware.

* * *

On September 29, 1918, General Ludendorff and Field Marshal Hindenburg informed the kaiser of the dire situation on the Western Front and recommended that armistice negotiations be initiated immediately. A few days later, a despondent Mann noted in his diary: "The catastrophe and worldwide defeat . . . is at hand. It is mine too."[82]

On the evening of October 6, he and Katia discussed the possibility of putting a stop to the publication of *Reflections*. What purpose would it serve now that Germany's defeat was all but assured? They quickly dispatched a telegram to Samuel Fischer asking that publication be delayed for the time being. Fischer responded the next morning that it was too late: copies of the book had already been delivered. "In God's name!" Mann remarked in the margin of the letter.[83]

Despite appearing at the most ironic moment for a book defending the Imperial Reich, to say nothing of its enormous length and idiosyncratic style, *Reflections on a Nonpolitical Man* turned out to be a modest success. The initial print run of six thousand copies sold out before the end of the year so that, by 1919, it had sold almost fourteen thousand copies.[84] Mann received a great many letters of support from all corners of Germany, as well as from friends like Bruno Frank and the composer Hans Pfitzner. When he took the tram into town and stopped by the bookseller Heinrich Jaffe, Jaffe himself "spoke in awestruck terms" about the sales of *Reflections*.[85]

Critical reactions, on the other hand, were largely disappointing. There were appreciative, at times even glowing, reviews in the conservative press, while the most important German newspapers, like the *Frankfurter Zeitung* or the *Berliner Tageblatt*, entirely ignored *Reflections*. Most painful of all was a long and critical essay by Paul Amann in the *Münchener Blätter für Dichtung und Grafik*, which Mann thought was "glib, nasty, and tactless." They wouldn't correspond again for another fifteen years.

Whatever the fate of *Reflections*, Mann's attention, like everyone else's, was directed now to the spectacle of the collapse of the German Empire. By early November, Germany was the only member of the Central Powers still at war. Bulgaria, the Austro-Hungarian Empire, and the Ottoman Empire had all been defeated and sued for peace. Despite these setbacks and the rapidly deteriorating military discipline, German forces were still holding the Western Front along a 120-mile line while armistice negotiations were ongoing. Meanwhile, fears of a Russian-style revolution at home led to the October constitutional reforms, transforming the German Empire into a parliamentary monarchy with Prince Max von Baden appointed Reich chancellor. "The self-abnegation, remorse, and penitence are boundless," Mann commented in his diary. "We now say that the enemy is in the right, admit that Germany needed to be reformed by such an enemy, and out of fear we declare ourselves reformed."[86]

The reforms, however, had come too late. Material deprivation, extreme war-weariness, and the shock of defeat turned ordinary Germans against their rulers. In Bavaria, there was a general sense of having been, as one liberal writer put it, "deceived and duped" by the central government:[87] 170,000 Bavarian soldiers had died in the war, 13,000 of them coming from Munich alone.[88] What's more, early hopes of a moderate peace "without victors or vanquished" were dashed when it became clear in the course of Germany's communications with President Wilson that the

Allies would set the terms of the armistice, not Germany.[89] As Mann rather prophetically put it in his diary on October 13: "There is a terrible danger that the Allies, drunk with victory, will come up with a dictated peace that will either have to be refused immediately as unacceptable, and will lead to horror like a last-ditch struggle or a revolution, or bring in its wake a latent state of war."[90]

* * *

On November 7, thousands of people converged on Munich's Theresenwiese fairground, the setting of the city's Oktoberfest, where the two social democratic parties—the Social Democrats and the Independent Social Democrats—were organizing a massive demonstration demanding an immediate end to the war. By late afternoon, the crowd had swelled to some sixty thousand demonstrators—party loyalists, union members, mutinous soldiers, Schwabing bohemians, and curious onlookers.[91] People waved red flags and banners, shouting, "Down with the war!" and "Long live the republic!"[92]

Standing on a soapbox that evening was a drama critic who, with his unruly beard and large balding head, looked like he'd walked straight out of the Old Testament. His name was Kurt Eisner. A Berlin-born Jew, Eisner had only recently been released from the Stadelheim prison, where he'd served an eight-month sentence for his role in the January 1918 munitions workers' strike. Now a parliamentary candidate for the Independent Social Democrats, he was about to lead a peaceful and successful one-man revolution.

Erhard Auer, the leader of the Majority Social Democrats, had given his assurances to the Bavarian Royal Government that no revolution would occur at the demonstration. But he was soon outmaneuvered by Eisner, who knew that the time for decisive action had come. While Auer was still speaking Eisner led his followers to the military barracks and munitions depot, where they encountered no resistance from the authorities. "The police seemed to have vanished," the writer Oskar Maria Graf recalled. "Inquisitive faces gazed down upon us from the many open windows in the houses. At every point fresh bands joined us, and now some were armed. Most of the people laughed and chattered, as though they were going to a fair."[93] Before long, all of Munich's garrisons and military barracks signaled their support for the revolution. A meeting convened at the Mäthaserbräu beer hall elected a Council of Workers, Soldiers, and Peasants over mugs of beer and plates of pork knuckle. Then word spread that Bavarian King Ludwig III, unable to count on any troops to defend him, had abandoned the Residenz Palace and escaped across the border to Austria with his family, effectively ending the Wittelsbach dynasty that had ruled Bavaria for nearly eight hundred years.

From the Mäthaserbräu, Eisner led his band of revolutionaries to the Bavarian parliament on Prannerstrasse, where he proclaimed the People's State of Bavaria, establishing a provisional government composed of members of both social democratic parties. The revolution had been entirely peaceful. At the end of the night, Eisner remarked to Wilhelm Herzog: "Isn't it wondrous that we made a revolution without spilling a drop of blood? That's never happened in history."[94]

Thomas Mann spent that evening at the Tonhalle, where he and Katia attended a concert by Hans Pfitzner. Rumors of unrest inevitably reached them, yet Mann refused to let the "absurd rabble" on the Theresenwiese prevent him from enjoying the evening's music.[95] There were songs by Haydn, Schumann, Brahms, and Weber, and though he found the singer of the *Oberon* overture "wretched," the concert had its "beautiful moments."[96] Afterward, the Manns agreed to dine at the home of the composer Walter Braunfels, but since there were no trams running they had to walk there. As they did, a few members of their party began discussing the events of the day and the general political situation. Mann was having none of it. He pointed to the starry sky above them, clear but moisture-laden. "Eternity puts one in a contemplative mood," he said. "Fundamentally, what is human is alien to politics."[97]

His mood was less sanguine the next morning. He awoke with a cold, received a phone call from his alarmed mother-in-law, and saw on the front pages of the local newspaper Eisner's declaration of the new Bavarian Republic. "I took it too lightly after all," he admitted to himself. During his noontime walk with Bauschan he passed a military vehicle with soldiers waving a red flag driving in the direction of Poschingerstrasse. He was relieved when he came across a poster bearing Eisner's signature that forbade looting of any kind.

The revolution was not confined to Munich. It had begun in Kiel on November 3, when sailors of the German High Seas Fleet mutinied against the Naval High Command's preposterous order to engage the British Royal Navy in a final battle in the English Channel. From there, it spread to other port cities along the German coast, including Bremen and Hamburg. It even reached Heligoland, a small archipelago in the North Sea some thirty miles off the coast of Germany. For anyone still hoping a German revolution could be prevented, the Kiel mutiny was a bitter corrective. As the historian Friedrich Meinecke put it in his diary: "The dam has broken."[98]

On November 9, following mass demonstrations on the streets of Berlin, as well as pressure from the Independent Social Democrats and other left-wing factions, the Majority Social Democrats broke with Chancellor von Baden and demanded the immediate abdication of the kaiser. Von Baden made several attempts to secure a declaration from Wilhelm II, who had instead abandoned his empire by fleeing Berlin for the military field headquarters in Spa, Belgium. At noon, without waiting for official authorization, von Baden declared the kaiser's abdication and recommended that Friedrich Ebert, the leader of the Majority Social Democrats, be appointed Reich chancellor. By evening, a provisional government consisting of three Majority Social Democrats and three Independent Social Democrats, called the Council of the People's Deputies, had been formed. The German Empire had officially been replaced by what became known as the Weimar Republic.

Given his wartime writings, Thomas Mann's attitude to the formation of a German republic proved surprisingly acquiescent: "My attitude toward the Greater German social republic that appears to be forming is completely reconciled and affirmative," he wrote in his diary on November 10. "The social republic is something well in advance of and superior to the idea of the bourgeois republic and plutocracy of the West; for the first time France will be forced to follow Germany's lead politically."[99] As Mann's biographer Hermann Kurzke points out, this was how nonpolitical men behaved in practice: "they are loyal to whatever is in existence."[100] Besides, Mann reserved his vitriol for the "victors" of the war, those "bourgeois imperialists, devotees of power politics, and stupid, revengeful devils" now imposing the terms of peace on Germany.[101]

That peace finally came two days later, on November 11. While the revolution unfolded in Berlin, the German armistice delegation, led by the Catholic Centre Party politician Matthias Erzberger, had traveled to Compiègne on November 8 to negotiate the terms of the armistice with Marshal Ferdinand Foch, head of the French delegation. At eleven o'clock on the morning of November 11, the guns fell silent at last.

The war had lasted 1,567 days. Over eight million soldiers had been killed, and more than twice that number wounded. Civilian deaths from war, disease, and malnutrition are estimated to have been as high as ten million. Four enormous empires—the German, the Russian, the Austro-Hungarian, and the Ottoman—had come crashing down, the European continent splintering into an unstable tapestry of nation-states, inflaming conflicts between national and ethnic groups. The world that now emerged from the war was more violent, dangerous, and unstable than the world that had preceded it. Far from being "the war that will end war," in H. G. Wells's famous phrase, it spawned a multitude of new wars instead. According to the historian Robert Gerwath, there were twenty-seven violent transfers of power in Europe between 1917 and 1920 alone.[102] As many as four million people died as a result of armed conflicts *after* the war.[103]

To the new German republic, the end of the war posed all manner of unhappy challenges. For starters, the roughly six million German soldiers still in arms on November 11 had to be brought back from the Western and Eastern Fronts, while another 2.7 million wounded or shell-shocked soldiers urgently needed to be cared for.[104] These millions would constitute Germany's "lost generation," as one historian has put it: men "who never quite felt at home anywhere, were unable to seize the initiative and get their lives on course, and were plagued by the uncertainty of the future."[105]

These returning men abound in the fiction of the Weimar era. There is the disfigured Doctor Otternschlag in Vicki Baum's novel *Grand Hotel* for whom "the world was a crumbling affair not to be grasped or held."[106] In Joseph Roth's *The Spider's Web*, a returning lieutenant, Theodor Lohse, suspects his mother and sister of resenting him for not dying "a hero's death" in the war: "A dead son would have been the pride of the family. A demobilized lieutenant, a victim of the revolution, was a burden to his womenfolk."[107] Most popular of all was Erich Maria Remarque's bestselling *All Quiet on the Western Front*, in which the main character, Paul Bäumer, prophesies that "the generation that has grown up after us will be strange to us and push us aside. We shall be superfluous even to ourselves."[108]

The country these soldiers were returning to was not, in their eyes, the same country they had fought for. Consequently, a rift opened up between troops stationed inside Germany, many of whom had participated in revolutionary soldiers' councils, and those returning from the Western Front. The fact that the German High Command had left it to civilian politicians to sign the armistice would turn out to be a cynical ploy to feed the so-called stab-in-the-back myth: the false idea that Germany had been defeated, not by enemies abroad, but by radicals at home.

Perhaps most pressing of all for the new German republic was the matter of politically uniting a starved country burdened by military loss and threatened by internal strife. As the historian Detlev J. K. Peukert has put it: "The beginning of the Republic was not marked by an event that served as an old-fashioned but politically unifying symbol of a pivotal moment in national history, along the lines of the American Declaration of Independence, the *quatorze juillet* in France or indeed Sedan Day after the creation of the German Empire in 1870–71. . . . The fact that the Republic had no legitimized founding ritual implies a lack of legitimacy in general: it suggests that there was a lack of active commitment to the new order."[109]

One individual who was nothing if not actively committed to the new order was Heinrich Mann. His novel *Man of Straw*, now published at last, became an instant success, going through seven editions in just six weeks, and was in some circles referred to as "the bible of the Wilhelmian epoch."[110] In early 1919 he dedicated his collection of political essays *Power and People* to the German republic. As a friend of Kurt Eisner's, he soon joined the Munich revolution as chairman of the Political Council of Intellectual Workers, dedicating himself to the moral and spiritual education of his fellow Germans. "We are here to do our part in the introduction of the moral laws of a liberated world into German politics," he said in an address to the council in late November. "Spiritual well-being is more important, for the fate of mankind is more determined by its way of feeling than by economic rules."[111]

Yet by prioritizing "spiritual well-being" over economic well-being, Heinrich revealed himself to be more than a touch naïve about the harsh realities facing the German public after four years of war economy and the dire consequences of the British blockade. It was admirable of him to believe that Germany could be reconciled with the world through the power of ideas, its people united in the spirit of "equal fraternity for all."[112] But unfortunately, as the coming months would show, such beliefs were shared by very few.

His younger brother certainly entertained no such illusions about the future. When Thomas Mann read the text of Heinrich's speech in the *Münchener Neueste Nachrichten* on December 1, he commented in his diary: "When will he have had his fill of it?" And yet Mann seemed despite this to be coming around to the idea that, as he put it, "the future belongs to the concept of socialism, even of communism, *as* an idea"—an idea he felt Germany ought to "take for its own, outwardly as well as inwardly."[113]

Though he spent most days working on a poem for his youngest daughter—eventually published in 1919 as *The Song of the Child: An Idyll*—Mann continued to try to make sense of what was happening, not just in Munich but in the country as a whole. He attended a discussion about the state of Germany at the München Herrenklub with, among others, Kurt Martens, Rainer Maria Rilke, and the Austrian writer Rudolf Kassner. He found it stimulating and was even tempted to take part in the debate but instead found himself absorbed in admiring an elegant young man with a "gracefully foolish, boyish face.... Was he a guest in the club, or will I meet him again? I readily admit to myself that this could turn into an experience."[114]

He longed above all to retreat from the realm of action and politics. Many of the letters flooding in from readers of the *Reflections* rubbed him the wrong way. A lieutenant stationed in Posen sent him "a rather confused and brooding gush of ideas about the fate of young people who have been through the war." The daughter of a Swiss Federal Council member sent a childish letter that was "excessively enthusiastic" about *Reflections*.[115] Worst of all was a registered letter from Elisabeth Förster-Nietzsche informing him that he had been awarded the Lassen Prize from the Nietzsche Archive in Weimar. "Mixed feelings," he noted in his diary, no doubt because of the increasingly rightward drift of the archive.[116] Where once it had attracted writers and thinkers from all over the world, during the war it had begun to nurture a militant, bastardized Nietzscheism that sanctioned war, violence, and ruthlessness. By the end of the 1920s, according to Nietzsche biographer Sue Prideaux, the archive would be "thick with Nazis."[117]

Germany's defeat in the war and the collapse of the old social order gradually pushed Mann to question his beliefs of the past four and a half years. What had been the point of the massive and agonizing undertaking of the *Reflections* if the people who now wrote to him were confused young soldiers or right-wing intellectuals? Once again, a cloud of isolation settled around him. "Realized that I live a solitary, withdrawn, brooding, peculiar, and sad existence," he wrote in his diary on December 29. "Heinrich's life, by contrast, is very sunny just now."

But at least he felt himself being drawn back toward fiction writing. Whatever else he now felt about his *Reflections*, it had lifted a leaden burden. In one of his last diary entries of the year, he remarked: "Made some good decisions yesterday with regard to the new beginning of *The Magic Mountain*."[118]

CHAPTER 5

Doubts and Considerations, 1919–1921

On April 9, 1919, Thomas Mann awoke from uneasy dreams and decided to cancel his afternoon appointment with his dentist. A wretched cough had kept him up until two in the morning; he felt tired and feverish. On the street outside his window, incredibly, not a trace remained of the heavy snowfall that had blanketed the city only a few days earlier. It was a very windy but mild spring day.

Mann went in to check on Katia, then almost nine months pregnant with the couple's sixth (and final) child. She felt no better than he did; she was still in bed and her voice was extremely hoarse. Downstairs, Mann took a phone call from the architect Gustav Ludwig, who provided a few updates on the city's ever-changing political situation. Newspapers were in the hands of the revolutionary government. Bank withdrawals were capped at a hundred marks a day. No jewels or valuables were to be removed, which meant that Katia's mother probably wouldn't see her pearls again. Mann thanked Ludwig and hung up the phone. Then, after a light breakfast, he cleared out his storage shelves and unpacked the handwritten pages of *The Magic Mountain* for the first time in almost four years.

His thoughts had been returning to the novel and the possibilities of its continuation and completion for many months now. In September 1914, the tone of Gogol's story "How the Two Ivans

Quarrelled" struck him as "just the right one for *The Magic Mountain*." In October, he reportedly "did some thinking about *The Magic Mountain* once again, and the problem of its conclusion."[1] By March, it had become clear that a reunion between author and novel was not far off: "Began studying the book about world freemasonry, pencil in hand, in connection with Settembrini. For now I am beginning to turn my thoughts back to *The Magic Mountain*, in which a whole world, a polyphony of themes, attractions, and ideas opens up for me once again."[2]

From the chain-dragging monomania of *Reflections* to the amiably peopled polyphony, the "pure, productive Goethean realm," of *The Magic Mountain*—this was itself a significant change.[3] The unhappy labor of his wartime writings, Germany's defeat and its subsequent plunge into revolution and chaos—not to mention the literary and political revival of Heinrich's career—all of these factors played their part in Mann's return to the terra firma of his fiction. The timing, Mann felt, was just right. "During the war it was too early," he noted in his diary. "The war had to clarify itself as the beginning of the revolution, and not only did it have to end, but the end had to become recognizable as only a pseudo-end." Sending Hans Castorp into the war, he continued, meant "sending him into the beginning of the struggle for the new."[4] But what kind of struggle did Thomas Mann imagine was now beginning?

* * *

The city in which Mann resumed writing his novel was almost unrecognizable from the city in which he'd written the novel's first chapters five years before. On the other side of the Isar, a bloody struggle for power was being waged that would determine the future, not only of Bavaria, but of the Weimar Republic as a whole.

The Bavarian parliamentary elections on January 12, 1919, had not gone down as Kurt Eisner hoped they would. The Independent Social Democrats suffered an unequivocal defeat, securing no more than 2.5 percent of the popular vote.[5] To a degree, this was a judgment on Eisner's apparent inability to solve the city's most pressing problems. Food shortages remained acute, inflation was rampant, and unemployment was high. Eisner's greatest folly, however, was his decision to leak documents he thought proved Germany's war guilt to the Allied victors. To his mind, this was a good-faith demonstration of the new Germany's break with its past. To the Bavarian middle classes, it was tantamount to treason.

Even had Eisner succeeded, the mostly conservative Bavarian populace simply didn't trust a Jew from Berlin. His brief tenure in office was marked by a pogrom-like atmosphere. On November 9, 1918, the occultist writer Rudolf von Sebottendorf, founder of the anti-Semitic Thule Society, delivered a speech in which he flat-out declared: "Now we need to speak about the German Reich, now we need to say that the Jew is our mortal enemy, and as of today we will act." A conspiracy theory claiming Eisner's real name was Kosmanowsky and that he was actually a Galician Jew was reprinted by the *Bayerische Kurier* and the *Münchner Neueste Nachrichten* and repeated by prominent politicians.[6] Even Thomas Mann, despite having married into a Jewish family and fathering six Jewish children, was not above the occasional anti-Jewish remark, though such language was at least confined to a few isolated and ill-tempered entries in his diary, such as his comment on November 8 that Munich was being run by "Jewish scribblers."[7]

As resistance to Eisner intensified, so did the viciousness of Munich's anti-Semitic elements. Hateful leaflets appeared in grocery stores or were pasted on walls around the city. The future Nazi ideologist Alfred Rosenberg arrived from Estonia, bringing with him the anti-Semitic fabrication *Protocols of the Elders of Zion*, published in a German translation in 1919. The Thule Society established a paramilitary organization, the *Kampfbund*, intending to overthrow the Bavarian government. Its members included Hans Frank, Rudolf Hess, and Rosenberg—all of whom would later rise to prominent roles in the Nazi Party.[8] Munich's Archbishop Michael von Faulhaber repeatedly refused to speak out against anti-Semitism despite being asked to do so by the rabbi Leo Baerwald, with whom he had served as military chaplain during the war.[9]

On Friday, February 21, while walking to the parliament building to submit his letter of resignation, Kurt Eisner was shot and killed by the twenty-two-year-old law student Count Anton Graf von Arco auf Valley. Incredibly, the assassination was immediately followed by an attempt on the life of Eisner's rival, the Social Democrat politician Erhard Auer. While delivering an impromptu eulogy for his murdered colleague, Auer was shot by Alois Lindner, an unemployed butcher, who stormed into the Landtag with a Browning rifle hidden under his coat. Auer survived, but the Bavarian People's Party politician Heinrich Osel and a young army major were both killed.[10]

As soon as she heard the news Katia burst into her husband's study. "Shock, horror, and disgust with the whole thing," Mann wrote in his diary. "What will the consequences be?" Bruno Walter's wife, Elsa, called several times to say that soldiers were searching nearby homes for weapons, while Klaus and Golo said their classmates applauded the news when they first heard it. Mann thought he heard cracks of gunfire and even the explosion of a grenade in the vicinity. "The situation is confused and dangerous," he wrote.[11]

The philologist Victor Klemperer, in a dispatch for the *Leipziger Neueste Nachrichten*, observed that all of Munich was changed in an instant by Eisner's assassination. "Before you even knew what had happened, you sensed the effects. Suddenly the streetcars stopped running, stores and restaurants closed, and students streamed out of the university and technical college, which were shut down."[12] The city that had so vehemently rejected Eisner as a politician now mourned his death to an almost bizarre degree. Hundreds gathered at the location of his death; some went so far as to dip their handkerchiefs in the pool of his blood. Soldiers erected a pyramid of rifles while others waved red flags adorned with a black ribbon. Heinrich Mann spoke at the memorial at the Odeon concert hall, claiming Eisner's short-lived government had brought "more ideas, more joys of rationality, more intellectual stimulation, than the fifty years that went before."[13]

A new coalition government led by the Social Democrat Johannes Hoffmann soon assumed power, but it too failed to address the city's mounting socioeconomic problems. Forty thousand people were out of work and the municipal debt was spiraling. According to the historian David Clay Large, "the capital's credit was so bad that state-run agencies like the post office had stopped accepting Munich's emergency currency."[14] Hoffmann's government encountered growing resistance from the left, where demands for a Soviet-style republic were rising in pitch.[15] A revolutionary demonstration on the Theresenwiese on March 1 was broken up by the Majority Social Democrats' militia, killing three people.[16] Later that month, news of Béla Kun's communist uprising in Hungary "hit Munich like a bomb," prompting Hoffmann's government to flee to the northern Bavarian town of Bamberg.[17] In its place, the Bavarian Soviet Republic was proclaimed, led by a Central Council consisting of, among others, the writers Ernst Toller, Erich Mühsam, and Gustav Landauer.

Munich's citizens looked on with stoic detachment as the city sank deeper and deeper into disarray. "Munich passively accepts its tragicomic fate," Victor Klemperer reported, "and even the apparently dominant proletariat is quite passive, allowing itself to be pushed hither and thither."[18] Revolutionaries bickered among themselves, hastening their own collapse. Even Ernst Toller had to admit the republic had been "a failure."[19] Workers went on strike, newspaper offices were occupied, the homes of the wealthy looted. There were instances of hostage-taking, occasional clashes in the streets, and rumors of an impending "liberation" by the ousted Hoffmann and his so-called White troops, who now controlled northern Bavaria. Everywhere one looked, people carried weapons: revolvers, rifles, hand grenades. "It looks more like the Wild West than Munich," Klemperer wrote.[20]

To a degree, this was true of Germany as a whole. In a bid to preserve order and win the support of the army, not to mention quell what it perceived to be a Bolshevik threat, Friedrich Ebert's government struck a deal with so-called Freikorps volunteers—paramilitary units consisting of former frontline troops and young right-wing students united by their hatred of communism (and, increasingly, of the republic they were supposedly defending). According to Robert Gerwarth, these were "explosive all-male subcultures in which brutal violence was an acceptable, if not desirable, form of political expression."[21] During the winter of 1918–19, when the communist Spartacus League led an uprising in Berlin, Freikorps troops marched on the city, leaving a trail of death and destruction in their wake. Two hundred people were killed, among them the Spartacist leaders Karl Liebknecht and Rosa Luxembourg. Their brutal deaths at the hands of right-wing paramilitaries sent shock waves around the world.[22]

But it was in Munich that the Freikorps played its most decisive role. Though he had rejected it at first, Hoffmann finally accepted the Reich government's offer to send thousands of regular troops to support his plan to "liberate" Munich from the revolutionaries. Additionally, he urged "all Bavarians" to help destroy the "Russian terror" in Munich, a call that naturally appealed to the most extreme nationalists. Yet even by the remorseless standards of the Freikorps, those who answered Hoffmann's call were some of the most brutal and antidemocratic forces in all of Germany. They were led by, among others, Franz von Ritter

Epp and Ernst Röhm, both of whom later joined the Nazi Party. Another Freikorps officer and future Nazi, Manfred von Killinger, put it this way: "Munich was under the rule of Red hordes. Levien, Leviné-Nissen, Mühsam, etc., what kind of people were these? Were they Bavarians? No! Jewish, internationalist riff-raff, Schwabing intellectuals."[23]

On April 30, in response to the murder of medical orderlies and unarmed soldiers by Freikorps troops in Starnberg and Dachau, a group of Bavarian "Red Army" soldiers decided to exact revenge by shooting ten hostages being held at the Luitpold Gymnasium (or School). One of them was a woman, a Jewish painter. When Ernst Toller heard what was happening, he sprinted to the school in a panic to prevent further bloodshed. He found another six hostages cowering behind a locked door and immediately released them, before attempting in vain to have a doctor come and remove the corpses. "The very sight of them would be enough to lash the Whites into an orgiastic frenzy of revenge," he later wrote.[24]

Just as Toller feared, the hostage murders were swiftly and effectively exploited to further inflame counterrevolutionary sentiment. Photographs of the corpses taken by Heinrich Hoffmann (Hitler's future private photographer) were splashed across newspapers everywhere.[25] "There are said to be ten of them, some townspeople and some aristocrats," Thomas Mann reported in his diary on May 1. "Tremendous rage among the bourgeois population." That same day, the army and the Freikorps troops moved in and began their decisive assault on the city. All throughout the afternoon the sound of machine-gun fire rattled through the air while explosions shook the windows. By early evening, Mann wrote, the city was "almost entirely in the hands of government troops."[26]

Despite encountering little resistance and being greeted with cheers by many of Munich's citizens, the army and Freikorps troops were out for blood. In their hunt for those responsible for

Bavaria's Soviet experiment they showed no mercy. Gustav Landauer was beaten half to death and then shot, his body dumped in a washhouse. The communist Eugen Leviné was captured, put on trial, and promptly executed. Ernst Toller went into hiding but was arrested a few weeks later, his life spared only when a few prominent writers, Thomas Mann included, managed to intervene on his behalf.[27] Hundreds of others were beaten, tortured, and summarily shot. So indiscriminate was the violence that, when a Freikorps unit came across a meeting of a Catholic society on May 6, they simply assumed they were communists and shot twenty-one innocent men in cold blood.[28]

On May 9, the *Münchner Neuesten Nachrichten* published an appeal against the ongoing violence, encouraging the city's bourgeoisie to recognize its common fate with the working people. "It is useless to ask now who was the first to shed blood and feel horror in this struggle: the only important thing is who will find a way out of it and into a fruitful future for the whole nation," the appeal read.[29] It was signed by, among others, Rainer Maria Rilke, Bruno Walter, and Heinrich and Thomas Mann.

It was a well-meaning but ultimately naïve letter. Worse, it gave the impression that the Reds and the Whites were somehow equally to blame for the violence. The reality was almost absurdly one-sided. In all, some six hundred people were killed during the White Terror, many of them civilians. More than twenty-two hundred were imprisoned or sentenced to death.[30] Did the Social Democrats in Berlin have any idea of the poison they'd just administered to their Bavarian patient? Gustav Noske, the Social Democrat army minister responsible for brokering the agreement between Ebert's government and the Freikorps troops, cheerfully cabled the White army's commanding officer: "I am extremely pleased with the discreet and wholly successful way in which you have conducted operations in Munich; please convey my thanks to your troops."[31]

DOUBTS AND CONSIDERATIONS

Munich, once lauded for its easygoing cheer, would never be the same. Its transformation from bohemian enclave to Nazi breeding ground had now commenced. Tens of thousands of government troops, Freikorps forces, and so-called *Einwohnerwehren,* or civil guards, now filled the streets and beer halls, enlisting in their ranks young men who had missed out on the war's action. "One can say that, in the bloody adventure of the council republic and its aftermath, the old and easygoing Munich zest for life came to an end," the poet Isolde Kurz observed.[32]

Many decided to leave Munich, the poet Rainer Maria Rilke among them. Rilke's apartment on Ainmillerstrasse had been searched twice when Ernst Toller was still in hiding, and he had even been suspected of producing communist propaganda. "Bitterness has increased enormously in all its many hiding places and will sooner or later become active again," he wrote. "One hears and sees nothing but departures; many of the most permanent residents are giving up their houses, here and there great moving vans spend the night before their gates."[33]

Thomas Mann, despite having "passed through all the storms virtually unaffected," as he put it, likewise thought of leaving. "I have had our good Munich up to here," he wrote to Phillip Witkop in May. "Now the bourgeoisie has come to the top again with outside help, but totally deceives itself about the lasting danger of the situation.... I am considering moving away."[34] But having sold Bad Tölz in 1917 and invested the fifty-three thousand marks he made from the sale in war bonds (a futile patriotic gesture: he never saw the money again), even the option of taking an extended break from the city seemed closed to him.[35] With a long novel to write and a house brimful of five children and a newborn son, Mann's need of an escape was beginning to feel especially acute.

A solution was offered by George Martin Richter, the American-born, German-raised, Munich-based art dealer whose daughter Mann would later become godfather to. In March 1919,

Richter had bought an English-style cottage in Feldafing, a small town on the west bank of Lake Starnberg. Nicknamed "Villino," the hip-roofed house was located just half a mile from the lake, and on clear, sunny days the snow-capped ridge of the Alps was visible beyond it.

For an investment of ten thousand marks, Richter would ensure that Mann had a bedroom, a study, and a housekeeper at his disposal whenever he desired. It was an opportunity he couldn't refuse. Between 1919 and 1923, Mann made at least fourteen trips to Feldafing, often staying for several weeks at a time in what he affectionately took to calling "the mousehole."[36] He went for long walks in the surrounding countryside, breakfasted in the arbor in the garden, and rowed on the broad lake in spring and summer months. The exterior facade of the nearby Hotel Kaiserin Elisabeth even reminded him of the Waldsanatorium in Davos.

But best of all was the gramophone Richter acquired for Villino. "The highlight of the visit," Mann wrote of one of his Feldafing sojourns in February 1920, "[was] Richter's superlative Gramophone, which I put to continuous use, either alone or with Katia or Richter." Mann could spend an entire evening listening to recordings of some of the most famous classical vocalists of the time, including Enrico Caruso, Mattia Battistini, Nellie Melba, and Titta Ruffo. He developed an "almost sinful passion" for the small cabinet-like electric device, and in *The Magic Mountain* he paid homage by describing its mechanism in exhaustive detail:

> When you lifted the gracefully beveled lid, a well-secured brass rod raised automatically to hold it in place at a protective angle, and inside you saw, set slightly lower, the turntable with its green cloth cover and nickel rim, plus the nickel spindle that fitted into the hole of the ebonite disks. At the front on the right was a device like the dial on a clock for regulating the turntable's tempo, to its left, the lever that started and stopped it; at the rear on the left, however,

was the sinuous, club-shaped nickel tube that had pliant, movable joints and ended in a flat, round sound-box equipped with a screw into which the needle was inserted. When you opened the double doors at the front, you saw a diagonal pattern of wooden louvers stained black—nothing more.[37]

Above all, Mann recognized immediately that the gramophone represented "a rich find both for its intellectual possibilities and its narrative value" with respect to *The Magic Mountain*.[38] It planted the seed of one of the novel's most unsettling questions: what if music, specifically the German love of music, could in fact lead to dark and dangerous consequences?[39]

* * *

The silence and solitude of Feldafing proved deeply beneficial to the progress of *The Magic Mountain*. Seated at his polished Biedermeier desk on the first floor of the house, Mann had only to produce his "daily quota," as he called it, about one-and-a-half handwritten manuscript sheets a day. He liked to use blue-lined graph paper with a tear-edge on the left, keeping very strictly to twenty-five lines per page, a system that enabled him to know at any given moment where exactly he was in the manuscript.[40]

Mann began by reading through and revising what he'd written prior to abandoning the novel in 1915, making significant changes to the material. Most crucial of all was his introduction of the theme of time, his sense that the years of the war marked a rupture in the fabric of world history, a transformation that could not, as he put it in the novel's foreword that he wrote in April, be measured in days or orbits around the sun. The narrator goes on: "The extraordinary pastness of our story results from its having taken place *before* a certain turning point, on the far side of a rift that has cut deeply through our lives and consciousness. It takes place, or, to avoid any present tense whatever, it took place back then, long ago, in the old days of the world before the Great War, with whose beginning so many things began whose beginnings, it seems, have not yet ceased."[41] As the critic Edwin Frank points out, by emphasizing the novel's taking place before the turning point of the war, the narrator is also reminding the reader that he is encountering the novel *after* that same turning point. "The book, in other words, is as much about after as before, bracketing the immensity of the war like a parenthesis," Frank comments.[42] The fact that Mann wrote the majority of the novel *after* the First World War adds another layer of meaning to the idea of *The Magic Mountain* as "a time-novel," as Mann called it. As much as he intended to portray European civilization as it existed before the war, the tumult of postwar Germany would increasingly come to impress itself on the manuscript. Tellingly, Mann at one point compared the manuscript to a sponge, capable of absorbing everything.[43]

Mann, of course, was not alone in grasping the rupture in historical time the war signified. A hitherto unknown intellectual by the name Oswald Spengler had spent the war years writing the first volume of *The Decline of the West,* a strange and unwieldy tome based on the idea that civilizations, like biological organisms, undergo life cycles. Though less an original work than "a great summing up of a half-century of historical pessimism and cultural discontent," Spengler's argument that the end of the liberal West was nigh found a receptive audience in Germany, reinforcing an already prevalent *Untergangsstimmung,* or declinist mood.[44] The young conservative sociologist Hans Freyer wrote a glowing review in *Die Tat,* a journal published by the *völkisch* Eugen Diederichs. Elisabeth Förster-Nietzsche was so impressed by the first volume that she awarded Spengler the Nietzsche Prize.

Mann first read Spengler's book in July 1919. Though his enthusiasm for *The Decline of the West* would prove to be short-lived, Mann was struck at once by Spengler's excursions on time and his belief that history is cyclical. "It makes a deep, mysterious impression on me to see what role the problem of time plays in Spengler's philosophy of history, since it has occupied me as a basic motif for *The Magic Mountain* since 1912 or 13, when Spengler's work was still in its early stages," he noted in his diary. Mann attributed this shared interest to his own "unusual sensitivity," since he felt himself to be largely ignorant of the prevailing intellectual fashions in the years before the war.[45]

Another pivotal reading experience that may have shaped some of Mann's thinking about *The Magic Mountain* took place later in that same summer of 1919. It was a novel called *Demian* by a writer no one had ever heard of before: Emil Sinclair. Serialized in *Die Neue Rundschau* between February and April and published in book form by Samuel Fischer in June, this novel became a surprise sensation, leading many readers to wonder at the author's identity. "Who is Emil Sinclair?" Mann wrote at once to Fischer. "How old is he? Where does he live?"[46] But all Fischer could tell him was that the author was young and sick and lived in Switzerland. Not until 1923 was it revealed that Emil Sinclair was a pseudonym, and that the real author was Herman Hesse, author of the popular 1904 novel *Peter Camenzind*, which had also been published by Fischer.

An unabashedly (and rather tediously) mystical novel, heavily influenced by C. G. Jung's disciple Dr. Josef Bernhard Lang, Hesse's *Demian* is the story of a young man's spiritual education in the years before the First World War at the hands of three mentors: Max Demian, a friend from school; Pistorius, a musician and theologian; and Demian's mother, the subtly-named Eve. Filled with tirades against the mediocrity of European society and premonitions of its destruction and collapse, Hesse's novel touched a nerve in a war-weary country longing for spiritual rebirth.

For Mann, the chief attraction of the novel was the thematic concerns it shared with *The Magic Mountain*: the ideals of the world before the war and what Hesse's narrator calls the problem of "two worlds, or half-worlds, one of light and one of darkness."[47] The fact that *Demian* was a kind of bildungsroman culminating with the outbreak of the war and a vision of "a new humanity" was significant.[48] Mann now knew that Hans Castorp, too, had to be a product of the old world before the war, that it was necessary to show him as "intellectually bound by his own time, reveal his mental and moral lassitude, his lack of faith, and hopelessness," as he wrote in his diary in early June.[49] Like Hesse's Demian, he would undergo a spiritual education at the hands of two mentors, Settembrini and Pastor Bunge (an earlier version of the character who would become Leo Naphta), characters "equally right and wrong in their viewpoints."[50]

The genre of the bildungsroman dates back to eighteenth-century Germany, a time of literary and cultural renewal wrought by the devastation of the Thirty Years' War and the political upheaval of the French Revolution. Novels like Karl Phillip Moritz's *Anton Reiser* (1785–90), Goethe's *Wilhelm Meister's Apprenticeship* (1795–96), and Ludwig Tieck's *Franz Sternbald's Wanderings* (1798) eschewed the picaresque mode in favor of an emphasis on inner development. In these novels, pliant young men go out into the world and grow spiritually and intellectually through their encounters with people and the world around them. Often regarded as "exuding an optimistic faith in the human potential for growth," the genre, Mann argued in 1916, could only survive in the twentieth century as parody.[51]

As Todd Kontje has shown, *The Magic Mountain* inverts the premises of the bildungsroman in that Hans Castorp is "seduced away from practical activity in the world" at the same time that it fulfills those same premises, since Hans Castorp would not have explored ideas had he returned to Hamburg and become an engineer instead.[52] Elsewhere, Kontje has challenged the overly simplistic understanding of the bildungsroman's alleged optimism, arguing that the novels of Goethe, Tieck, and Moritz, among others, were as much a critical commentary on the social and cultural transformations of the late eighteenth century as they were artistic examples of it.[53] With its disquisitions on time, biology, and music, and above all in the debates between Naphta and Settembrini, *The Magic Mountain* pushes this feature of the genre even further, into the direction of what David S. Luft calls philosophical essayism, thereby blurring the boundaries of fiction and nonfiction.[54] Far more than just a parody, then, *The Magic Mountain* is also a self-conscious continuation of, and challenge to, the genre of the bildungsroman.

* * *

One pastoral summer day in July 1920, Klaus and Erika Mann surprised their father by biking the nearly twenty-five miles from Poschingerstrasse to Villino with their friend Richard Hallgarten. Delighted by this unexpected visit, Mann at once had lunch prepared for them in the garden's grove and then took them rowing on the lake in the direction of Tutzing, a town just a few miles south of Feldafing. When the intense heat overwhelmed them, they bathed along the shore, perhaps in sight of Schloss Garatshausen, a small castle dating back to the sixteenth century. At one point, beholding his thirteen-year-old son frolicking in the water, Mann thought to himself that Klaus looked "terribly handsome in his swimming trunks." Later, in his diary, he wrote: "Find it quite natural that I should fall in love with my son." A few days later, on Friday, July 23, Mann took the new express train back to Munich, traveling in third class. He struck up a short but "very pleasurable" conversation with an attractive young man in white trousers seated next to him. In his diary that night he wondered: "It seems I am once and for all done with women?"[55]

Mann resumed writing *The Magic Mountain* at a difficult time in his sexual life. The last section he'd written before abandoning the manuscript in 1915 was the "Hippe" subchapter; revisiting it now, he felt the "distinctly ticklish" subject required "tact": "Every detail must be examined to see whether it only touches upon the verge of aestheticism or oversteps the limit."[56] His diary records that in April 1919, he witnessed "a sensually exciting spectacle" while taking a walk that made him think of "the motif of forbidden love in *The Magic Mountain*."[57] A few months later, he received a letter from Paul Ehrenberg, the object of Mann's youthful romantic interest, that brought back memories: "I loved him, and [it] was something akin to requited love."[58] On that same day, he began reading the first volume of Hans Blüher's *The Role of Eroticism in Masculine Society*, published in 1917. In it, Blüher envisaged a homoerotic state in which men were free to cast off the burden of daily life, believing "that masculine creativity could flourish only among male camaraderie and that the family destroyed man's spirit."[59]

Blüher's book touched a nerve. Whenever Mann returned from his Feldafing retreats, after days or weeks of living in the "self-indulgent ambience of a bachelor household," he found domestic life difficult to readjust to. There were taxes to pay, children to scold, housemaids to reprimand, and an igloo of mail waiting on his desk. "I am suffocating from all the letters I owe, my nerves being destroyed by the world's pressures and importunities," he complained.[60] His diaries also record that he and Katia were having sexual problems. "Grateful to Katia for her unwavering love for me even though she no longer awakens my desire," he wrote on October 17, 1920. Months later, in May 1921, he once again notes "the goodness with which she accepts my sexual problems."[61]

Compounding Mann's difficulties was the sexual awakening of Klaus, who first became aware of his own erotic attraction to boys around this time, a development for which he was "completely unprepared," he later wrote.[62] One day in May 1920, Katia came across Klaus's diary lying open in his room and was shocked and disturbed by what she read in it. Thomas, for whom Klaus's feelings were anything but unfamiliar, did his best to reassure and comfort Katia. "I will never play the infuriated father," he observed in his diary the same evening. "There is nothing the boy can do about his nature, which is not of his own making." A few days later, he made a point of hugging Klaus and telling him to be of good cheer even if "life isn't always easy."[63]

Mann lived out his complicated sexual life against a broader crisis of masculinity among European intellectuals. The dramatic social and cultural upheavals of the late nineteenth century brought about a transformation in attitudes toward sexuality. In the first decades of the twentieth century, no figure represented this transformation more brilliantly than Sigmund Freud, whose *Three Essays on the Theory of Sexuality* first appeared as a pamphlet in 1905.

Though Mann thought highly of Freud and wrote about him on several occasions, he never gave the same answer when asked about his first encounter with the Viennese doctor's work. He claimed to first have read him in 1925, when he was beginning his research for the *Joseph* novels, but that same year he told an Italian newspaper that *Death in Venice* "originated under the immediate influence of Freud."[64] (The inconsistency of his answers can be interpreted, in Freudian terms, as proof of a resistance to psychoanalysis.) Whatever the case, Mann was clearly "prepared," as he put it, for Freud's theories from his readings of Schopenhauer, whom even Freud had to admit grasped the importance of sexuality and knew "the mechanism of repression."[65] But Mann would also have been prepared for Freud's ideas from reading Nietzsche, Jacobsen, and the Austrian playwright Hermann Bahr, whose famous essay "The Irretrievable Self," with its claim that "man was nothing but a mass of highly unstable perceptions creating the impression of personality," formed an artistic correlative to Freud's basic insights.[66]

DOUBTS AND CONSIDERATIONS

Whatever Mann's knowledge of Freud during his writing of *The Magic Mountain*, he knew enough about psychoanalysis to be able to explain, in a 1926 article for the *Almanach der Psychoanalyse*, that he viewed it as "something great and admirable, a bold discovery [and] extension of our knowledge of man." And yet, characteristically, he also worried that it could be "an instrument of malicious enlightenment, a mania for debunking and discrediting, dangerous to our deep cultural roots."[67] Perhaps he felt that there was such a thing as knowing too much about oneself, or that such knowledge, even if it were attainable, would not be desirable. In his preface to *The Joyous Science*, Nietzsche admired the Greeks for their modesty in turning away from the pursuit of truth at any cost, preferring instead to "stay on the surface, the fold and the skin, to worship appearance, to believe in forms, tones and words, in the whole Olympus of appearance!" Put a little differently: no superficiality, no art.[68]

* * *

Mann's ambivalence about psychoanalysis is manifested in *The Magic Mountain* in the figure of Dr. Edhin Krokowski, Director Behrens's psychoanalytic assistant. Hans Castorp first hears of him on the day he arrives in Davos. "A very savvy character," Joachim Ziemssen explains to his cousin. "They make a special note of his services in the brochure. He dissects the patients' psyches."[69] Hans Castorp responds by bursting into an uncontrollable fit of laughter, which, as described in the original German—"Er war ihrer gar nicht mehr Herr"[70]—seems to recall Freud's famous dictum that "the ego is not the master of his own house" ("dass das Ich nicht Herr sei in seinem eigenen Haus"), thereby validating the most basic insight of Freudian psychoanalysis.[71]

The reader first encounters Dr. Krokowski a few pages later, after Hans Castorp and his cousin have partaken of their inaugural evening meal together. They stumble on the doctor in the lobby, sitting by the fireplace reading the newspaper: "He was about thirty-five years old, broad-shouldered, stout, considerably shorter than the two men across from him, so that he had to tip his head back to look them in the eye, and extraordinarily pale—there was almost a translucence, even phosphorescence, to his pallor, and it was enhanced by dark, glowing eyes, black eyebrows, and a rather long beard that already showed a few gray strands and ended in two diverging points." This sinister and unsavory impression is reinforced by Dr. Krokowski's black smock and "yellowish teeth," as well as his tendency to thrust his head forward "at a derisive slant" when engaging in conversation. Upon learning that Hans Castorp is only visiting his cousin and is "perfectly healthy," Krokowski sardonically responds: "You don't say! . . . In that case you are a phenomenon of greatest medical interest. You see, I've never met a perfectly healthy person before."[72]

Dr. Krokowski is clear about the merits of his "psychic dissection": "He spoke of hidden suffering, of shame and affliction, of the redemptive effects of analysis; he praised the effects of light piercing the dark unconscious."[73] (Freud himself referred to psychoanalysis as a "bringing to light" the buried facts of a given case.)[74] For all that he is associated with darkness, Krokowski is also a man of enlightenment, a scientist, someone who, in Mann's words from 1926, extends our knowledge of the human being.

In the subchapter "Analysis," which directly follows Hans Castorp's recollection of the pencil episode with Pribislav Hippe, Dr. Krokowski delivers one of his fortnightly lectures in the dining hall. Bearing the title "Love as a Force Conducive to Illness," it is often assumed to be a parody of Freud's *Three Essays on the Theory of Sexuality*, though it functions primarily as a metaphor for Hans Castorp's particular situation, since Dr. Krokowski argues that "any symptom of illness was a masked form of love in action"—the body's response to repressed desire.[75] For the reader as for Hans Castorp, this is indeed enlightening stuff.

Much later in the novel, however, Krokowski's lectures take a decidedly unsettling turn. Suddenly their focus is no longer on masked forms of love or the transformation of illness back into conscious emotion—none of the "bringing to light" of Freudian psychoanalysis. Instead, Krokowski now lectures the Berghof patients about hypnotism, somnambulism, telepathy, second sight, and "the very riddle of life itself, which, so it appeared, might be more easily approached along very uncanny paths of illness, than by the direct road of health."[76]

Krokowski, whose field of study "had always been concerned with those dark, vast regions of the human soul that are called the subconscious," has now embraced parapsychology and the occult. When a young Danish patient, Elly Brand, astounds the Berghof with her psychic abilities, Dr. Krokowski quickly places a "scientific embargo" on her.[77] Behind the assistant doctor's back a group of patients, Hans Castorp among them, nevertheless begin conducting séances with Elly. Hans Castorp's curiosity, the narrator writes, triumphs over his morality: "It was the unconditional curiosity of the tourist thirsty for knowledge ... a curiosity that displayed something of a military character by not trying to evade something forbidden if it might offer itself."[78]

The description of the "military character" of Hans Castorp's curiosity foreshadows, not only his volunteering to fight in the First World War, but also what he is about to see. For during the course of the séances with Elly, eventually conducted by Dr. Krokowski himself, it is revealed that Elly possesses the ability to communicate with and even summon the dead. At Hans Castorp's request, she summons the ghost of Joachim Ziemssen, who, in a hair-raisingly creepy passage, suddenly materializes, sitting cross-legged in a chair in Dr. Krokowski's room in the basement where the séance is being conducted. Dressed, strangely, in the achromatic military uniform and steel helmet of the German soldiers of the First World War, his emaciated face stamped with suffering, Joachim is staring quietly at his cousin, at Hans Castorp, whose eyes fill with tears as he whispers to himself—"forgive me"—before bringing an end to the séance in a decidedly Settembrini-like manner: "with a flick of the hand, he turned on the white light."[79]

The supernatural and the occult enjoyed considerable public interest in the years after the First World War, at one point even attracting high-profile Nazis like Heinrich Himmler. Since the unimaginable had already happened, people were prepared to believe in anything. Even Mann was not immune to its lure and attended a number of séances at the home of Baron Albert von Schrenck-Notzing, a German psychiatrist and psychical researcher (who was also an expert in "contrary sexual feelings").[80] In February 1920, in a similar spirit of research and curiosity, Mann visited Dr. Gottfried Boehm at the university hospital on Ziemsensstrasse in February 1920 to watch patients undergo X-ray examinations—an experience as close to the supernatural as you could get. "Was outfitted with a white hospital smock and taken into the X-ray laboratory, where I watched while a resident and his assistant took various pictures of lungs and one of a knee joint, both men and women," he observes in his diary.[81] He was shown photographs of diseased lungs and stomach ulcers and even had his own hand X-rayed, an experience he found fundamentally indecent. When Director Behrens points out Joachim Ziemssen's heart during the X-ray examination early in *The Magic Mountain*, Hans Castorp is "stung by secret doubts whether it might not be somehow abnormal after all, doubts about whether it was permissible to stare like this amid the quivering, crackling darkness."[82]

* * *

Meanwhile, Germany's political situation continued to deteriorate. The Weimar Republic was severely tested early in 1920 by a plot to overthrow Ebert's government. On February 29, defense minister Gustav Noske, under pressure from the Allied victors, ordered the disbandment of two Freikorps paramilitary units stationed outside Berlin: the Baltikum Brigade, led by General von der Goltz, and the Naval Brigade, led by Captain Hermann Ehrhardt. Outraged by the order to demobilize, the Ehrhardt Brigade marched on Berlin on the night of March 12, intending to overthrow Ebert's government. With white swastikas painted on their helmets, the paramilitary troops were greeted at the Brandenburger Tor by the extremist Nationalist Association, a group whose leaders included the Prussian government official for whom the coup was named, Wolfgang Kapp, the commander of the Berlin Military District, Walther von Lüttwitz, and General Ludendorff, the embodiment of the old Wilhelmine military ethos.[83]

When they eventually caught wind of the Kapp Putsch, as it became known, the government appealed to the army for assistance, only to be rebuffed. "There can be no question of ordering the Reichswehr to fight the Freikorps," General Hans von Seeckt, the army's chief of staff, bluntly informed the defense minister. So shattered was Noske by this betrayal that he contemplated suicide.[84] The government quickly fled to Dresden, where in response to the attempted coup, Ebert proclaimed a general strike on March 14, the largest in German history.

The impact was immediate. In Weimar, 155 miles southwest of Berlin, the writer and composer Alma Mahler observed that the streets were thick with the stench of unemptied sewers. "But the worst thing is that the workers have prevented the burial of the dead. Students who tried to sneak up to the cemetery wall where bodies were simply dumped were driven away by the greater numbers of workers who stood guard there. As a result, dead bodies have lain outside, unburied, for days."[85] Combined with the political incompetence of the conspirators, the strike brought about a swift end to the putsch. It had lasted just five days.

DOUBTS AND CONSIDERATIONS

Despite its failure, the Kapp Putsch emboldened far-right elements across the country, and nowhere more so than in Munich, where in March 1920 the Bavarian People's Party politician Gustav von Kahr successfully ousted Hoffmann and his cabinet. The conservative monarchist Kahr was subsequently appointed Bavaria's new minister-president, turning Munich into a safe haven for counterrevolutionaries and right-wing extremists. While Weimar-era Berlin flourished as a mecca for alternative lifestyles and modernist counterculture, Munich emerged as its polar opposite: "a cell of order," as Kahr put it, in which the republic's domestic enemies schemed and plotted while the authorities looked the other way.[86]

Several high-profile Kapp putschists descended on Munich, including General Ludendorff, whose home in the suburb of Ludwigshöhe became "a kind of *völkisch* Lourdes," and Captain Ehrhardt, who helped establish Organization Consul, a shadowy terrorist network whose sole purpose consisted in murdering supporters of the republic.[87] For example, in October 1920 the OC murdered a young woman, Marie Sandmayr, who stumbled across a cache of illegal arms and reported it to the authorities, as the Disarmament Commission required. For obeying the law, she was strangled and hung from a tree with a sign reading: "You lousy bitch, you have betrayed your Fatherland. The Black Hand has judged you."[88] In general, right-wing organizations could rely on the tacit, if not outright, approval of Munich's authorities: whereas Bavarian courts handed down more than eighteen hundred prison sentences to left-wing revolutionaries, not a single Freikorps member was ever held responsible for the violence of the crushing of the Munich revolution in 1919.[89] Asked by a concerned citizen if he was aware that political assassination groups were thriving in Munich, the chief of police Ernst Pöhner sarcastically remarked: "Yes, but not enough of them."[90]

The fact that some of the leading Munich revolutionaries had been Jewish was used to justify the implementation of new anti-Semitic measures. East European Jewish immigrants were singled out for harassment and deportation. Chillingly, Pöhner even suggested interning them in Landsberg or Plassenberg: "Mere expulsions aren't enough; these people will come back," he claimed.[91] Gustav Kahr did not go quite that far, though on March 20, 1920—four days after taking office—he ordered the expulsion of "unwelcome foreigners" from Bavaria within five days.[92]

Perhaps just as ominously, in the middle of the Kapp debacle the right-wing German Workers' Party (DAP), founded just one year earlier by Anton Drexler, rebranded itself as the National Socialist German Workers' Party (NSDAP), or the Nazi Party. Its new party program was announced on February 24 at the Hofbräuhaus am Platzl, an occasion attended by some two thousand people. It might have been a forgettable evening if not for Adolf Hitler, the party's "star speaker," who thundered against the Treaty of Versailles, Jewish profiteers, and Minister of Finance Matthias Erzberger. The decorated young corporal whipped the crowd into an absolute frenzy.[93] "There was often great tumult and I was convinced fights were going to break out at any moment," a police observer noted.[94]

At the time, Hitler was still a "political education agent" in the Army Intelligence Division, but his oratorical skills persuaded his superiors to encourage him in his political work. They eventually discharged him in March 1920. That September, Captain Karl Mayr, Hitler's former superior, wrote to Wolfgang Kapp, who since the failed coup had fled to Sweden, that the NSDAP would "provide the basis for the strong assault troop we envision and that they had a profound "motivational force" in the party's young leader, as NSDAP membership showed: it now stood at two thousand, compared to less than a hundred just one year earlier.

Outside Nazi circles, however, few people suspected "the little corporal with the big mouth" of being any different from the many other obscure and disgruntled rabble-rousers stirring crowds in beer halls across Germany.⁹⁵ In Joseph Roth's 1923 novel, *The Spider's Web*, the right-wing character meets Hitler and decides he looks "no different" than he himself does, the implication being that Hitler was hardly a unique figure in Germany at the time.⁹⁶ Still, as the American ambassador to Germany wrote in his diary: "Something is brewing in Bavaria, and no one seems to know what it is."⁹⁷

Where did Thomas Mann stand politically in all this? His response to the Munich revolution in 1919 had been characteristically ambivalent. "He flipped sides a dozen times," the biographer Anthony Heilbut writes.⁹⁸ When the right-wing *Bonner Zeitung* claimed the author of *Reflections of a Nonpolitical Man* was a supporter of the Independent Social Democrats, Mann didn't entirely disagree. "I have a growing sympathy for what is healthy, human, national, anti-Entente, anti-political within Spartacism, Communism, Bolshevism. The rumor of my 'joining the USPD' is not meaningless," he wrote.⁹⁹ At the same time, Mann still hoped conservatism could be saved from its far-right elements. "Nothing is more important than the task of giving German conservatism an intellectual and spiritual element," he wrote to the philosopher Hermann Graf Keyserling.¹⁰⁰ Though "keyed up" by the political unrest of the Kapp Putsch, Mann admitted in his diary that he would be "glad if something is achieved on the political plane, assuming good sense and order were followed and the conservative ideal is not compromised."¹⁰¹

As the bodies kept piling up, however, any hope that German conservatism would not be compromised by the violence of the far right looked more and more naïve. On June 9, 1921, Organization Consul shot and killed Karl Gareis, a Bavarian Independent Social Democratic politician who, in a speech in the Bundestag, had demanded an end to right-wing paramilitary lawlessness. Then, on August 21, Matthias Erzberger—"the most hated man in all of Germany," as the theologian Ernst Troeltsch described him—was gunned down near the Black Forest town of Bad Griesbach while on vacation with his family. "Erzberger, who negotiated the shameful peace of Versailles, has gotten his just desserts as a traitor to the fatherland," one newspaper reported.[102] It was a high-ranking member of the Erhardt Brigade, Manfred von Killinger, who gave the order to carry out the assassination. Local police soon learned the identities of the two gunmen, yet by the time they arrived in Munich to make the arrests the assassins had fled to Hungary using false passports provided by Chief of Police Pöhner. Von Killinger was arrested, but a sympathetic judge soon acquitted him. Killinger would later play an instrumental role in facilitating the Holocaust in Romania.

* * *

In May 1921 Thomas Mann reluctantly set aside *The Magic Mountain*'s manuscript once more. The occasion this time was an invitation he'd received back in March to give a lecture in Lübeck as part of the city's first-ever Nordic Week celebration in early September. He initially considered choosing Knut Hamsun as his subject—Mann had read the Nobel Prize winner's novel *The Growth of the Soil* in 1919 with rapturous enthusiasm—but ultimately decided that Goethe and Tolstoy would be better suited to his own needs and interests. The lecture, which would be repeated in Berlin on September 10, would give him and Katia a chance to revisit the home of Mann's ancestors and spend their summer holiday with Ernst Bertram at Villa Oda in Timmendorf, a seaside resort northeast of Lübeck. "Too bad that *The Magic Mountain* has to be put aside again, but one must take life as it comes," he noted in his diary on May 31.[103]

At the time he put it aside, the manuscript consisted of a little over half the novel, or what would amount to the first volume of the published version: chapters 1 through 5, concluding with the "Walpurgis Night" section in which Hans Castorp and Clavdia Chauchat converse in French. Mann hoped to be able to resume work on the manuscript in late September and then "finish it all in one go" in the winter, as he explained to the writer Adele Gerhard.[104]

On September 2, 1921, Thomas and Katia arrived in Lübeck after three weeks of vacation in Timmendorf and Wenningstadt. They were guests of Mann's old friend, the Hamburg-born novelist and newspaper columnist Ida Boy-Ed, who lived in the historic customs house next to the city gate, the Burgtor. Mann was flattered by the enthusiastic welcome he received. There were lavish dinners, garlands of flowers, and interviews with journalists from Germany and Scandinavia. Mann was especially gratified to learn that the city of Lübeck had recently purchased his family's old home on Mengstrasse, intending to restore it and open a "Buddenbrook Book Shop" on the first floor.

Mann had spent several months working on his lecture, compiling a hundred pages of handwritten notes in the process: long quotations from Tolstoy and Goethe, as well as passages from the work of Turgenev, Dostoevsky, Schiller, not to mention biographies by Pavel Biryukov and Albert Bielschowsky. Mann was initially worried the lecture would draw him away from *The Magic Mountain*, yet the more he read and the more notes he took, the more he began to realize that it would form an "appropriate, full-fledged counterpart to the novel."[105]

"Goethe and Tolstoy" is a masterful portrayal of the two famous writers of its title, a searching account of their tendency to autobiography and confession, their drive to make themselves public, which is what finally distinguishes them as the healthy pedagogues of humanity, in Mann's view. By contrast, Schiller and Dostoevsky are "sickly" temperaments, writers who lack the "extraordinarily vital sense of self" of a Goethe or Tolstoy. A great writer, Mann argues, is never more magnanimous than when he seems most self-centered; his egotism is the key that unlocks his ability to give his life literary form—"to show his development," making subjective experience "objective for others, for the world."[106] In a sentence that must have seemed a little strange coming from Thomas Mann, standing there in his bourgeois disguise, he declared: "Self-denial can be the most shameful form of lying."[107]

Though he admired Schiller and Dostoevsky deeply, Mann identified more obviously with the self-preservational temperaments of Goethe and Tolstoy, and clearly aspired to "the dignity and consecration of advanced years" they both attained.[108] Reading their works and accounts of their lives in the summer of 1921 provided him with a clearer understanding of his role as a writer. Goethe's *Faust* and *Wilhelm Meister* in particular ballasted the growing manuscript of *The Magic Mountain*. These were "educational poems, presentations of human development," Mann wrote, musing on this theme of education so central to the genre of the bildungsroman. He admired the way Goethe in *Wilhelm Meister* had transformed personal and adventurous self-development into an ideal of human education. He was struck, too, by its similarity to Tolstoy's educational maxims, his belief in school as an "educational laboratory wherein experiment creates a firm basis for pedagogical science."[109] Or as a certain fictional Italian humanist and pedagogue is fond of saying: "*Placet experiri*," it is pleasant to experiment.[110]

As Mann's first major artistic statement since *Reflections*, "Goethe and Tolstoy" also marked a turning point. Though he still believed in the Western decline that was common currency among German conservatives—"Don't we have the feeling," Mann asked in the lecture, "that for the European West . . . an era is ending, the middle-class, humanistic, liberal era, born in the Renaissance and achieving power with the French Revolution?"—he now looked beyond the prospect of this decline, wondering about the possibility of "love for others, for the world, for mankind." Mann admired Tolstoy's putting "himself in the service of the community" and lauded Goethe's "perception of the necessity for improvement, for perfection, this awareness of one's own self as a *task*." He ended the lecture with a far more conciliatory vision of Germany as a "many-sided national organism, articulated into parts and yet unified, full of respect and community, genuineness and presence, loyalty and boldness, preserving and creative, diligent, dignified, happy, the model of peoples—a dream worthy of being dreamed, worthy of being believed."[111]

Returning to Munich and *The Magic Mountain* in mid-September, he at once began writing a new subchapter of the novel. He titled it: "Changes."

CHAPTER 6

Changes, 1922–1923

For Heinrich Mann, 1922 began with the threat of death. A sudden stomach pain in January landed him in the hospital, where he was diagnosed first with appendicitis, then with peritonitis. Stomach surgery was required and performed, but then bronchial complications seemed to augur the worst. He was almost fifty-one years old, the same age his father had been when he died.

On January 28, 1922, newspapers reported that Heinrich's situation was "serious, but by *no means hopeless*."[1] When Mimi, Heinrich's wife, called the Poschingerstrasse household in despair, breaking a silence of seven years, Katia at once went to see her. A few days later, on January 31, Thomas Mann sent his older brother a bouquet of flowers along with a note that read:

Dear Heinrich,
With these flowers accept my warm greetings and best wishes—I was not allowed to send them to you earlier.
Those were difficult days that lie behind us, but now we are over the hill and will go on better—together, if you feel as I do.
T.[2]

A week later, he was permitted to visit Heinrich in the hospital. Standing at his bedside, there was no point in trying to hide the emotion. The brothers clasped hands and then embraced. "Let us never lose each other again," Heinrich said.[3]

In a letter to Ernst Bertram on February 2, Mann announced the cautious resumption of brotherhood. It wouldn't be easy; he was under no illusion about that. "The monuments of our dispute still stand," he wrote. And yet, had they not been moving toward each other intellectually since the end of the war? "I feel this may have happened when I realize that the thought which truly dominates my mind these days is of a new, personal fulfillment of the idea of humanity."[4]

Before the news of Heinrich's illness reached them, Thomas and Katia had spent the month of January traveling in eastern and central Europe—Prague, Brunn, Budapest, Vienna—where Mann delivered his "Goethe and Tolstoy" lecture. Other than being robbed at the Hotel Imperial in Vienna ("our losses were trifling," Mann said), the most memorable part of the trip was meeting Georg Lukács, the thirty-six-year-old Hungarian Marxist critic and author of *The Theory of the Novel* (1916). A supporter of the Hungarian Soviet Republic of 1919, Lukács had served Béla Kun's communist government as commissioner for education as well as a theoretician of red terror. When the republic was overthrown he was forced to flee to Vienna, only to be arrested by Austrian authorities. His extradition back to Hungary and an almost certain death was prevented thanks to a protest signed by a group of German and Austrian writers, including Thomas and Heinrich Mann.

Their meeting in Mann's luxurious room at the Hotel Imperial in Vienna was a strange one. Katia recalled that Lukács at once began regaling them with his literary and political theories, speaking for a whole hour while Mann sat patiently and listened.[5] Many years later Mann himself would recall how Lukács had "explained his theories to me for an hour. For as long as he spoke, he was right. And even if after his talk there remained with me an impression of almost uncanny abstractness, I also felt his clarity and intellectual generosity."[6]

What exactly had Lukács droned on about? Enough, apparently, for an idea to take root in Mann's mind: the idea to replace *The Magic Mountain*'s Pastor Bunge with a different, and decidedly more modern, character. For despite his being an atheist there was something "quasi-religious" about Lukács; he was "imbued with a longing for absolute salvation and redemption," according to the intellectual historian Judith Marcus. Some of his essays from this period border on the mystical even as they propound an earthly utopia, as in "Tactics and Ethics" from 1919: "The salvation of society is a mission which only the proletariat ... can achieve."[7] In another essay, "Bolshevism as a Moral Problem," Lukács spoke of the "fervor of ... messianism" necessary for the proletariat to become "the agent of the social salvation of mankind."[8] As Marcus comments: "Because socialism had presented the solution, Lukács was presented his salvation."[9]

It is more likely, however, that what struck Mann most about Lukács was his intellectually intense yet unnervingly calm manner of speaking. He wasn't foaming at the mouth or wildly gesticulating when he told his comrades things like: "Bolshevism rests on the metaphysical assumption that the bad can engender the good"; or, "If we take advantage of the given possibility for the realization of our goal, we have to accept dictatorship, terror, and the class oppression that goes with it."[10] Ervin Sinkó, a fellow party member, recalls that even in the heat of the fiercest debates, the "astonishing phenomenon called Lukács" would sit in studied silence, his glasses perched on the bridge of his aquiline nose, and calmly wait his turn to speak. Another contemporary is supposed to have exclaimed of Lukács: "Damn him, he is right about almost everything, and that means that we must be wrong!"[11]

It was this combination of asceticism and fanaticism that made such a strong impression on Mann—more so, at any rate, than the content of Lukács's ideas. And this was the remarkable thing about Mann, as Katia would later observe: "He didn't observe people for the sake of portraying them afterward. Once he had seen someone, he had a mental image of him, and when a fictional figure came along with whom this someone matched, the someone popped up again, but not intentionally."[12]

Mann scrapped the idea of the character Pastor Bunge around the time he met Lukács. His eventual replacement was first announced in a letter to Ernst Bertram in June: Leo Naphta, a "half-Jewish Jesuit pupil" whose constant disputes with Settembrini will one day lead to a pedagogical duel, Mann explained.[13] Many years later, when someone suggested to Lukács that Naphta's resemblance to him was primarily physical, he responded: "So what if I lent [Thomas Mann] my nose? He did so much for me—I am happy I could do that much in return!"[14]

* * *

Sometime after the events of "Walpurgis Night," accepting that he will never again be well enough to return to the world of work, Settembrini decides to leave the Berghof and moves into a small studio above a tailor's shop in the village. On the floor below him, in elegant, silk-clad furnishings, lives Leo Naphta, a Jewish-born Jesuit from a small Galician border town (it could have been Brody, the birthplace of Joseph Roth) whose father was brutally murdered during a pogrom.

The introduction of Naphta, one of Mann's most memorable fictional creations, marks a shift in *The Magic Mountain*. It raises the novel's ideological temperature. For the next several hundred pages, the reader, like Hans Castorp, listens with rapt attention as Naphta and Settembrini "cross intellectual swords," debating science, religion, philosophy, and politics—disputes as wide-ranging as they are irresolvable, which is perhaps why, as the poet Adam Zagajewski once put it, we are still dealing with Naphta's demonic whisper and Settembrini's humanitarian discourse a hundred years later.[15]

Naphta is a character of Dostoevskian disquiet. We would hardly be surprised to see him come crawling out of an ill-lit boarding room in St. Petersburg, say, or to learn that he has murdered his landlady for some minor slight. And yet Hans Castorp (and the reader) are drawn to him precisely because a life dedicated to the permanent daylight of reason and good health is, somehow, a life only half-lived. We, too, are drawn to the night, to the darkness that lives inside us, to a sympathy with death. Naphta speaks to us from what Nietzsche called the "unexplored realm of dangerous knowledge," which is why Settembrini warns Hans Castorp against his influence.[16]

What exactly does Naphta believe? Steeped in the scholasticism of medieval Europe, he affirms the supremacy of the Catholic Church over the secular state and bluntly justifies the use of terror and violence to bring humankind back under divine rule. In his disputes with Settembrini he is unsparing in his attacks on the Italian's worldview, which, in a Nietzschean flourish, he finds guilty of "robbing life of all its difficult and deadly serious aspects."[17] Against Settembrini's bourgeois humanism, his belief in science and reason and the individual human being, Naphta heralds the coming of "newer, less namby-pamby social concepts, ideas of submission and obedience.... The mystery and precept of our age is not liberation and development of the ego," he says. "What our age needs, what it demands, what it will create for itself, is—terror."[18]

Curiously, Naphta sees the principles of the Church resurrected in the modern idea of communism, which he praises for its opposition to private ownership and "bourgeois-capitalist rot."[19] Viewing it as a temporary expedient on the path to the kingdom of heaven, he declares a communist "proxy dictatorship" necessary: "The proletariat has taken up Gregory the Great's task, his godly zeal burns within it, and its hands can no more refrain from shedding blood than could his. Its work is terror, that the world may be saved and the ultimate goal of redemption be achieved: the children of God living in a world without classes or laws."[20]

It is in this apparently confusing constellation of Naptha's ideas that the prescience of Mann's characterization resides. Despite his medievalism, Naphta is an unmistakably modern thinker: a "revolutionary of reaction," as Hans Castorp perceptively calls him. The structure of his ideas aligns with Mark Lilla's description of the reactionary mind as one that is "shipwrecked": "Where others see the river of time flowing as it always has, the reactionary sees the debris of paradise drifting past his eyes. He is time's exile."[21]

Since Naphta's sympathies with communism are only superficial, or at best opportunistic, critics have rightly viewed his belief in absolute rule and terroristic violence as fascistic. As Lilla puts it, Naptha's sympathies for communism "could just as well have been for fascism."[22] This is not as strange as it sounds. As Jean-Michel Palmier has shown, the conditions and aspirations that led some writers in the Weimar Republic to embrace communist ideas were the same that led others to believe in conservative revolution. Many intellectuals of the time "had in common the experience of war, hatred for capitalism, a certain contempt for bourgeois culture, and the expectation of a new world," Palmier writes.[23] Far from being divided into clearly delineated camps, the intellectual scene in the Weimar Republic was sometimes dizzyingly heterogenous, leading to surprising or unusual ideological constellations. What made Mann such a perceptive analyst of this intellectual hodge-podge was that he recognized it in himself.

In the temporary absence of Clavdia Chauchat, Leo Naphta instantly awakens Hans Castorp's—and the reader's—curiosity and interest. "I find him more than a little intriguing," Hans Castorp tells his cousin when they first meet him. "We definitely have to go find out what we can learn from all this."[24] ("*Placet experiri!*" as Settembrini puts it.) Before long, the two cousins become regular guests of Naphta's, while Settembrini attempts to provide a "pedagogic counterweight" and even warns them of the spiritual dangers of entering the fray unarmed and exposing themselves to "the influences of this half-fanatic, half-malicious humbug."[25]

But Hans Castorp, who says he will "refrain from taking sides or endorsing any viewpoint," is hardly unarmed. As we've seen, in the year or so since his arrival, he has already come a long way. Sitting on a bench in a meadow of the valley, he takes seriously those "metaphysical questions" with which his time in the sanatorium has confronted him, questions he was unaware of when he first arrived.[26] What Settembrini condemns as Hans Castorp's "wanton experiments with the powers of unreason" are actually experiences of a positive dialectical nature, as the scholar Børge Kristiansen has argued.[27] They are a measure of Hans Castorp's growing independence and the development of his critical faculties, a view of education consistent with the one laid out in Mann's "Goethe and Tolstoy" lecture.

In this way, Mann was actually resuscitating some of the main arguments of his *Reflections,* in which writing is seen as "a witness to and expression of ambivalence, of here and there, of yes and no, of two souls in one breast, of an annoying richness in inner conflicts, antithesis, and contradictions."[28] By lending his ear to both Naphta and Settembrini, Hans Castorp is exposing himself—and the reader—to conflicting ideologies and points of view, honing his critical faculties and eventually drawing his own conclusions.

The Magic Mountain is thus the artistic illustration of what Mann, in *Reflections,* calls "aestheticism"—his term for the dialectical nature of art, its negative capability. Not to be confused with art for art's sake, Mann argues that aestheticism "lies in art's lively ambiguity, its deep lack of commitment, its intellectual freedom." The true artist, he goes on, "*never takes* spiritual and intellectual things *completely seriously,* for his job has always been rather to treat them as material and as playthings, to represent points of view, to deal in dialectics, always letting the one who is speaking at the time be right."²⁹ It is by virtue of being so aesthetically open that *The Magic Mountain* can be seen as an atonement for the crude politicizing of *Reflections*. Fascinating and intellectually rich though it may be, the essay of 1918 is also a spectacular failure of precisely the aesthetic point of view it affirms. It bears the dubious distinction of making the master of contradictions sound like the servant of a single position.

Only the novel form could accommodate Mann's fierce self-interrogation, his many revisions and contradictions. Unburdened by the closure of argument, the novel's intellectual duels are permitted to remain unresolved. For many readers, they never end. The Polish poet Czeslaw Milosz recalled that when he first read *The Magic Mountain* as a student in the early 1930s, he almost regarded the quarrel between Naphta and Settembrini as "more important than the story of Hans Castorp"—an exaggeration, to be sure, but one that speaks to the novel's intellectual vibrancy.

* * *

In Weimar Germany, Naphta's terroristic prophesy was proving all too accurate. On the morning of June 24, 1922, Walther Rathenau, the recently appointed German foreign minister and former minister of reconstruction, not to mention a leading industrialist, renowned writer, and assimilated Jew, left his stately villa in Berlin's Grunewald suburb for his offices in the Foreign Ministry in downtown Wilhelmstrasse. Just before the intersection of Wallotstrasse and Erdenerstrasse, a dark-gray Mercedes-Benz Tourenwagon intercepted Rathenau's chauffeured convertible. A young man reared up from the car and fired at the foreign minister with an MP-18 submachine gun, hitting him five times, while another man lobbed a hand grenade into the backseat. As the Tourenwagon sped off, a passing nurse raced to the stricken Rathenau's aid; she was holding the fifty-four-year-old foreign minister's head in her lap when he bled to death.³⁰

The threats had accompanied him for several years. Ever since he was appointed minister of reconstruction and handed the thankless task of negotiating an agreement on reparations with the Allied victors, Rathenau had become subject to increasingly virulent attacks from the German right. It didn't matter that he was a committed patriot and internationally respected politician; he exemplified "the presence and success of Jews in German life," in the words of Fritz Stern, and for that he was hated.[31] His failure—in the eyes of his critics—to obtain financial concessions from the West during his brief stint as foreign minister only served to inflame this hatred. He was a frequent target of Hitler's beer hall abuse, accused of "selling out and betraying the German people," and on the day before his death denounced as a traitor in the Reichstag by Karl Helfferich, the leader of the German Nationalist Party.[32] Rathenau was urged to take security precautions more seriously, but when he got in the backseat of his car on the morning of June 24, he did so without protection of any kind.

The third high-profile political assassination carried out by Organization Consul in just over twelve months, the murder of Rathenau was the most consequential. "Panic broke out, shaking the entire Reich," Stefan Zweig, one of Rathenau's many prominent literary friends, recalled.[33] Half a million people marched in Berlin to mourn his death in a demonstration organized by the trade union movement. In a special session of the Reichstag, right-wing parties were denounced, as Chancellor Wirth, pointing toward Karl Helfferich and the German Nationalists, bluntly declared: "the enemy stands on the right."[34] In purely numerical terms, Wirth was absolutely correct: the statistician Emil Julius Gumbel, writing in October 1922, estimated that the far right had committed 354 political murders since November 9, 1918; the far left's toll stood at 22.[35]

For Thomas Mann, Rathenau's murder marked the decisive moment when he gave up hoping for the "spiritualization" of German conservatism. The man who could write, in 1920, that he believed "the conservatives will again have the greatest say in Germany," that "nothing is more important than the infusion of intelligence into German conservatism," now realized how out of step he had been with respect to what was actually happening to the country. The conciliatory vision he had laid out in "Goethe and Tolstoy" would remain just that: a vision, a Fata Morgana, not the political and social reality playing out before him.

He would now not only abandon his hope for German conservatism, however; he would go one step further and urge Germany's youth to embrace the Weimar Republic. As he explained in a letter to Ernst Bertram on July 8:

> I am gradually coming to see the dangers of history, the way it obscures the uniqueness of a situation by false analogies and leads a certain kind of youth astray into mad acts. The distortion of the German countenance causes me acute suffering. I am thinking of turning a birthday article on Gerhart Hauptmann into a kind of manifesto in which I appeal to the conscience of the young people whose ear I have. I am not going back on the *Reflections*, and I am the last to demand that young people should be enthusiastic about things like democracy and socialism which their inner development has left far behind. But I have already on a previous occasion called mechanical reaction sentimental coarseness, and the new humanity may perhaps after all flourish no worse on the basis of democracy than on that of the old Germany. It is all a matter of shying and rebelling at words. As if "the Republic" were not still the German Reich, which is in fact today placed in all our hands to a much greater extent than it was when historical forces which had degenerated into banal theatricality throned over it—and that precisely is democracy.[36]

Not exactly the tone of the author of "Thoughts in Wartime" or *Reflections of a Nonpolitical Man*. Far from thinking democracy poisonous or alien to German culture, the disillusioned conservative now recognized that a democratic republic might actually serve Germany's future as well as any other form of government—and with democracy, well, the German people had a greater say in what kind of country they wanted to live in than ever before. As T. J. Reed has pointed out, Mann accepted parliamentary democracy "in its simplest terms, as participation and responsibility."[37] This is where Mann differed from the many other so-called *Vernuftrepublikaner,* or common-sense republicans: the professors, industrialists, and politicians whose hatred of the Nazis finally triumphed over their hostility to the Weimar Republic. According to the historian Peter Gay, "they learned to live with the Republic, judged its advent a historical necessity, and respected some of its leaders, but they never believed in its future."[38]

By contrast, the future was precisely what troubled Mann most. His preparations for the "Goethe and Tolstoy" lecture had made clear to him the importance of "being at one with time and the future."[39] More and more he felt it his duty to set aside whatever private apprehensions he still had about parliamentary democracy and "place himself in the service of the community," as he had put it in the lecture.[40] The "idea of humanity" he mentioned in his letter to Ernst Bertram at the time of his reconciliation with Heinrich was his term for this sense of civic responsibility and friendliness toward the future. What's more, it was an idea he found inspiration for from an unexpected source: the American poet Walt Whitman.

In August, Thomas and Katia left Munich for their summer vacation in Ahlbeck, a popular seaside resort on the island of Usedom in the Baltic Sea. Mann spent his mornings working on his birthday address to Gerhart Hauptmann or swimming in the ocean. Like his young hero Hans Castorp, he had always had "a great partiality" for the sea, where "time drowns in the monotony of space."[41] We can imagine him setting out one evening from

Ahlbeck's stately pier, listening to the "husky song" of the sea's to and fro, looking up at the sky and, like Walt Whitman's speaker, thinking of "the clef of the universes and of the future":

> All nations, colors, barbarisms, civilizations, languages,
> All identities that have existed or may exist on this globe, or any globe,
> All lives and deaths, all of the past, present, future,
> This vast similitude spans them, and always has spann'd,
> And shall forever span them and compactly hold and enclose them.[42]

Whitman had been much on Mann's mind. When Samuel Fischer published Hans Reisiger's two-volume translation of the works of Whitman in the spring, Mann had written a rapturous open letter to Reisiger in the *Frankfurter Zeitung*. "It is truly a service of the highest order that you have rendered us," Mann said, adding that "as someone who has inwardly busied himself with the idea of *Humanity* for years, laboring with a slowness uniquely my own ... this book has been nothing less than a gift from heaven, for now I really see that what Whitman calls '*democracy*' is nothing other than what we, in an old-fashioned usage, call 'humanity.'" What's more, in order to achieve what Mann, with an eye to the future, called "the new humanity," Germany could not rely on Goethe alone: "a shot of Whitman will be necessary," he wrote.

Mann could hardly have been more explicit: Germany needed the bard of American democracy, a great poet who shared with Goethe something Mann referred to, mysteriously, as "the sensual element."[43] What he meant by this exactly would not become clear until the fall, when at last he delivered his birthday address to Hauptmann in Berlin. He knew it would not go unnoticed by the broader culture, so in advance of the festivities he made sure to read the address to a few friends in Munich first, his brother Heinrich among them. Then, once more, Thomas Mann stepped into the breach.

Gerhart Hauptmann, the great dome of his forehead wreathed with a halo of wispy white hair—looking, Klaus Mann recalled, "like Goethe in a state of intoxication"—was the grand old man of interwar German letters.[44] A once controversial writer and exponent of naturalism who provoked the ire of the kaiser himself, Hauptmann had since come to be "revered as an incarnation of the German national spirit," according to Tobias Boes.[45] With a Nobel Prize for literature to his name, decades of success as a playwright and novelist, and a large summer home on the island of Hiddensee, he was now sunk in the respectable eminence of advancing years. The occasion of his sixtieth birthday on November 15, 1922, was celebrated with an almost excessive fanfare and pomp. Samuel Fischer issued a massive special edition of his collected works. Reich President Friedrich Ebert awarded him the inaugural Eagle Shield of the German Reich for his artistic achievements. The city of Breslau declared Hauptmann an honorary citizen during a festival that lasted ten days. For a young republic desperately in need of some national unity, the politically obtuse but universally loved Hauptmann more than fit the bill.

In this respect, it made sense for Thomas Mann to use the occasion of one of the many celebrations in Hauptmann's honor to speak about the republic. But even so, when he took the stage on October 15 in Berlin's Beethovensaal before an audience of over a thousand people, no one was prepared for what they were about to hear. Thomas Mann's opening words were as follows:

> May I remind you, Gerhart Hauptmann, that you were among the audience when I gave a lecture, at the University of Frankfurt during the Goethe Week celebrations, about belief and education, or about humanity? You were seated in the first row, and the auditorium behind you was filled to the rafters with students. It was a lovely

occasion, and I hope that this one today will prove likewise. In my imagination, I can see you before me now, just as you were then, and address you as a distinguished man on your birthday; and when I raise my glance a bit higher, I can also see the youth of Germany in the hall, listening attentively, for I want to talk to them again today, and also talk about them, and yet again talk *with them*, to borrow a phrase that appears in a locution such as "to have a bone to pick with them." I have to speak, in short: about you, whose birthday we're celebrating today, and about other, more wide-ranging concerns, or yet once again about issues concerning humanity—issues that will always receive a receptive response from German young people, or else they would cease to be German.[46]

Mann went on to deliver what amounted to a full-throated defense of the Weimar Republic in which his aim, as he put it, was to "win over" Germany's youth to the side of the republic. "*Republic*—how do you like that word coming, as it does, from my lips?" Mann asked, anticipating the disbelief of his audience. He went on to disparage the Wilhelmine Empire as a farcical embarrassment, declaring the time when political and national life were two separate things to be over. No longer could writers and artists regard the affairs of state with "fatalist resignation": "The state, whether we like it or not, has fallen into our hands, and that means into the hands of every individual. It has become our affair, one that we now have to make good on, and that is just what the Republic is—nothing more."[47]

He didn't hold back in condemning the "sentimental obscurantism" of the political reactionaries now disgracing the country with their "disgusting and crackbrained assassinations." Nor, significantly, did he spare himself: Mann freely admitted his fear that, in his pursuit of intellectual freedom, he had "put weapons into the hands of obscurantism."[48] And yet he wasn't "recanting anything essential," he claimed. At most, he was attempting to draw a clear line—for himself, as much as for his audience—from his *Reflections* to his support for the republic. He achieved this, or tried to, by dissenting from the view that the Weimar Republic was born of defeat by foreign powers. Nonsense, Mann said: the German Republic was born not in 1918 but in 1914. It was *then* that a new age dawned in the hearts of the German people, and it was *then* that the old powers of the state began to die away. And if Germany now stood humiliated on the world stage—Mann, of course, did not deny that this was the case—then it would be "an act of cowardice to leave it in the lurch, instead of lending a helping hand, instead of supporting it. . . . It would be cowardice to concoct every conceivable difficulty for the Republic, acting as if you were old men who no longer understand life and could only show fidelity to the good old days."[49]

Mann proceeded with an unusual reflection on the concept of humanity, in which his recent readings of Whitman and Novalis—readings undertaken "in connection with an artistic project," he said—were deployed to unite the idea of democracy with German Romanticism, to fuse Whitman's "social eroticism" with Novalis's "mysticism," as he put it: "It is a union of the life of the state with intellectual and national life, a union that for so long we did not experience, but that once again we hope to see. In a word, it is the Republic."[50] Mann now distanced himself from Oswald Spengler's "extreme inhumanity" and "harmful, deadly work"—not because it prophesied the decline of Western civilization, but because, in so doing, Spengler was *willing* that decline and urging his readers to do the same.[51]

Against this iron-fisted fatalism, Mann, no doubt raising a few eyebrows among his listeners, began to speak of an "erotic-political emotion, modelled after certain loving friendships of antiquity," against which society was finally beginning to relax its taboo.[52] He wondered if "from the experiences of comradeship in blood and death, of hard and exclusive masculinity" during the war, there might not rise up out of it a love of the organic, of humanity, an eros from which it might be possible to create a state. Are they so different, Mann asked, "Whitman's worship of boys"—his "phallically healthy, phallically brimming inspiration"—and Novalis's "sympathy with death"? Be careful with notions of health and sickness, he cautioned his audience: "Interest in death and disease, in decadence and the pathological, is only an expression of interest in life, in man, as the humanistic discipline of medicine proves. Whoever takes an interest in the organic, in life, will also take an interest in death. Perhaps a bildungsroman will strive to show that the experience of death is ultimately an experience of life, that it leads toward the human."[53] A few minutes later, Mann concluded his speech with a rousing affirmation: "Long live the Republic!"

Contemporary reactions to Mann's speech can be gleaned from a famous headline in the conservative newspaper *Das Gewissen* on October 23: "Mann Overboard," it read. The article's author, Otto Werner, began by quoting Mann's owns claim from *Reflections* that the German people will never accept democracy, and then declared the author's apparent volte-face "embarrassing."[54] Friends, too, found Mann's change of tack incomprehensible. Ida Boy-Ed sent him a letter accusing him of apostasy and self-betrayal, to which Mann responded by explaining that his lecture was "the direct continuation of the essential line of [*Reflections*], I assure you! In the name of German humanitarianism, I took arms against the revolution when it was starting. Today, out of the same impulse, I take arms against the reactionary wave which is sweeping over Europe just as one did after the Napoleonic wars ... and which seems to me not a whit more agreeable where it takes a fascistic-expressionistic form."[55]

He'd picked an inauspicious time to defend the republic. In January 1923, the stability of the young German democracy was once again severely challenged when French and Belgian troops occupied the Ruhr region in response to Germany's inability to meet its reparations payments. "Our Frenchmen are behaving brilliantly," Mann wrote to Heinrich. "They seem determined to give the lie to everyone in Germany who urges moderation."[56] Indeed, nationalists "exploded with rage and humiliation," the historian Richard J. Evans has written, engaging in widespread campaigns of civil disobedience and passive resistance. Adolf Hitler exploited the situation in a speech in Munich's Zirkus Krone on January 11 by once again blaming the "November criminals," who, by "stabbing the army in the back," had left Germany utterly defenseless.[57]

To make matters worse, the inflation that had been a reality of German society since 1914 began spiraling out of control in the months after Rathenau's assassination. By the time of the French occupation, it simply defied belief. Golo Mann would later admit that he'd never read a convincing explanation of the "mad occurrence" of hyperinflation—and he was hardly alone.[58] Overnight, it seemed, the value of the German mark plummeted, and continued to plummet, until the very idea of even having money ceased to make any sense whatsoever. The journalist and war veteran Victor Klemperer reported paying 12,000 marks for coffee and cake one day and 104,000 marks for the same thing a week later.[59] The Reichsbank had to issue paper currency in ever larger denominations to keep up, culminating in the absurdity of a one-hundred-trillion-mark note on November 2, 1923, at which point a single U.S. dollar was worth 4.2 trillion marks.[60] As an article in the *Berliner Illustrirte Zeitung* put it, life had become a race to turn a near-worthless piece of paper into something one could eat before it lost what little value it had.[61]

For Mann, the period of German hyperinflation primarily meant that he had to spend the first half of 1923 bowling around Europe, reading and lecturing in a desperate bid for foreign income. Between January and June, he was invariably to be found in Switzerland, Austria, Hungary, Czechoslovakia, or Spain. "It is a mad life," he wrote to Kurt Martens, especially with a novel "crying out to be finished," but as a pater familias of many he needed to make a living.[62]

A particularly important source of income came from the wealthy American poet and art collector Scofield Thayer, editor of *The Dial* magazine. Under Thayer's stewardship, *The Dial* had already established itself as "a lighthouse of the modernist movement," publishing T. S. Eliot's *The Waste Land*, as well as works by Maxim Gorky, Khalil Gibran, Marianne Moore, Hugo von Hofmannsthal, William Butler Yeats, and Jorge Ortega y Gasset, among others.[63] In 1922, Thayer had asked Thomas Mann to serve as *The Dial*'s German correspondent, an offer Mann gladly accepted.

Mann's association with *The Dial* and his widely publicized lectures across the continent helped build his reputation abroad as the preeminent representative of the German cultural tradition. He forged personal connections with some of the most esteemed writers in Europe, including Hugo von Hofmannstahl, George Bernard Shaw, Robert Musil, H. G. Wells, Stefan Zweig, André Gide, Georg Brandes, and Arthur Schnitzler. According to Tobias Boes, Mann also helped introduce non-German authors to the Weimar Republic, for a time even serving as coeditor of a book series called Novels of the World.[64] In coming years, he would speak in venues throughout the continent—London, Florence, Paris, Warsaw, Vienna, Copenhagen—at the invitation of such organizations as PEN International and the Carnegie Foundation for International Peace. As Mann put it in a letter to the German scholar Ernst Robert Curtius, "In the absence of effective political action, the thought that writers might lead the way toward European reconciliation may not have seemed quite as unrealistic as it does today."[65]

On March 10, 1923, in the middle of all the national uncertainty, Thomas Mann was roused from his determined stupor in

CHANGES

Feldafing by a phone call informing him that his mother probably wouldn't make it through the night. He hastened back to Munich to meet Heinrich, and together the two brothers drove to Wessling to join their younger siblings, Julia and Viktor, at their mother's deathbed to say their final goodbyes.

She was buried a few days later, in a plot next to her daughter Carla in Munich's Waldfriedhof cemetery. How strange, Mann reflected, that the woman who was now laid to rest in Munich had first seen light six thousand miles away, in Paraty in Brazil, where her childhood was spent walking barefoot on the beach. He thought of the chapter he'd been writing when he was interrupted by the phone call, a chapter set in the snow. For some reason, these two images—the image of his mother as a child walking in the sand, and the image of his hero lost in the snowy Alps—struck him as somehow related. Could it be, he wondered, that life on the shore was really so different from life in the snow?

* * *

We are still no more than two years into Hans Castorp's stay at the Berghof when he decides to try his hand at skiing. Enraptured by life in the snow, whose "primal monotony" reminds him of the ocean, Hans Castorp longs to escape the society of the Berghof and "be alone with his thoughts to 'play king,'" a term he uses to describe a childhood game in which he would imagine looking on the world from above.[66] Encouraged by Settembrini, Hans Castorp flouts the house rules of the sanatorium, which strictly forbid athletic activities given that the air, though easy to breathe, makes "great demands on the heart," and after purchasing a pair of skis at a shop on the promenade in Davos begins practicing in his own time, well away from the winter season tourists.[67]

Hans Castorp is attracted to the "cottony nothing" of the snow for the same reason he is attracted to the ocean: it offers a respite from the burdens of organic, conscious life. "It was primal silence to which Hans Castorp listened as he stood there, leaning on one pole, his head tilted to the side, his mouth open; and silently, unrelentingly the snow went on falling, drifted down in a gentle hush," the narrator tells us.[68] We recall that tilting one's head to the side is one of the novel's many leitmotifs; it is the same position Hans Castorp assumes when listening to music, which is to say: when he is contemplating death.

And it is precisely death that is foremost on Hans Castorp's mind as, one day, he takes his skis up in the cable car to the top of Schatzalp and is "abducted into a world of shimmering, powdery slopes, sixty-five hundred feet above sea level."[69] There, far from the civilization of the flatlands, hundreds of feet above the society of the sanatorium, Hans Castorp engages in his game of "playing king," reflecting on his discussions with the "windbag and organ-grinder" Settembrini and "that caustic little Jesuit and terrorist" Naphta, both of whom, he reflects, have been battling pedagogically for his soul like "God and the Devil struggling over a man in the Middle Ages."[70]

Before long, however, Hans Castorp is engulfed in a snowstorm and loses his way in the frozen wilderness, pressing on and becoming increasingly fearful, until he realizes that he has been trying to lose his way all along.[71] (The subchapter here begins to function as an approximation of Hans Castorp's journey in the novel as a whole.) As the blizzard moves in, he continues skiing onward even though he no longer knows whether he is making progress or not: "Whether it was purposeful movement, movement in the right direction, or whether it might have been better to stay where he was (which, however, did not seem feasible), that remained to be seen."[72]

On the slopes of the same mountains that he first saw on his arrival from Hamburg, Hans Castorp's physical exhaustion is overpowering. A "merciful self-narcosis" sets in, the temptation to lie down and sleep beckons, and yet he decides that one must "fight against such things" unless one means to succumb to death, which Hans Castorp's "feeling of duty" toward life prevents him from doing.[73] Dizzy and disoriented, he seeks shelter by a shed and takes a swig of port from a bottle he has brought with him—a mistake, he decides, because the alcohol only serves to make his head heavy, muddling his thoughts. Standing there gazing into the white void, he begins to dream of young men and women—"children of the sea and sun"—frolicking on the sun-drenched rocks or riding horses into the glistening Mediterranean Sea. At the sight of the friendliness and courteousness with which this "intelligent, cheerful, beautiful, young humanity" treats one another, Hans Castorp's "whole heart opened wide—painfully, lovingly wide." Despite never having been to either Naples or Sicily or Greece, his vision of "sunny, civilized happiness" has the intimate force of memory.[74]

Then, just as quickly, his dream darkens. A young man standing off to the side stares back at Hans Castorp with a "smile of courteous, brotherly deference," until, looking somewhere beyond him, his "beautiful, finely chiseled" face takes on a grave expression of "deathlike reserve." Looking now in the same direction, Hans Castorp notices a temple gate flanked by huge columns. There is a stairway he heavy-heartedly descends. Then more stairs, more columns, until finally he comes across the gruesome sight of two half-naked old women dismembering a child above a basin: "They devoured it piece by piece, the brittle little bones cracking in their mouths, blood dripping from their vile lips." When they suddenly spot Hans Castorp, they damn him "soundlessly with the filthiest, lewdest curses of his hometown dialect."[75] Horrified, Hans Castorp desperately tries to pull away as the old women curse and shake their fists at him, only to slip and fall against a column, at which point he awakens to find himself lying in the snow with his skis still strapped to his feet.

Hans Castorp's eerie dream-vision explicitly recalls Nietzsche's *The Birth of Tragedy*, particularly its third chapter, in which

Nietzsche tells us that "we must level down, stone by stone, as it were, the elaborate construction of Apolline culture until we can see its underlying foundations." Only then, he writes, does "the Olympian magic mountain [open] up before us, revealing all its roots."[76] One of Nietzsche's central claims in *The Birth of Tragedy* is that the Greeks created the "dream-birth" of the Olympian gods in order to endure a life burdened with the knowledge of "the fears and horrors of existence."[77] But where Nietzsche sees the Apollonian impulse to veil and conceal the horrors of existence, Hans Castorp's dream suggests that the "gentle reverence" with which the sunny people treat one another springs from their "silent regard for the bloody banquet."[78] In other words, it is in their acknowledgment of the horrors of existence that these people have erected a civilization whose "deep-seated ideals" bind them all together. The dignity and good cheer of their sunny, civilized happiness is based on an awareness of the fears and horrors of existence lurking somewhere beneath them.

Babbling aloud to himself, still only half-conscious, Hans Castorp movingly reflects: "I have experienced so much among the people up here, about kicking over the traces, about reason. I have passed on with Naphta and Settembrini into these dangerous mountains. I know everything about humankind. I have known flesh and blood. I gave Pribislav Hippe's pencil back to ailing Clavdia. But he who knows the body, who knows life, also knows death. Except that's not the whole thing—but merely a beginning. You have to hold it up to the other half, to its opposite. Because our interest in death and illness is nothing but a way of expressing an interest in life."[79] Hans Castorp decides that he will take neither Settembrini's nor Naphta's side. "Death or life—illness or health—spirit or nature. Are those really contradictions?" he wonders. He knows they are not: earlier in the novel, sitting on his balcony with a shelf's worth of books on anatomy, physiology, and biology, he asked himself what exactly life was, of what it consisted, until deciding that it's "the existence of what, in actuality, has no inherent ability to exist, but only balances with sweet, painful precariousness on one point of existence in the midst of this feverish, interwoven process of decay and repair. It was not matter, not spirit. It was something in between the two."[80]

Now, atop the magic mountain, surrounded by cottony nothingness, Hans Castorp utters a truth the search for which, he realizes, was what brought him to these mountains in the first place: "Man is the master of contradictions, they occur through him, and so he is more noble than they. More noble than death, too noble for it—that is the freedom of the mind. More noble than life, too noble for it—that is the devotion of his heart." He vows to keep faith with death in his heart, but also to remember that "if faithfulness to death and to what is past rules our thoughts and deeds, that leads only to wickedness, dark lust, and hatred of humankind. *For the sake of goodness and love, man shall grant death no dominion over his thoughts.*"[81]

Hans Castorp thus rejects Clavdia Chauchat's exhortation to seek morality "in sin, in abandoning oneself to danger, to whatever can harm us, destroy us."[82] He has overcome his innate "sympathy with death," refusing to yield to his desire to lie down in snowy nothingness and die, recognizing instead his "feeling of duty" toward life. At the same time, he also rejects Settembrini's anemic rationalism, his meager reason, as an insufficient counterpoint to death, just as he rejects Naphta's malicious mysticism.

Instead, Hans Castorp's dream-vision has made him conscious that it is only love—love understood as a community of human beings—that can stand opposed to death: "Only love, and not reason yields kind thoughts. And form, too, comes only from love and goodness: form and the cultivated manners of man's fair state, of a reasonable, genial community—out of silent regard for the bloody banquet."[83]

Hans Castorp's dream and subsequent realization that "man is the master of contradictions" thus functions as a kind of allegory of the humanism Thomas Mann was beginning to articulate for himself in the years after the end of the war and the publication of *Reflections*. (When Hans Castorp says that "our interest in death and illness is nothing but a way of expressing an interest in life," he is paraphrasing Thomas Mann's 1922 address to Gerhart Hauptmann.) And yet the chapter is layered with irony as thick as the falling snow. Hans Castorp's ethical demand to choose life *"for the sake of goodness and love"* remains ambiguous, not only by virtue of its being a dream, but by being a dream that has already begun to fade at the end of the chapter: "By bedtime he was no longer sure what exactly his thoughts had been."[84]

And yet, by ironizing Hans Castorp's dream-vision, *The Magic Mountain* affirms its metaphorical power; that is, by remaining "just" a metaphor, the dream-vision eschews the closure of argument for the sake of aesthetic openness. If life, as Hans Castorp's anatomical and physiological studies have taught him, is "organic multiplicity," is "prohibited from understanding itself," then any life-truth that is not ambiguous would be inherently false.[85] "I've long been searching for that truth," Hans Castorp thinks to himself, even as the novel is busy contradicting him.

* * *

Despite the traveling, the inflation, and his mother's passing, Thomas Mann completed "Snow" in the early summer of 1923, shortly before the one-year anniversary of Walther Rathenau's assassination. On that occasion, Mann delivered a speech at a memorial service in Munich organized by a group of pro-republican students. It was subsequently printed in the *Frankfurter Zeitung* on June 28. In it, he paid tribute to the slain Rathenau and the republic for which he died, a republic Mann again celebrated as "the fulfillment of German humanity."

Distancing himself from Germany's conservative intellectuals, Mann argued that he did not consider German humanity as "something finished, closed, and final," but rather as an open-ended process of *becoming* whose greatest artistic expression is the bildungsroman, this genre that is "aimed at the cultivation, shaping, deepening, and perfection of one's self." Using *Wilhelm Meister* as his example, Mann argued that Goethe's novel is "a marvelous anticipation of German progress from inwardness to objectivity, to politics, to republicanism."[86] This was the fate of Germanness, Mann hoped: that those who still believed democracy foreign to German culture would, in time, come to see it as the completion, the improvement, of that culture.

He understood, he said, the objective political and historical obstacles standing in the way of this happening. With sympathy for the economically suffering populace, and with anger at the French whose occupation only served to reinforce the worst elements in German political life, he acknowledged the outdatedness ideas like individuality and democracy might evoke compared to "the iron-bound allegiance, absolute command, and terror" being preached to the German youth from the political extremes. He feared, he said, that this youth "may be driven into the arms of political obscurantism—that is, into reaction." Against this threat, he concluded his speech with a rousing vision of a "Third Reich of religious humanity, a new idea of the human being that stands beyond optimism and pessimism—something that is more than an idea, an expression of passion and love: a truly educative love that assures its followers the loyalty of an entire world youth."[87] This was a vision that did not sound very different from Hans Castorp's in the snow.

But the only movement that seemed to be gaining any followers was National Socialism, a movement in which the idea of a "Third Reich" would come to mean something radically different from what Mann imagined. The Nazi Party proved to be the sole beneficiary of hyperinflation, attracting as many as thirty-five thousand new members between February and November 1923 alone.[88] In their brown shirts and jackboots and swastika armbands, they were a ubiquitous menace in the streets of Munich, beating up political opponents and threatening the city's Jews. Stefan Zweig even recalled their members spilling into the nearby villages of Berchtesgaden and Reichenhall, where they marched and sang and hung garish posters on building fronts.[89]

As Heinrich Mann wrote to a friend, "You won't believe how desolate Munich has become in spiritual and artistic matters."[90] The city's increasingly illiberal cultural and political climate convinced many artists and writers to leave, among them Berthold Brecht, Bruno Walter, and Lion Feuchtwanger. In his third "German Letter" for *The Dial,* published in October 1923, Thomas Mann—who in years to come would likewise consider leaving—simply declared Munich to be "the city of Hitler, the leader of the German *fascisti.*"[91]

He had no idea just how right he was.

CHAPTER 7

Fullness of Harmony, 1923–1924

Shortly after eight o'clock on the evening of November 8, 1923, the ponderous figure of Gustav Kahr, now Bavaria's state commissioner general, rose to address the approximately three thousand people who had gathered in the cavernous Bürgerbräukeller in Munich for a political meeting. For some time, tensions between Bavaria and the national government in Berlin had been escalating. Kahr, along with the Bavarian regional commander of the army, Otto von Lossow, had openly defied orders from the newly appointed Reich chancellor, Gustav von Stresemann, to shut down the Nazi Party's newspaper, the *Völkische Beobachter*. There was ongoing talk in nationalist circles of attempting a coup in Berlin, or perhaps even engaging in armed confrontation with the French in the Ruhr. So far, however, talk was all it had amounted to; no one could agree on how to proceed or on who could be relied on to stage a coup.

But one man decided the time for talk was over. Forty-five minutes into Kahr's speech, ex-corporal Adolf Hitler stormed into the beer hall flanked by steel-helmeted *Sturmabteilung* (SA) troops under the command of the fighter pilot ace Hermann Göring, whose many medals could be heard clinking against his chest. Clad in a dark tailcoat that made him look like "a cross between Charlie Chaplin and a headwaiter," Hitler quickly mounted the podium, fired his pistol into the ceiling, and proclaimed a national revolution.[1] "The Bavarian government has been deposed," he shouted. "The Reich government has been deposed. A provisional government has been formed."[2]

Outside, several truckloads of heavily armed SA troops had already surrounded the beer hall and covered all the exits. Even the fifty-eight-year-old General Ludendorff, whom Hitler believed would be able to restore the German army to its glory, had turned up to lend the coup his credibility. Meanwhile, at the Löwenbraukeller, nearer the city center, the former German military officer Ernst Röhm and a detachment of SA troops awaited the order to begin taking command of the army headquarters and thereby thwart any countermeasures the government might take.

But the coup was a fiasco from the start. While Göring tried to calm the outraged audience, Hitler ushered Kahr, Lossow, and chief of police von Seisser into an adjoining room, where, foaming at the mouth and waving about his pistol, he failed to persuade any of the three men to support him in exchange for posts in his provisional government. When he threatened them with death, an outraged Kahr responded: "You can arrest me, have me shot, or shoot me yourself. I don't care whether I live or die."[3] Frustrated, Hitler reentered the giant hall and finally managed to win over the audience with a rousing speech, at which point Kahr, Lossow, and Seisser had no choice but to reluctantly signal their support. Victorious, Hitler triumphantly addressed the crowd: "In the coming weeks and months, I intend to fulfill the promise I made myself five years ago to the day as a blind cripple in an army hospital: never to rest or relax until the criminals of November 1918 are brought to the ground!"[4]

Unfortunately for them, Röhm and his troops had only managed to seize control of a single local army commando; the crucial army barracks complexes remained in government hands. As Hitler left the beer hall to try and work things out, he left Ludendorff in charge of Kahr, Lossow, and von Seisser. When Hitler returned, Kahr, Lossow, and von Seisser were gone; Ludendorff had let them go. When an irate Hitler demanded to know what in God's name he was thinking, Ludendorff calmly explained that he'd only let them go because they assured him they would honor the agreement. But instead of doing as Hitler had instructed, Kahr, Lossow, and von Seisser immediately set about coordinating with the police and military to oppose the insurrectionists. At which point the putsch was destined for failure.

After a long night spent agonizing over how to proceed, Hitler was eventually swayed by Ludendorff's proposal to march to the center of the city. With a force of about two thousand men, they set out around noon on November 9 with no particular notion of where to go. In front of the Feldherrnhalle at Odeonsplatz, they were met with police resistance. Someone fired a shot and then all hell broke loose. In just over thirty seconds, eighteen people—fourteen putschists and four policemen—were killed. Hitler, despite a dislocated shoulder, managed to flee the scene but was arrested two days later in a villa near Uffing, a village forty-odd miles south of Munich. He was taken to the Landsberg prison and charged with high treason.

* * *

Relief washed over Munich. Parts of it, anyway. The failed coup occurred just as a period of relative stability for the Weimar Republic was beginning. Throughout the fall, Stresemann's government had at last managed to stabilize the economy by introducing a new currency and had even negotiated the withdrawal of the French troops from the Ruhr in exchange for a guarantee that Germany would fulfill its reparations payments. This eventually led to the creation of the Dawes Plan, a temporary measure drawn up by the American diplomat and financial expert Charles Dawes that enabled Germany to make its payments according to a staggered schedule. The beleaguered Weimar Republic, it seemed, had survived its most serious threat yet.

Still, the damage that hyperinflation had wreaked on the social fabric of German society could not be ignored. "Life seemed to be a game of chance, survival a matter of the arbitrary impact of incomprehensible economic forces," Richard J. Evans writes.[5] Klaus Mann, who had turned seventeen in 1923, recalled that "nobody had the faintest idea what would happen next. Sometimes it looked as if utopia were around the corner: in other moments we anticipated the collapse of all values and institutions."[6]

In *Doctor Faustus,* Serenus Zietblom recalls the "blithe satisfaction" with which many intellectuals at the time described the inadequacies, failures, and coming end of Weimar democracy—a satisfaction often accompanied by "smug, intellectually amused laughter."[7] He probably had in mind the likes of Oswald Spengler; though Mann had been briefly fascinated by the first volume of *Decline of the West* when he read it in the aftermath of the Munich revolution, he now bristled at its fatalism, its "malicious demonstration of hostility toward the future, in the guise of scientific ruthlessness." In an essay printed in the *Allgemeine Zeitung* on March 9, 1924, Mann described Spengler as a repellent snob and "defeatist of humanity" who actively willed the decline he claimed to have diagnosed: "Though we may envisage but darkly the fate of mankind, thinking it doomed to suffer through endless ages; though we may shroud ourselves in the profoundest skepticism and refuse to believe in any hypothetic future happiness; yet we shall not thereby relish the more, by a single grain, the schoolmasterish insensibility of the Spenglerian brand of pessimism."[8]

Mann defended his own pessimistic humanism against Spengler's willful fatalism by asserting that "pessimism is not lovelessness"—that is, the skepticism and sense of foreboding with which he, Mann, envisaged the future did not prevent him from hoping for a better future. On the contrary the task, as Mann now understood it, was to affirm democracy *despite* all that could be said against it. As Theodor Adorno later put it: "Not least among the tasks now confronting thought is that of placing all the reactionary arguments against Western culture in the service of progressive enlightenment."[9]

With the failure of the Beer Hall Putsch, many suspected that National Socialism's moment had come and gone. In Hitler's absence, party leadership became plagued by internecine struggles and petty feuds, most of them reflecting geographical divisions within the party. Meanwhile, the Bavarian government made efforts to have Hitler deported back to Austria on his release from prison, though the Austrian chancellor made it clear he would not be welcome there. Even Gustav Kahr, now loathed by the far right for betraying Hitler, was forced to resign; he was replaced in early 1924 by the Catholic politician Heinrich Held, who immediately went about reconciling Bavaria with the federal government. Along with the stabilization of the economy, these developments brought "a calming tendency" to the city.[10] "The name of Adolf Hitler lapsed into oblivion," Stefan Zweig later wrote. "No one thought of him as a potential political force anymore."[11]

* * *

As political temperatures in Munich cooled, Thomas Mann was at last beginning his descent from *The Magic Mountain*. Since 1920, a few individual subchapters of the novel had started appearing at regular intervals in newspapers and magazines, the most recent, "Snow," in *Die Neue Rundschau* in December 1923. Samuel Fischer had already started printing the parts of the manuscript he'd received, even though Mann still wasn't done and warned it had reached "monstrous dimensions."[12]

An especially crucial eleventh-hour development occurred during the fall of 1923, when Thomas and Katia decided to spend their October holidays at the Hotel Austria in Bolzano in South Tyrol, where none other than Gerhart Hauptmann also happened to be staying. Mann wrote to Heinrich that he and the "good old man" went drinking together every evening, occasions on which Hauptmann consumed the lion's share, if *The Magic Mountain* is anything to go by.[13] For in those unguarded moments Hauptmann unwittingly supplied Mann with the voice, the mannerisms, and the boozy human camaraderie of Mynheer Peeperkorn, one of *The Magic Mountain*'s most memorable characters. As Mann would explain later in an apologetic letter to Hauptmann, dated April 11, 1925: "I was seeking a character vital to my novel and long since provided for in its scheme, but whom I did not see, did not hear, did not hold. Uneasy, anxious and perplexed, I came to Bolzano—and there, over wine, was unwittingly offered what I should never, never have allowed myself to accept, speaking in human and personal terms, but which in a state of lowered human responsibility I did accept, imagined I had the right to accept."[14]

Mynheer Peeperkorn, who appears in the novel's seventh and final chapter, is a sixty-year-old coffee planter from Java, an Indonesian island and former Dutch colony. He arrives at the Bergdorf escorted by—who else?—Clavdia Chauchat, much to the initial confusion of Hans Castorp, who nevertheless is quick to warm to the Dutchman. Unlike the majority of the patients at the Berghof, Mynheer Peeperkorn does not suffer from tuberculosis but from quartan fever, a form of malaria where the onset of a fever occurs every three days and lasts four—another example of the novel's number symbolism. And unlike Settembrini and Naphta, he does not possess great linguistic gifts: his incoherent speech is pocked with repetitions, interruptions, and half-finished sentences:

> "Ladies and gentlemen. Fine. How very fine. That *set*-tles it. And yet you must keep in mind and never—not for a moment—lose sight of the fact that—but enough on that topic. What is incumbent upon me to say is not so much *that*, but primarily and above all *this:* that we are duty-bound, that we are charged with an *inviolable*—I repeat with all due emphasis—inviolable obligation—*No!*

No, ladies and gentlemen, not that I—oh, how very mistaken it would be to think that I—but that *set*-tles it, ladies and gentlemen. Settles it completely. I know we are all of one mind, and so then, to the point!"[15]

Peeperkorn bursts open the hermetically sealed world of the Berghof with the sheer life force of his outsized personality. The entire sanatorium is swept up in the gyre of his grand commanding gestures. In the subchapter "Ving et un," he leads the patients in a drunken bacchanalian feast, a kind of Dionysian Last Supper, in the course of which Hans Castorp, in spite of his initial jealousy, cannot help but befriend Peeperkorn, much to Clavdia Chauchat's annoyance. In the narrator's words, deploying a phrase that is repeated during Elly Brand's séances, Hans Castorp "lets the power of that personality work upon him the way new sights work upon a tourist thirsty for knowledge."[16]

One of the most oft-quoted incidents involving Peeperkorn is the excursion of the Dutchman, Hans Castorp, Frau Chauchat, Naphta, Settembrini, and a few others to a waterfall in the vicinity of the Berghof. Picnicking in the midst of the water's deafening tumult, the company is suddenly startled when Peeperkorn, a goblet of port in hand, stands up and begins to speak. Despite no one being able to hear him over the sound of the water, they are spellbound by the sight of the "tyrannical and autocratic" Peeperkorn, whose hands make "compelling, riveting, cultured gestures that demanded their attention."[17] It is hard not to think of Max Weber here; in his famous lecture "Politics as a Vocation," which he delivered to a group of university students in Munich in 1919, Weber emphasized the power of speech among those political leaders who appealed to the masses by emotional means alone, even going so far as to describe the present situation as a "dictatorship based on exploiting the masses' emotions."[18] Mann, by demonstrating the impotence of Peeperkorn's authoritarian charisma against the forces of nature, is at the same time demonstrating a verbal mastery that is superior to the nonverbal and super-rational by virtue of being able to describe their effects—that is, by putting it into the sequential, forward-moving medium of prose, Mann is neutralizing Peeperkorn's charisma.

Hans Castorp, too, maintains a certain distance from Peeperkorn. Though at first his friendship with the Dutchman deepens the critical distance with which he has come to regard both Settembrini and Naphta. He regards them now as "little chatterboxes," borrowing the Dutchman's vocabulary (always a sure sign of Hans Castorp's sympathy), recognizing that a life consecrated by intellect alone is a life unlived in some vital sense. At the same time, however, Hans Castorp does not fall under Peeperkorn's spell the way he did Settembrini's or Naphta's; his spiritual education is advanced enough that Peeperkorn represents for him values "suitable for our earnest consideration," as he explains to Settembrini, but nothing more.[19] In these considerations of Peeperkorn, he demonstrates a psychological shrewdness and self-awareness that shows the extent of his pedagogical development.

But Mynheer Peeperkorn is also a tragic figure, since his insatiable appetite and lust for life is undermined by his own deteriorating physical state. "Life, young man, is a woman," he tells Hans Castorp on the night of the bacchanal, "a woman sprawled before us [who] demands our most urgent response, the proof or collapse of our resilient manly desire." Hans Castorp sees in Peeperkorn's eyes a flicker of fear, of existential dread, the terror of "failure of feeling in the face of the classic gifts of life," as the Dutchman puts it.[20] In other words, what Peeperkorn fears is his own sexual inadequacy, the attenuating powers of his potency. The inability to perform, the failure of feeling, is for Peeperkorn tantamount to a kind of religious betrayal of life: "it is an eruption of divine disgrace, it is the defeat of God's manly vigor, a cosmic catastrophe, a horror that never leaves the mind."[21] It is a fear, moreover, for which he has long been prepared: when he suddenly commits suicide, he does so by way of a carefully engineered syringe he has been carrying with him for some time, designed to replicate the bite of a snake.

As Hans Castorp explains to Clavdia Chauchat, paraphrasing his own insights from the "Snow" subchapter, "the love of death leads to the love of life and humanity. That is how it is. It came to me up on my balcony, and I am delighted to be able to tell it to you. There are two ways to life: the one is the regular, direct, and good way. The other is bad, it leads through death, and that is the way of genius."[22] These words suggest that Hans Castorp has not forgotten the content of his snowy vision after all. Intimacy with death, recognition of its siren song, is a necessary, if dangerous, step toward a truer affirmation of life—a love that carries death within it, since death is part of and inseparable from life. That Hans Castorp claims to have come to this insight on his balcony and not during his skiing misadventure suggests that life and death are what have truly preoccupied him during all his time at the Berghof, and that he has, now, finally become aware of it.

Shortly after Peeperkorn's departure, there follows the subchapter "Fullness of Harmony," in which Hans Castorp is spellbound by quite another sound: the Berghof's newly acquired gramophone, and in particular with a recording of "The Linden Tree," a song from Franz Schubert's 1828 song cycle *The Winter Journey*, a masterpiece of Romantic alienation and gloomy death-longing in which a lovelorn young man sets out at night through a winter landscape. Considered "Schubert's most famous song," the tenor Ian Bostridge writes, "Der Lindenbaum" opens with an arpeggiated figure resembling a gentle rustling, which is then interrupted by horn calls, "the Romantic sound par excellence, the call of the past, of memory, sensuality at a distance."[23] The song's lyrics—written by the poet Wilhelm Müller—describe the wanderer coming across a linden tree that whispers to him: "Come here to me, old chap, / Here you find your rest."[24]

Listening to "The Linden Tree" in solitude one night, Hans Castorp imagines how Settembrini might rebuke him for spending his time in this way, only to dismiss the idea that Schubert's "sweet, lovely, fair song," although it's a song of death, should in any way be "sick," or liable to lead to any sort of intellectual backsliding. Oddly, the song is then compared to a fruit: "a fresh, plump, healthy fruit, that was liable, extraordinarily liable, to begin to rot and decay at that very moment, or perhaps the next; and although it was purest regalement of the spirit when enjoyed at the right moment, only a moment later and it could spread rot and decay among those who partook of it."

The narrator goes on tell us that although Hans Castorp considers the song "a miracle of the soul," he also regards it with mistrust, looking at it with the "responsible eye of someone 'playing king,' who affirmed life and loved its organic wholeness. Both a miracle and, in response to the final compelling voice of conscience, the means by which he triumphed over himself." There follows a puzzling passage:

> In the solitude of night, Hans Castorp's thoughts, or intrusive half-thoughts, soared high as he sat before his truncated musical coffin ... ah, they soared higher than his understanding, were thoughts enhanced, forced upward by alchemy. Oh, it was mighty, this enchantment of the soul. We were all its sons, and we could all do mighty things on earth by serving it. One need not be a genius, all one needed was a tree to become an enchanter of souls, who would then give the song such vast dimensions that it would subjugate the world. One might even found whole empires upon it, earthly, all-too-earthly empires, very coarse, very progressive, and not in the least nostalgic ... his truncated musical coffin, inside which the song decayed into some electrical gramophone music. But the

song's best song may yet have been the young man who consumed his life in triumphing over himself and died, a new word on his lips, the word of love, which he did not yet know how to speak. It was truly worth dying for, this song of enchantment. But he who died for it was no longer really dying for this song and was only a hero only because ultimately he died for something new—for the new word of love and for the future in his heart.[25]

At first glance, the passage appears to be foreshadowing *The Magic Mountain*'s ending: Hans Castorp will indeed vanish from sight with Schubert's song on his lips. But there is something else going on. Commenting on the passage, the critic Alex Ross questions what music the narrator is actually describing. He brings attention to the fact that Mann in November 1924—just a few weeks before the publication of *The Magic Mountain*—gave a lecture on Nietzsche's relationship to Wagner in which he recited the passage above with no indication that it was from his forthcoming novel. Ross, like Hans Rudolf Vaget before him, thus makes the point that the music being described is Wagner's and the young man "triumphing over himself" is Nietzsche.[26] That Mann uses Schubert's "miracle of the soul" to very subtly invoke Nietzsche's rejection of Wagner thus constitutes a buried criticism of the German Empire and its cult of music, as Vaget has shown.[27]

For any modern reader of the novel, the narrator's description of "earthly, all-too-earthly empires, very coarse, very progressive" will also, of course, bring to mind Nazi Germany, in which the ideological exploitation of music reached its zenith. It speaks to the depth of Mann's insight into the lure of German Romanticism that he saw the potential for this rot so clearly. On this particular point, at least, his own views were consistent with Settembrini's: in a short essay from 1911, Mann admitted he found Wagner both "suspect" and "deeply questionable."[28]

FULLNESS OF HARMONY

* * *

In February 1924, Katia was whisked off yet again to a sanatorium, this time in Clavadel, Switzerland, not far from Davos. She remained there for six weeks, leaving the children at the mercy of their governess and the remote and preoccupied "Magician." While Erika, now eighteen, would shortly graduate high school and depart for Berlin to study acting with Max Reinhardt, Klaus, age seventeen, had recently decided he wanted nothing more to do with school or with his private tutors and that he intended to go to Berlin to become a dancer—"like Nijinsky," he said.[29] Thirteen-year-old Monika, meanwhile, was briefly and hastily transferred to an all-girls school following an "impermissible" incident of some sort with a male teacher and would eventually join her brother Golo at a boarding school in Salem.[30] The two youngest, Michael, age five, and Elisabeth, age four, had both recently had their appendixes removed.

Everyone breathed a sigh of relief when Katia returned at the beginning of April, no one more so than her husband, who in the meantime had come down with the flu. By early May, however, Thomas and Katia were both well enough to travel to London, where they were guests of honor at a dinner hosted by the PEN Club, where they met John Galsworthy, H. G. Wells, and George Bernard Shaw, among others. *Buddenbrooks* had recently been translated into English and published by Alfred A. Knopf in New York and Martin Secker in London. In 1921, Knopf and his wife Blanche had traveled to Germany on the recommendation of the cultural critic and journalist H. L. Mencken and secured from Samuel Fischer the exclusive rights to all of Mann's work. Mann found the translation "extraordinarily sensitive and accomplished" and visited his English-language translator in Oxford. Her name was Helen Tracy Lowe-Porter, and she hailed from the small town of Towada, Pennsylvania. In addition to translating

Mann, she was raising the three daughters she had had with her paleographer husband, Elias Avery Lowe, who taught at Oxford. Mann and Lowe-Porter's meeting was cordial enough, though ever so slightly strained by social awkwardness and language barriers. Mann's English was not yet conversational, and Lowe-Porter later said she'd felt nervous and insecure. She also recalled that Mann, in his dark-blue pinstripe suit, gave the impression of "a businessman, like Hans Castorp's Uncle-Cousin James. His manner was rather dry and stiff, though kindly."[31]

All eight members of the Mann family were reunited that summer in Kloster on the Baltic island of Hiddensee, where they stayed at the hotel Haus am Meer, or House on the Sea. They were joined by Frank Wedekind's daughter Pamela, a friend of Klaus's, which made it feel like one big summer camp. They were entertained one evening by Gerhart Hauptmann, the "King of Hiddensee," as Mann called him, who read to them from the manuscript of his novel *Till Eulenspiegel*. The following evening, Hauptmann asked Mann to read from *The Magic Mountain*, which he politely refused to do, saying he did not wish to dim the light of the previous evening's impressions. Hauptmann persevered. "You are wrong," he empathetically told Mann. "In my father's house are many mansions."[32]

From Kloster, the family moved east along the mainland coast to Bansin for two weeks, before concluding their Baltic holiday with a stay at Haus Heimdahl in Ahlbeck. Even with the summer crowds and busy itinerary, Mann wrote to Ernst Bertram that his manuscript was "steadily reducing, for I never work more smoothly and more productively than after my morning devotions in the sea."[33]

Mann also wrote a warm letter to the French novelist André Gide, thanking him for sending copies of his two latest books, *Corydon* and *Incidences*, which had finally reached him in Ahlbeck. "I shall perhaps be able to reciprocate shortly, around November, by sending you my new novel, which I am just finishing and which is called *The Magic Mountain*. But I assure you that I do not in the least expect you to read it. It is a highly problematical and 'German' work, and of such monstrous dimensions that I know perfectly well it won't do for the rest of Europe."[34]

A little over a month later—on September 28, 1924—Mann wrote *Finis operis* on the last page of his manuscript. Twelve years, a world war, and a social revolution after he first conceived of it, *The Magic Mountain* was finished at last.

* * *

The great stupor into which Hans Castorp and the other patients sink toward the end of the novel reflects the stasis—"the dead standstill"—described by many in the years before the First World War. In a desperate bid to pass the time, the residents of the Berghof take up amateur photography, stamp collecting, Esperanto, solitaire—anything to break the monotony of a life without time. Eventually, the stupor degenerates into petulance, "a love of quarrels ... a universal penchant for nasty verbal exchanges and outbursts of rage, even for fisticuffs."[35] A paranoid and anti-Semitic businessman who subscribes to a newspaper called *The Aryan Light* taunts his way into a fistfight with a Jewish patient, Sonnenschein, so that employees from the management office have to separate them. Everyone who witnessed the fight, the narrator tells us, "was still quivering hours later."[36]

Inevitably, perhaps, the ideological rift between Settembrini and Naphta, too, comes to a head. The nihilism and political sickness of the times inflames them, too. Naphta in particular scales the heights of "unparalleled aggressiveness" in his remarks. He claims to loathe "the bourgeois state and its love of security"; considers the sinking of the *Titanic* "most refreshing; it was handwriting on the wall"; and thinks "the universal lust for war ... quite honorable" in comparison to the "the weak-willed humanitarianism [and] villainy of slaughter on the economic battlefield known as the bourgeois state."[37]

Eventually, during a particularly heated argument, Naphta challenges Settembrini to a duel. That the Italian humanist consents to such an atavistic ritual is proof that even reason and humanism has been trumped by the irrationality and barbarism of the times. Hans Castorp reflects that "Settembrini's words seemed calm and logical, and yet they sounded strange and unnatural coming from him." In the heat of battle, however, Settembrini fires his pistol into the air—a final act of humanistic defiance. "I shoot in whatever direction I choose," the Italian counters when Naphta demands he take the duel seriously and fire again. Settembrini refuses, at which point Naphta reaches the logical conclusion of his irrational and terroristic worldview—and shoots himself.[38]

The Magic Mountain concludes as it must—as the reader has always known it would—with the outbreak of the First World War, a "thunderbolt that bursts open the magic mountain and rudely sets its entranced sleeper outside the gates." Settembrini, now almost entirely bedridden, musters up enough strength to bid Hans Castorp goodbye at the station as "life's problem child" departs Davos to serve his country in that "deafening detonation of great destructive masses of accumulated stupor and petulance," as the narrator describes the war.[39]

Our final glimpse of Hans Castorp occurs amid a gouged and barren former farmland, where tree trunks jut into cold rain and signposts have been ripped to shreds. "It is the flatlands—this is war," the narrator declares. Hans Castorp is caked with mud and sludge, advancing with his bayoneted rifle at his side as shells howl and explode around him. He accidentally steps on the hand of a fallen comrade, his hobnailed boots pressing the dead flesh deeper into muck. As he disappears from our sight, he is singing to himself, lines from Shubert's "The Linden Tree."

We are reminded of the "Snow" subchapter, in which Hans Castorp resisted the temptation to give in and surrender to his sympathy with death—he overcame it, in fact. "I do not intend, my stormily pounding heart does not intend, to lie down and be covered by stupid, precise crystallometry," he said then.[40] And yet he will almost certainly die this time, as Germany failed to adequately overcome its own Romanticism, its terrible sympathy with death. In 1925, when Thomas Mann heard that General von Hindenburg, the man who had led the German army during the war, was standing as a candidate for the presidency, he commented: "The candidacy of Hindenburg is 'Lindenbaum'—to put it mildly." In other words, Hindenburg's candidacy was a sign of Germany's unhealthy sympathy with death. He denounced "this shameful exploitation of the German people's romantic impulses" in an article in the *Neue Freie Presse*.[41] A few weeks later, in a letter to Hans Pfitzner, the composer whose political sympathies Mann no longer shared, he wrote: "The modest hero of my last novel is occasionally called 'a problem child of life.' All of us artists are life's problem children, but we are children of life all the same, and whatever the romantic license of the musician may be, a literary artist who in such a moment of European history as the present did not choose the party of life and the future as against the fascination of death would truly be an unprofitable servant."[42] *The Magic Mountain* thus ends with the suggestion, the possibility, that Hans Castorp has triumphed over his sympathy with death and chosen the party of life, even as he disappears into a war his country's sympathy with death partly caused.

* * *

The Magic Mountain was published in two volumes by Samuel Fischer Verlag on November 28, 1924. Having received approximately five thousand preorders, Fischer had to print an initial twenty thousand copies, a first print run that sold out in three months, earning Mann enough money to buy his first car, a six-seater Fiat.[43] Clearly, his concern that the novel's length and complexity would compromise its readability proved unfounded.

The novelist Jakob Wassermann, author of *Caspar Hauser*, wrote to Mann and told him he'd read *The Magic Mountain* in just four days while staying in Davos—at the source, as he put it—and considered it "a stupefying achievement" and "a crystallization of all the intellectual events of the past twenty years."[44] Even Walter Benjamin, who "hated [Thomas Mann] like no other writer," said he was deeply moved by it. In a letter to Gershom Scholem, Benjamin perceptively wrote: "I can only imagine that an internal change must have taken place in the author while he was writing. Indeed, I am certain this was the case."[45] Robert Musil, on the other hand, found the novel intellectually glib and exasperating. "What does his problem child, Castorp, do in all that time on the Magic Mountain?" he asked in his notebook. "Obviously he masturbated! But [Mann] removes the private parts from his characters as if they were plaster-of-Paris statues."[46]

Contemporary critical reviews of *The Magic Mountain*, even the most favorable, bore unmistakable signs of bafflement. No one seemed to know how exactly to categorize it. Was it a novel? A fairytale? A satire? One reviewer shared the story of a reader returning the novel to her bookseller in exchange for *The Count of Monte Cristo*, since both novels were about the same length but Dumas's novel at least had some action in it.[47] Writing to André Gide, Mann reported that he "kept hearing the most scathing judgments of [*The Magic Mountain*], mostly to the effect that it is not a novel, not a creative work, but a product of intellect and criticism."[48]

It was against this last point that Mann was moved most passionately to defend himself. In a letter to the German dramatist Julius Bab, he wrote of his use of Schubert's "The Linden Tree" at the end of the novel: "I do after all have a little of the poet in me, in spite of the intellectualism with which I have 'ruined the novel.' "⁴⁹ He was similarly defensive in a letter to Gerhart Hauptmann, in which he claimed he had "much more of the artist-child in me than is suspected by those who rattle on about my 'intellectualism.' "⁵⁰

Predictably, given Mann's recent defense of the Weimar Republic, the most pointed criticism came from the right. The writer and veteran Franz Hedwig called the novel "unmanly," while the Expressionist playwright (and Nazi sympathizer) Hanns Johst lamented its "smell of intellectuality."⁵¹ Friedrich Georg Jünger, the brother of Ernst Jünger, went so far as to prophesy that, "We shall one day soon see a team of bold, young men move into action against the magic mountain, with long-handled broad-bladed logging axes in their hands, and with these splendid axes smash the whole magic mountain into splintering ruins."⁵² In 1930, the Jünger brothers would join the playwright Arnolt Bronnen in interrupting a pro-democracy lecture by Mann in Berlin.

For many contemporary readers, then, *The Magic Mountain* became synonymous with Mann's embrace of democracy and his growing international stature, an impression strengthened by the fact that the novel was soon translated into Danish, Swedish, English, Hungarian, Polish, Czech, Yiddish, and French. In fact, as the literary scholar Karolina Watroba rightly points out, *The Magic Mountain* "began its life in translation even before it was published in German": the Swedish and Hungarian translators began their work while Mann was still finishing the manuscript.⁵³

One of the languages that counted most, of course, was English. Curiously, however, Mann was not sure that Helen Lowe-Porter was the right person to translate *The Magic Mountain*, despite his favorable impression of her version of *Buddenbrooks*. He felt that his novel would make serious psychological and intellectual demands on the translator—"demands which I sometimes deem would be more readily met by a male rather than a female temperament," as he put it in a letter to her.⁵⁴ That a writer so often accused of being effete or unmanly should worry about a "female temperament" taking on his novel was an irony apparently lost on Mann.

Writing to Alfred Knopf, Mann said he would prefer to name as his translator Herman George Scheffauer, the eccentric former protégé of Ambrose Bierce and a poet, dramatist, and literary mischief-maker to boot. (In 1899, Scheffauer had staged a hoax by tricking the *San Francisco Examiner* into printing what they thought was an unpublished poem by Edgar Allen Poe.) Scheffauer had translated Mann's *Bashan and I* in 1923 and was eager to take on *The Magic Mountain*. Knopf gently tried to dissuade Mann, explaining that "Mr. Scheffauer's reputation is nothing like as important or noticeable, outside perhaps of Germany today, as you would seem to think."⁵⁵ Eventually, Mann let himself be persuaded to accept Lowe-Porter. The matter was in any case settled definitively when Scheffauer murdered his private secretary and lover, Katherine von Meyer, cut his own throat and wrists, and then threw himself from his third-floor apartment in Berlin.

Helen Tracy Lowe-Porter's translation of *The Magic Mountain* was published in two volumes by Knopf in New York in May 1927. It received a full-page review in the *New York Times*, complete with an illustration by Max Liebermann and a headline calling it a "record of profound mental and spiritual experience," setting the stage for Mann's popularity of the 1930s and 1940s, when he emigrated to the United States and became the world's most famous antifascist writer.⁵⁶ Much of this was due to Alfred Knopf's pioneering marketing skills and ability to exploit American cultural conditions in his and his authors' favor. In Tobias Boes's words, Knopf's promotional material highlighted "the use value of [*The Magic Mountain*] for the practical life of modern man." It was advertised in *Publisher's Weekly* as "a *Divine Comedy* for our disastrous age," and elsewhere as "a *Pilgrim's Progress* for the physical and psychic life of modern man." Knopf even used as a promotional slogan the novel's most famous line: *"for the sake of goodness and love, man shall let death have no sovereignty over his thoughts."*⁵⁷

Among *The Magic Mountain*'s earliest American readers of note was the novelist Charles R. Jackson, author of *The Lost Weekend* (1944) and *The Fall of Valor* (1946). Jackson first read Mann's novel in 1928 in a New York hospital while waiting for admission to a tuberculosis sanatorium in New Mexico. After reading the novel, he decided to go to Davos instead. When Jackson explained to his new German doctor why he'd come all the way to Switzerland for the cure, the doctor was aghast. "You read *Der Zauberberg* and *then* came to Davos? . . . Crazy American!" Jackson even persuaded himself that he'd encountered several real-life inspirations for the novel's characters, including "the original of Settembrini."⁵⁸ In *The Lost Weekend*, which was adapted into an Academy Award–winning film by Billy Wilder, Jackson's alcoholic protagonist frequently references Thomas Mann, and at one point compares himself to Hans Castorp lost in the snow.

The American reception of *The Magic Mountain* was further elevated by the appearance, in 1933, of the Yale University scholar Hermann J. Weigand's book-length study, *Thomas Mann's Novel "Der Zauberberg": A Study*, the first of its kind in any language, and one that remains an invaluable resource for students of the novel. In 1938, thanks to the graduate student Joseph Warner Angell, Yale University also announced the establishment of its Thomas Mann collection of the author's papers and manuscripts, including rejected pages from the lost manuscript of *The Magic Mountain*.

By 1928, *The Magic Mountain* had been through more than one hundred reprints and sold over a hundred thousand copies in German alone.⁵⁹ It came as no great surprise when it was announced a year later that Thomas Mann was being awarded the Nobel Prize for literature, even though Frederik Böök, one of the judges, felt *The Magic Mountain* was a poor representation of the German cultural heritage. Mann recounted the episode in a letter to André Gide: "The most amusing part of it is that the Stockholm critic and professor of literature Böök, who usually has a decisive influence upon the choice of the Nobel Prize winner, publicly proclaimed [*The Magic Mountain*] an artistic monstrosity and said I was receiving the prize exclusively, or at any rate chiefly, for my early novel *Buddenbrooks*."[60] In its official citation, the Swedish Academy thus awarded the prize to Mann "principally for his great novel, *Buddenbrooks*, which has won steadily increased recognition as one of the classic works of contemporary literature." Although it had by then sold over a million copies, *Buddenbrooks* was almost three decades old in 1929.

Even so, the Nobel Prize and the international success of *The Magic Mountain* etched Thomas Mann's name into the pantheon of the twentieth century's greatest authors. At Harvard University in the 1940s, the influential scholar and critic Harry Levin taught an enormously popular course on "Joyce, Proust, and Mann," three names that formed a kind of literary shorthand for the best of European modernism. Indeed, For many young students at the midcentury, reading *The Magic Mountain* counted as an intellectual rite of passage. The literary scholar Stanley Corngold recalls that "the feat of reading and loving *The Magic Mountain* as a teenager was not rare in the 1950s," and that the novel served him and his fellow students as "an introduction to European intellectual history and its leading idea of dialectical process."[61] Susan Sontag described her first encounter in similar terms. When she picked up her copy of the novel at Pickwick Bookstore in Hollywood, she said, "all of Europe fell into my head."[62]

As Corngold's and Sontag's remarks suggest, *The Magic Mountain* is a quintessentially European novel, if by "European" we use Milan Kundera's definition as "one who is nostalgic for Europe"; that is, Mann's novel seems to harken back to an idea of Europe as something more than just a tapestry of competing nationalisms.[63]

In this respect, *The Magic Mountain* is surely one of the greatest expressions of European humanism. And yet, at the same time, the novel is a curious one-off that has almost nothing in common with the other major modernist novels (least of all their predominantly urban setting). It is a magical, mysterious, even alchemical book. To put it in its own language, *The Magic Mountain*'s brilliance is produced by instability attempting to preserve form, by a process of ceaseless dissolution and renewal of itself.

* * *

All of the above still lay far in the future. On New Year's Eve at the end of 1924, *The Magic Mountain* had only just begun its stratospheric ascent. Thomas Mann, as he ceremoniously prepared his annual ritual of changing the calendar pages, looked back on a journey that had begun twelve years earlier, when he first traveled to Davos to visit Katia. He'd been a young man then, he thought, whereas now he faced the prospect of soon turning fifty, a year younger than his father had been when he died in 1891.

But let's banish those thoughts of death and decay; let's assume a vertical position and leave the horizontal life to Hans Castorp. Can we imagine Thomas Mann hopeful instead? Knowing what we know with all the benefit of hindsight and history, can we—if only for a brief moment—allow Mann, in his understandable ignorance of the future, a flicker of optimism, a glimmer of hope? Was there not after all cause for hope, as those last few minutes of 1924 died away? Adolf Hitler, though he'd recently been released from prison, was yesterday's news, and his National Socialist movement appeared to have lost momentum. The Weimar Republic had survived hyperinflation and was negotiating the withdrawal of French troops in the Ruhr. Cultural traffic between the battered nations had resumed, as Mann's lecture tours across the continent suggested. Most importantly, he'd made amends with Heinrich after a silence of seven years.

And what of himself? Hadn't Mann triumphed over his sympathy with death? His *Reflections*, he now understood, was too much a product of that sympathy, that head-tilting temptation to kick over the traces and surrender to the permanent horizontal position. But it had been necessary, he thought: his love of humanity had more depth as a result of his having gazed into the abyss. Only by facing death can we choose life. It was, he'd decided, the way of genius.

EPILOGUE

They're still with us, Hans Castorp and Joachim Ziemssen, Naptha and Settembrini (those two especially), even Clavdia Chauchat and Mynheer Peeperkorn. Their world up at the Berghof may not be ours, not quite, but it's impossible to read *The Magic Mountain* a hundred years after it was first published and not feel a shiver of recognition. This great swan song of a bygone European epoch confronts us with our own nihilism and political backsliding, with the suspicion that faithfulness to death and to what is past rules the thoughts and deeds of humankind today, and with the all-too-real possibility of a new, more terrible thunderbolt shaking the foundations of the earth.

The pessimistic humanism that grew out of Mann's writing of *The Magic Mountain* deserves our attention because it is open to the possibility of its own failure, which means it is also open to the possibility of enrichment. This was Mann's idea of education and democracy: a continuing process with no end point of perfection. For this reason, his occasional claim that Hans Castorp's words—"*For the sake of goodness and love, man shall grant death no dominion over his thoughts*"—constitute *The Magic Mountain*'s message, or that he ought to have placed the "Snow" subchapter at the novel's conclusion, are misguided. *The Magic Mountain*, this masterpiece of ambiguities, is not reducible to a political slogan. Fittingly, Mann is contradicted by his own great creation, a novel whose "radical openness" eschews the closure of conviction.[1]

EPILOGUE

No, Hans Castorp's famous words constitute not a message but a metaphor—"a poem of humankind," as he calls it. His resolution to "remember" the content of his dream-vision thus invites the reader to do so with him, and this invitation is all the more powerful, and moving, for being open to the possibility of our rejection. It is a metaphor we are again requested to consider in the novel's last line: "And out of this worldwide festival of death, this ugly rutting fever that inflames the rainy sky all around—will love rise up out of this too?"

To read *The Magic Mountain* today is to be confronted with this metaphor anew. It reminds us that we, too, are entranced sleepers sitting outside the gates, sheepishly rubbing our eyes, wondering how on earth our compulsive consumption of news and information failed to sufficiently warn us.

Already the world in which I began writing this book seems to belong to another era. Those seven weeks I spent in the snow happened to someone else, somewhere else, in another time. What happens next, what this rupture in time will mean, falls to us to imagine. For the sake of the future, we had better find a way of answering *The Magic Mountain*'s final question in the affirmative.

NOTES

PROLOGUE

1. Susan Sontag, *Reborn: Journals and Notebooks, 1947–1963*, ed. David Rieff (New York: Farrar, Straus & Giroux, 2008), 57.
2. Elizabeth Hardwick, *The Collected Essays of Elizabeth Hardwick*, ed. Darryl Pinckney (New York: New York Review of Books Classics, 2017), 416.
3. Susan Sontag, "Tea with Thomas Mann," *New Yorker*, December 21, 1987, 39.
4. Sontag, *Reborn: Journals and Notebooks*, 6.
5. Susan Sontag, "Pilgrimage," *New Yorker*, December 21, 1987.
6. Thomas Mann, *The Magic Mountain*, trans. John E. Woods (New York: Alfred A. Knopf, 1995), 8.
7. Ibid., xxxv.
8. Quoted in Karin Verena Gunnemann, *Heinrich Mann: Heinrich Mann's Novels and Essays; The Artist as Political Educator* (Rochester, NY: Camden House, 2003), 79.
9. Thomas Mann, *Order of the Day: Political Essays and Speeches of Two Decades*, trans. H. T. Lowe-Porter (New York: Alfred A. Knopf, 1942), 105.
10. Thomas Mann, *Letters of Thomas Mann, 1889–1955*, ed. Richard Winston and Clara Winston (New York: Alfred A. Knopf, 1971), 119.
11. Hans Rudolf Vaget, ed., *Thomas Mann's The Magic Mountain: A Casebook* (Oxford: Oxford University Press, 2008), 15.
12. Jenny Erpenbeck, "Will I Come to a Miserable End? Jenny Erpenbeck on Thomas Mann," trans. Kurt Beals, *Literary Hub*, September 3, 2020.
13. George Orwell, *An Age Like This, 1920–1940*, ed. Sonia Orwell and Ian Angus (Boston: David R. Godine, 1968), 19.
14. Mann, *Letters of Thomas Mann*, 641.

15. Adam Zagajewski, *A Defense of Ardor: Essays*, trans. Clare Cavanagh (New York: Farrar, Straus & Giroux, 2004), 18.

ONE. ARRIVAL

1. Ian Bostridge, *Schubert's Winter Journey: Anatomy of an Obsession* (New York: Alfred A. Knopf, 2015), 3.
2. Susan Barton, *Healthy Living in the Alps: The Origins of Winter Tourism in Switzerland, 1860–1914* (Manchester: Manchester University Press, 2008), 10.
3. Quoted in Rodney Symington, *Thomas Mann's "The Magic Mountain": A Reader's Guide* (Newcastle upon Tyne: Cambridge Scholars Publishing, 2011), 7.
4. Karl Turban, "Practical Hints for Doctors Sending Patients to Davos," in *Davos as Health-Resort: A Handbook* (Davos, Switzerland: Davos Printing Company, 1906), 294.
5. Quoted in Thomas Dormandy, *The White Death: A History of Tuberculosis* (New York: New York University Press, 2000), 155.
6. Quoted in Barton, *Healthy Living in the Alps*, 22.
7. Thomas Mann, *The Magic Mountain*, trans. John E. Woods (New York: Alfred A. Knopf, 1995), 53.
8. Helen Bynum, *Spitting Blood: The History of Tuberculosis* (Oxford: Oxford University Press, 2012), 4.
9. Susan Sontag, *Illness as Metaphor and AIDS and Its Metaphors* (New York: Doubleday, 1990), 16.
10. Ibid., 25.
11. Quoted in Thomas Goetz, *The Remedy: Robert Koch, Arthur Conan Doyle, and the Quest to Cure Tuberculosis* (New York: Avery Publishing, 2014), 93.
12. Quoted in Richard Winston, *Thomas Mann: The Making of an Artist, 1875–1911* (New York: Alfred A. Knopf, 1981), 116.
13. Thomas Mann, *Death in Venice and Other Stories*, trans. David Luke (London: Vintage Books, 1998), 94.
14. Katia Mann, *Unwritten Memories*, ed. Elisabeth Plessen and Michael Mann, trans. Hunter and Hildegaard Hannum (New York: Alfred A. Knopf, 1975), 68.
15. Quoted in H. L. Reider, "Ninety Years after *The Magic Mountain*: World Literature Inspired by a Misdiagnosis; A Tribute to Christian Virchow," *International Journal of Tuberculosis and Lung Disease* 18, no. 7 (July 1, 2014): 761–62.

16. Hans Wysling, ed., *Letters of Heinrich and Thomas Mann, 1900-1949*, trans. Don Reneau (Berkeley: University of California Press, 1998), 112.

17. Quoted in Inge and Walter Jens, *Frau Thomas Mann: Das Leben der Katharina Pringsheim* (Hamburg: Rowohlt Verlag, 2012), 92-93.

18. Hans Bürgin and Hans-Otto Mayer, *Thomas Mann: A Chronicle of His Life*, trans. Eugene Dobson (Tuscaloosa: University of Alabama Press, 1969), 29.

19. Wysling, ed., *Letters of Heinrich and Thomas Mann*, 114.

20. Sue Prideaux, *I Am Dynamite! A Life of Nietzsche* (New York: Tim Duggan, 2018), 181.

21. Friedrich Nietzsche, *Selected Letters of Friedrich Nietzsche*, trans. Christopher Middleton (Indianapolis: Hackett Publishing, 1996), 174.

22. Richard Wagner, *Tannhaeuser* (Boston: Oliver Ditson, 1925), 4.

23. Quoted in Hermann Kurzke, *Thomas Mann: Life as a Work of Art; A Biography*, trans. Leslie Wilson (Princeton, NJ: Princeton University Press, 2002), 4.

24. Marcel Reich-Ranicki, *Thomas Mann and His Family*, trans. Ralph Manheim (London: Fontana Press, 1990), 35.

25. Richard Winston, *Thomas Mann: The Making of an Artist, 1875-1911* (New York: Alfred A. Knopf, 1981), 189.

26. Wysling, ed., *Letters of Heinrich and Thomas Mann*, 77.

27. Arthur Schopenhauer, *The World as Will and Representation*, vol. 1, trans. E. F. J. Payne (New York: Dover Publications, 1969), 352.

28. Thomas Mann, *A Sketch of My Life*, trans. H. T. Lowe-Porter (New York: Alfred A. Knopf, 1960), 25.

29. Quoted in Wysling, ed., *Letters of Heinrich and Thomas Mann*, 83.

30. Thomas Mann, *Stories of Three Decades*, trans. H. T. Lowe-Porter (New York: Alfred A. Knopf, 1936), 289.

31. Quoted in Donald Prater, *Thomas Mann: A Life* (Oxford: Oxford University Press, 1995), 12.

32. Ronald Hayman, *Thomas Mann: A Biography* (New York: Scribner, 1995), 99.

33. Thomas Mann, *Letters of Thomas Mann, 1889-1955*, ed. Richard Winston and Clara Winston (New York: Alfred A. Knopf, 1971), xv.

34. Quoted in Tobias Boes, *Thomas Mann's War: Literature, Politics, and the World Republic of Letters* (Ithaca, NY: Cornell University Press, 2019), 24.

35. Thomas Mann, *A Sketch of My Life*, trans. H. T. Lowe-Porter (New York: Alfred A. Knopf, 1960), 3.

36. Viktor Mann, *Wir waren fünf: Bildnis der Familie Mann* (Frankfurt am Main: Fischer Taschenbuch Verlag, 1994), 29.

37. Winston, *Thomas Mann*, 252.

38. Quoted in Frederic Spotts, *Cursed Legacy: The Tragic Life of Klaus Mann* (New Haven: Yale University Press, 2016), 300.

39. Wysling, ed., *Letters of Heinrich and Thomas Mann*, 48.

40. Mann, *Death in Venice and Other Stories*, 31.

41. Thomas Mann, *Buddenbrooks: The Decline of a Family*, trans. John E. Woods (New York: Alfred A. Knopf, 1994), 410.

42. Ibid., 462.

43. Hari Carel, *Phenomenology of Illness* (Oxford: Oxford University Press, 2016), 218.

44. Friedrich Nietzsche, *On the Genealogy of Morals*, trans. Michael A. Scarpetti (New York: Penguin Books, 2013), 87.

45. Mann, *Letters of Thomas Mann*, 50.

46. Mann, *Buddenbrooks*, 680.

47. Adam Kirsch, "Art over Biology," in *Rocket and Lightship: Essays on Literature and Ideas* (New York: W. W. Norton, 2015), 5.

48. Mann, *Death in Venice and Other Stories*, 159.

49. Friedrich Nietzsche, *The Birth of Tragedy*, trans. Shaun Whiteside (New York: Penguin Books, 1993), 39.

50. Clayton Koelb, ed., *Thomas Mann's "Goethe and Tolstoy": Notes and Sources*, trans. Alcyone Scott and Clayton Koelb (Tuscaloosa: University of Alabama Press, 1984), 230.

51. Lionel Trilling, *The Moral Obligation to Be Intelligent: Selected Essays*, ed. Leon Wieseltier (New York: Farrar, Straus & Giroux, 2000), 99.

52. Mann, *Death in Venice and Other Stories*, 157.

53. Wysling, ed., *Letters of Heinrich and Thomas Mann*, 85.

54. Quoted in Reich-Ranicki, *Thomas Mann and His Family*, 124.

55. Wysling, ed., *Letters of Heinrich and Thomas Mann*, 55.

56. Ibid., 17.

57. Nigel Hamilton, *The Brothers Mann: The Lives of Heinrich and Thomas Mann, 1871–1950 and 1875–1955* (London: Secker & Warburg, 1978), 102.

58. Mann, *Buddenbrooks*, 259.

59. Ibid., 563.

60. Thomas Mann, *At erkende dybt og gestalte smukt*, trans. Karin Højersholt (Copenhagen: Multivers, 2022), 20.
61. Mann, *Buddenbrooks*, 296.
62. Wysling, ed., *Letters of Heinrich and Thomas Mann*, 68.
63. Anthony Heilbut, *Thomas Mann: Eros and Literature* (London: Papermac, 1997), 16.
64. Quoted in Dirk Heisserer, *Im Zaubergarten: Thomas Mann in Bayern* (Munich: C. H. Beck, 2005), 179.
65. Hayman, *Thomas Mann*, 70.
66. Andrea Weiss, *In the Shadow of the Magic Mountain: The Erika and Klaus Mann Story* (Chicago: University of Chicago Press, 2008), 4.
67. Katia Mann, *Unwritten Memories*, 154.
68. Quoted in Inge and Jens, *Frau Thomas Mann*, 45.
69. Katia Mann, *Unwritten Memories*, 69–70.
70. Ibid., 69–71.
71. Quoted in Hans Rudolf Vaget, ed., *Thomas Mann's "The Magic Mountain": A Casebook* (Oxford: Oxford University Press, 2008), 17.

TWO. SYMPATHY WITH DEATH

1. Thomas Mann, *Diaries, 1918–1939*, trans. Richard Winston and Clara Winston (London: Robin Clark, 1984), 103.
2. Ibid., 111.
3. Thomas Mann, *Letters of Thomas Mann, 1889–1955*, ed. Richard Winston and Clara Winston (New York: Alfred A. Knopf, 1971), 68.
4. Mann, *Magic Mountain*, 8.
5. Dirk Heisserer, *Thomas Manns Zauberberg: Einstieg, Etappen, Ausblick* (Würzburg: Verlag Königshausen & Neumann, 2006), 17.
6. Hans Bürgin and Hans-Otto Mayer, *Thomas Mann: A Chronicle of His Life*, trans. Eugene Dobson (Tuscaloosa: University of Alabama Press, 1969), 34.
7. Thomas Mann, *The Magic Mountain*, trans. John E. Woods (New York: Alfred A. Knopf, 1995), 34.
8. Ibid., 34–35.
9. Ibid., 39.
10. Ibid., 58.
11. Ibid., 45.
12. Alexander Nehamas, *The Art of Living: Socratic Reflections from Plato to Foucault* (Berkeley: University of California Press, 1998), 23.

13. Stephen D. Dowden, ed., *A Companion to Thomas Mann's Magic Mountain* (Rochester, NY: Camden House, 1999), xii.

14. Mann, *Magic Mountain*, 312.

15. Ibid., 40.

16. Hermann Broch, *The Sleepwalkers*, trans. Willa Muir and Edwin Muir (New York: Vintage Classics, 1996), 448.

17. Børge Kristiansen, *Thomas Mann—Digtning og tankeverden* (Copenhagen: Forlaget Rosenkilde og Bahnhof, 2013), 330.

18. Friedrich Nietzsche, *The Will to Power*, trans. R. Kevin Hill and Michael A. Scarpitti (New York: Penguin Books, 2017), 12-15.

19. See Nolen Gertz, *Nihilism* (Cambridge, MA: MIT Press, 2019), 37-57.

20. Mann, *Magic Mountain*, 31.

21. T. J. Reed, *Thomas Mann: The Uses of Tradition* (Oxford: Oxford University Press, 1974), 228-29.

22. Bürgin and Mayer, *Thomas Mann: A Chronicle*, 34.

23. Thomas Mann, *Stories of Three Decades*, trans. H. T. Lowe-Porter (New York: Alfred A. Knopf, 1936), 440.

24. Quoted in Bürgin and Mayer, *Thomas Mann: A Chronicle*, 34.

25. Hayman, *Thomas Mann: A Biography* (New York: Scribner, 1995), 235, 268.

26. Ibid., 178.

27. Hans Wysling, ed., *Letters of Heinrich and Thomas Mann, 1909-1949*, trans. Don Reneau (Berkeley: University of California Press, 1998), 118-19.

28. D. H. Lawrence, *Phoenix: Posthumous Papers, 1936*, ed. Edward D. McDonald (London: Penguin Books, 1978), 308-13.

29. Thomas Mann, *Death in Venice and Other Stories*, trans. David Luke (London: Vintage Books, 1998), 201-7.

30. Thomas Mann, *Essays of Three Decades*, trans. H. T. Lowe-Porter (New York: Alfred A. Knopf, 1976), 73.

31. Ibid., 83.

32. Thomas Mann, *Late Essays*, trans. Richard Winston, Clara Winston, Tania Stern, and James Stern (New York: Alfred A. Knopf, 1959), 181.

33. Thomas Mann, "Address at the Dedication of the Thomas Mann Collection at Yale University," *Yale Review* 27 (1938): 705.

34. Quoted in Nigel Hamilton, *The Brothers Mann: The Lives of Heinrich and Thomas Mann, 1871-1950 and 1875-1955* (London: Secker & Warburg, 1978), 128.

35. Wysling, ed., *Letters of Heinrich and Thomas Mann*, 99.
36. Karin Verena Gunnemann, *Heinrich Mann's Novels and Essays: The Artist as Political Educator* (Rochester, NY: Camden House, 2002), 4.
37. Heinrich Mann, "Geist und Tat," *Pan* I, no. 5 (January 1911): 143.
38. Heinrich Mann, *Man of Straw*, trans. Ernest Boyd (London: Penguin Books, 1979), 44.
39. Quoted in Hamilton, *Brothers Mann*, 139.
40. Mann, *Letters of Thomas Mann*, 54.
41. Wolf Lepenies, *The Seduction of Culture in German History* (Princeton, NJ: Princeton University Press, 2006), 15.
42. Christopher Clark, *The Sleepwalkers: How Europe Went to War in 1914* (New York: HarperCollins Publishers, 2013), 205.
43. Mann, *Death in Venice and Other Stories*, 208.
44. Wysling, ed., *Letters of Heinrich and Thomas Mann*, 118–19.
45. Mann, *Magic Mountain*, 43–44.
46. Ibid., 160–61.
47. Ibid., 7.
48. Ibid., 70.
49. Ibid., 300.
50. Ibid., 161.
51. Ibid., 58.
52. Ibid., 179.
53. Ibid., 26.
54. Ibid., 107.
55. Ibid., 288.
56. Ibid., 57.
57. Ibid., 95–98.
58. Ibid., 111–12.
59. Friedrich Nietzsche, *Basic Writings of Nietzsche*, trans. Walter Kaufmann (New York: Modern Library, 1992), 639.
60. Friedrich Nietzsche, *The Birth of Tragedy*, trans. Shaun Whiteside (New York: Penguin Books, 1993), 10.
61. Mann, *Magic Mountain*, 197–98.
62. Arthur Schopenhauer, *The World as Will and Representation*, vol. 2, trans. E. F. J. Payne (New York: Dover Publications, 1966), 469.
63. Thomas Mann, *Buddenbrooks: The Decline of a Family*, trans. John E. Woods (New York: Alfred A. Knopf, 1994), 635.
64. Mann, *Death in Venice and Other Stories*, 207, 224, 265.

65. Quoted in Peter de Mendelssohn, *Der Zauberer: Das Leben des deutschen Schriftstellers Thomas Mann*, vol. 2 (Frankfurt am Main: S. Fischer Verlag, 1975), Kindle edition.

66. Thomas Mann, *Reflections of a Nonpolitical Man*, trans. Walter D. Morris (New York: New York Review Books, 2021), 352.

67. See Steven Cerf, "Georg Brandes' View of Novalis: A Current within Thomas Mann's *Der Zauberberg*," *Colloquia Germanica* 14, no. 2 (1981): 114–29.

68. Georg Brandes, *Main Currents in Nineteenth Century Literature*, vol. 2, *The Romantic School in Germany* (New York: Macmillan, 1902), 189.

69. Ibid., 184–85.

70. Quoted in Rüdiger Safranski, *Romanticism: A German Affair*, trans. Robert E. Goodwin (Evanston, IL: Northwestern University Press, 2014), 75.

71. Hermann J. Weigand, *Thomas Mann's Novel "Der Zaubeberg": A Study* (New York: A. Appleton-Century, 1933), 43.

72. Ibid., 47–48.

73. Mann, *Magic Mountain*, 7.

74. Ibid., 16.

75. See Paul Ricoeur's lengthy discussion of *The Magic Mountain* as a time-novel in *Time and Narrative*, vol. 2, trans. Kathleen McLaughlin and David Pellauer (Chicago: University of Chicago Press, 1985), 112–30.

76. Mann, *Magic Mountain*, 642.

77. Hayman, *Thomas Mann*, 252.

78. Ernst Bertram, *Nietzsche: Attempt at a Mythology*, trans. Robert E. Norton (Urbana: University of Illinois Press, 2009), 41.

79. Thomas Mann, *Past Masters and Other Essays*, trans. H. T. Lowe-Porter (New York: Alfred A. Knopf, 1933), 151.

80. Hermann Kurzke, *Thomas Mann: Life as a Work of Art; A Biography*, trans. Leslie Wilson (Princeton, NJ: Princeton University, 2002), 91.

81. Walter Benjamin, *The Storyteller Essays*, trans. Tess Lewis (New York: New York Review of Books, 2019), 58.

82. Mann, *Reflections*, 17.

83. Charles Neider, ed., *The Stature of Thomas Mann* (New York: New Directions, 1947), 80.

84. Katia Mann, *Unwritten Memories*, ed. Elisabeth Plessen and Michael Mann, trans. Hunter and Hildegaard Hannum (New York: Alfred A. Knopf, 1975), 43.

85. Klaus Mann, *The Turning Point: Thirty-five Years in This Century* (New York: Markus Wiener Publishing, 1984), 8.

86. Thomas Mann, "The Making of *The Magic Mountain*," in *The Magic Mountain*, trans. H. T. Lowe-Porter (New York: Modern Library, 1992), 751.

87. Alex Ross, *Wagnerism: Art and Politics in the Shadow of Music* (New York: Alfred A. Knopf, 2021), 35.

88. Mann, *Magic Mountain*, 71.

89. Ibid., 316.

90. James Wood, "Thomas Mann: The Master of the Not Quite," *The Broken Estate: Essays on Literature and Belief* (New York: Random House, 1999), 113.

91. Mann, *Magic Mountain*, 27.

92. Ibid., 37.

93. Ibid., 210.

94. Ibid., 118.

95. Ibid., 210, 127.

96. Ibid., 191.

97. Ibid., 326.

98. Ibid., 323.

99. Ibid., 326.

100. Rodney Symington, *Thomas Mann's "The Magic Mountain": A Reader's Guide* (Newcastle upon Tyne: Cambridge Scholars Publishing, 2011), 201.

101. Mann, *Magic Mountain*, 262.

102. Ibid., 269.

103. Ibid., 289.

104. Ibid., 111–12, 152, 157.

105. Ibid., 334.

106. Ibid., 336–37.

107. Ibid., 338.

108. Charles Neider, ed., *The Stature of Thomas Mann* (New York: New Directions, 1947), 79.

109. Klause Mann, *Turning Point*, 9.

110. Neider, ed., *Stature of Thomas Mann*, 59.

111. Klaus Mann, *Turning Point*, 7–8.

112. Neider, ed., *Stature of Thomas Mann*, 60.

113. Ibid., 77.

114. Quoted in Ivo de Figueiredo, *Henrik Ibsen: The Man and the Mask*, trans. Robert Ferguson (New Haven: Yale University Press, 2018), 493.

115. Quoted in David Clay Large, *Where Ghosts Walked: Munich's Road to the Third Reich* (New York: W. W. Norton, 1997), xiii.

116. Michael Brenner, *In Hitler's Munich: Jews, the Revolution, and the Rise of Nazism*, trans. Jeremiah Riemer (Princeton, NJ: Princeton University Press, 2022), 19.

117. Large, *Where Ghosts Walked*, xxiii–xxiv.

118. Mann, *Magic Mountain*, 675.

119. Fritz Stern, *The Politics of Cultural Despair: A Study in the Rise of the German Ideology* (Berkeley: University of California Press, 1961), 167–69.

120. Large, *Where Ghosts Walked*, xxv.

121. Ibid., 39.

THREE. THE THUNDERBOLT

1. Joseph Roth, *The Radetzky March*, trans. Michael Hofmann (London: Granta Books, 2002), 324.

2. Stefan Zweig, *The World of Yesterday* (Lincoln: University of Nebraska Press, 1964), 216.

3. Klaus Mann, *The Turning Point: Twenty-five Years in This Century* (New York: Markus Wiener Publishing, 1984), 18.

4. Robert Musil, *The Man without Qualities*, trans. Sophie Wilkins and Burton Pike (London: Picador, 1995), 390.

5. Quoted in Hayman, *Thomas Mann: A Biography* (New York: Scribner, 1995), 280.

6. Margaret MacMillan, *The War That Ended Peace: The Road to 1914* (New York: Random House, 2013), xxviii.

7. Klaus Mann, *Turning Point*, 28.

8. Thomas Mann, *Doctor Faustus*, trans. John E. Woods (New York: Alfred A. Knopf, 1997), 316.

9. See Jeffrey Verhey, *The Spirit of 1914: Militarism, Myth, and Mobilization in Germany* (Cambridge: Cambridge University Press, 2000).

10. Jörn Leonhard, *Pandora's Box: A History of the First World War*, trans. Patrick Camiller (Cambridge, MA: The Belknap Press of Harvard University Press, 2018), 113–15.

11. Verhey, *Spirit of 1914*, 34.

12. Ernst Toller, *I Was a German: The Autobiography of Ernst Toller*, trans. Edward Crankshaw (New York: William Morrow, 1934), 63.

13. Quoted in David Clay Large, *Where Ghosts Walked: Munich's Road to the Third Reich* (New York: W. W. Norton, 1997), 48.

14. Volker Ullrich, *Hitler: Ascent, 1889-1939*, trans. Jefferson Chase (London: Bodley Head, 2016), 54.

15. Ernst Jünger, *Storm of Steel*, trans. Michael Hofmann (London: Penguin Books, 2004), 5.

16. Zweig, *World of Yesterday*, 26.

17. Leonhard, *Pandora's Box*, 103.

18. Ibid., 129.

19. Paul Fussell, *The Great War and Modern Memory* (Oxford: Oxford University Press, 1975), 7.

20. Philipp Blom, *The Vertigo Years: Europe, 1900-1914* (New York: Basic Books, 2008), 268.

21. Friedrich Nietzsche, *The Will to Power*, trans. R. Kevin Hill and Michael A. Scarpitti (New York: Penguin Books, 2017), 7.

22. Quoted in Verhey, *Spirit of 1914*, 127.

23. Quoted in Hans Kohn, *The Mind of Germany: The Education of a Nation* (New York: Scribner's, 1960), 299.

24. Modris Eksteins, *Rites of Spring: The Great War and the Birth of the Modern Age* (New York: Houghton Mifflin, 2000), 92.

25. Roy Pascal, *From Naturalism to Expressionism: German Literature and Society, 1880-1918* (New York: Basic Books, 1973), 105.

26. "To the Civilized World," *North American Review* 210, no. 765 (August 1919): 284-87. The letter was originally published in all the major German newspapers on October 4, 1914.

27. Wolf Lepenies, *The Seduction of Culture in German History* (Princeton, NJ: Princeton University Press, 2006), 9.

28. Quoted in ibid., 17.

29. Thomas Mann, *The Magic Mountain*, trans. John E. Woods (New York: Alfred A. Knopf, 1995), 365.

30. Ibid., 366-67.

31. Ibid., 373.

32. MacMillan, *War That Ended Peace*, 286-90.

33. Christopher Clark, *The Sleepwalkers: How Europe Went to War in 1914* (New York: HarperCollins, 2013), 362.

34. Quoted in MacMillan, *War That Ended Peace*, 576.

35. Mann, *Magic Mountain*, 246.

36. Christopher Middleton, ed., *Selected Letters of Friedrich Nietzsche* (Indianapolis, IN: Hackett Publishing, 1996), 67.

37. Mann, *Magic Mountain*, 699.

38. Golo Mann, *The History of Germany Since 1789*, trans. Marian Jackson (New York: Frederick A. Praeger, 1968), 289.

39. Hans Wysling, ed., *Letters of Heinrich and Thomas Mann, 1900–1949*, trans. Don Reneau (Berkeley: University of California Press, 1998), 120–21.

40. Ibid., 121.

41. Quoted in Nigel Hamilton, *The Brothers Mann: The Lives of Heinrich and Thomas Mann, 1871–1950 and 1875–1955* (London: Secker & Warburg, 1978), 159.

42. Evelyn Juers, *House of Exile: The Lives and Times of Heinrich Mann and Nelly Kroeger-Mann* (London: Penguin Books, 2012), 77.

43. Wysling, ed., *Letters of Heinrich and Thomas Mann*, 101.

44. Ibid., 123.

45. Leonhard, *Pandora's Box*, 131–33.

46. Eksteins, *Rites of Spring*, 100.

47. Leonhard, *Pandora's Box*, 153.

48. Viktor Mann, *Wir waren fünf: Bildnis der Familie Mann* (Frankfurt am Main: Fischer Taschenbuch Verlag GmbH, 1994), 313.

49. Quoted in Evelyn Juers, *House of Exile: The Life and Times of Heinrich Mann and Nelly Kroeger-Mann* (London: Penguin Books, 2012), 70.

50. Thomas Mann, *Reflections of a Nonpolitical Man*, trans. Walter D. Morris (New York: New York Review Books, 2021), 505.

51. Thomas Mann, *Letters of Thomas Mann, 1889–1955*, ed. Richard Winston and Clara Winston (New York: Alfred A. Knopf, 1971), 72.

52. Thomas Mann, *Death in Venice and Other Stories*, trans. David Luke (London: Vintage Books, 1998), 158–59.

53. Mann, *Reflections*, 496.

54. Ibid.

55. *Letters of Thomas Mann*, 72.

56. Sue Pridaux, *I Am Dynamite! A Life of Nietzsche* (New York: Tim Duggan Books, 2018), 373.

57. Lepenies, *Seduction of Culture in German History*, 9.

58. Mann, *Reflections*, 500.

59. Eksteins, *Rites of Spring*, 144.

60. Leonhard, *Pandora's Box*, 819–20.

61. Quoted in Hayman, *Thomas Mann*, 281.

62. Laird Easton, ed., *Journey to the Abyss: The Diaries of Count Harry Kessler, 1888–1918* (New York: Alfred A. Knopf, 2011), 679.

63. Quoted in Hermann Kurzke, *Thomas Mann: Life as a Work of Art; A Biography*, trans. Leslie Wilson (Princeton, NJ: Princeton University, 2002), 217.

64. Erich Heller, *Thomas Mann: The Ironic German* (Cambridge: Cambridge University Press, 1958), 120.

65. Kurzke, *Thomas Mann*, 217.

66. Herbert Wegener, ed., *Thomas Mann: Letters to Paul Amann*, trans. Richard Winston and Clara Winston (Middletown, CT: Wesleyan University Press, 1960), 33.

67. Zweig, *World of Yesterday*, 246.

68. Kurzke, *Thomas Mann*, 217–18.

69. Mann, *Death in Venice and Other Stories*, 259.

70. Mann, *Reflections*, 174.

71. Mann, *Death in Venice and Other Stories*, 204.

72. Hamilton, *The Brothers Mann*, 160.

73. Hayman, *Thomas Mann*, 285.

74. Frederic Spotts, *Cursed Legacy: The Tragic Life of Klaus Mann* (New Haven: Yale University Press, 2016), 14.

75. *Letters of Thomas Mann*, 75.

76. Mann, *Stories of Three Decades*, trans. H. T. Lowe-Porter (New York: Alfred A. Knopf, 1936), 443.

77. Hans Rudolf Vaget, "The Making of *The Magic Mountain*," *Thomas Mann's The Magic Mountain: A Casebook*, ed. Hans Rudolf Vaget (Oxford: Oxford University Press, 2008), 19.

78. Wegener, ed., *Letters to Paul Amann*, 42–43.

79. Hamilton, *Brothers Mann*, 168.

80. Quoted in Tobias Boes, *Thomas Mann's War: Literature, Politics, and the World Republic of Letters* (Ithaca, NY: Cornell University Press, 2019), 34.

FOUR. A GOOD SOLDIER

1. Peter de Mendelssohn, *Der Zauberer: Das Leben des deutschen Schriftstellers Thomas Mann*, vol. 2 (Frankfurt am Main: S. Fischer Verlag, 1975), Kindle edition.

2. Jörn Leonhard, *Pandora's Box: A History of the First World War*, trans. Patrick Camiller (Cambridge, MA: The Belknap Press of Harvard University Press, 2018), 414.

3. Herbert Wegener, ed., *Thomas Mann: Letters to Paul Amann*, trans. Richard and Clara Winston (Middletown, CT: Wesleyan University Press, 1960), 58.

4. Nigel Hamilton, *The Brothers Mann: The Lives of Heinrich and Thomas Mann, 1871–1950 and 1875–1955* (London: Secker & Warburg, 1978), 164.

5. Thomas Mann, *Diaries, 1918–1939*, trans. Richard Winston and Clara Winston (London: Robin Clark, 1984), 186.

6. Hans Wysling, ed., *Letters of Heinrich and Thomas Mann, 1900–1949*, trans. Don Reneau (Berkeley: University of California Press, 1998), 77.

7. Hamilton, *Brothers Mann*, 166.

8. Ibid., 165.

9. Heinrich Mann, "Zola," *Die Weissen Blätter* (Leipzig) 1, no. 11 (November 1915): 1312–82.

10. Hamilton, *Brothers Mann*, 172.

11. Hayman, *Thomas Mann: A Biography* (New York: Scribner, 1995), 289.

12. Wysling, ed., *Letters of Heinrich and Thomas Mann*, 26.

13. Hayman, *Thomas Mann*, 300.

14. Leonhard, *Pandora's Box*, 464.

15. Ibid., 656.

16. Ernst Toller, *I Was a German: The Autobiography of Ernst Toller*, trans. Edward Crankshaw (New York: William Morrow, 1934), 131.

17. Klaus Mann, *The Turning Point: Twenty-five Years in This Century* (New York: Markus Wiener Publishing, 1984), 37.

18. Golo Mann, *Reminiscences and Reflections: A Youth in Germany*, trans. Krishna Winston (New York: W. W. Norton, 1990), 21.

19. Klaus Mann, *Turning Point*, 39.

20. Golo Mann, *Reminiscences*, 25.

21. Mann, *Letters to Paul Amann*, 63.

22. Klaus Mann, *Turning Point*, 39.

23. Thomas Mann, *Reflections of a Nonpolitical Man*, trans. Walter D. Morris (New York: New York Review Books, 2021), 5–7.

24. Ibid., 352.

25. Ibid., 47, 210, 434.

26. Ibid., 6.

27. Thomas Mann, *Briefe, 1889–1936*, ed. Erika Mann (Frankfurt am Main: S. Fischer Verlag, 1961), 148.

28. Mann, *Reflections*, 245.
29. Ibid., 91.
30. Ibid., 44.
31. Rüdiger Safranski, *Romanticism: A German Affair*, trans. Robert E. Goodwin (Evanston, IL: Northwestern University Press, 2014), 220.
32. Mann, *Reflections*, 7.
33. Ibid., 57.
34. Ibid., 31.
35. Ibid., 486.
36. Thomas Mann, *Letters of Thomas Mann, 1889-1955*, ed. Richard Winston and Clara Winston (New York: Alfred A. Knopf, 1971), 82.
37. Romain Rolland, *Above the Battle*, trans. C. K. Ogden (Chicago: Open Court Publishing, 1916), 115.
38. Mann, *Diaries*, 12.
39. Mann, *Reflections*, 453.
40. Eskil Elling, "Reflections of a Nonpolitical Man," *The Point* 26 (Winter 2022): 185.
41. Mann, *Reflections*, 379.
42. Hayman, *Thomas Mann*, 288.
43. Ibid., 287.
44. Katia Mann, *Unwritten Memories*, ed. Elisabeth Plessen and Michael Mann, trans. Hunter and Hildegaard Hannum (New York: Alfred A. Knopf, 1975), 30.
45. "The truth is that civilization's literary man does not denigrate war when it is waged in the service of civilization," Mann wrote in *Reflections*, 51.
46. Ibid., 40.
47. Thomas Mann, *The Magic Mountain*, trans. John E. Woods (New York: Alfred A. Knopf, 1995), 241.
48. Mann, *Diaries*, 96.
49. Friedrich Nietzsche, *Beyond Good and Evil: Prelude to a Philosophy of the Future*, trans. R. J. Hollingdale (New York: Penguin Classics, 1990), 72.
50. Mann, *The Magic Mountain*, 153.
51. Ibid., 241.
52. Ibid., 154.
53. Leonhard, *Pandora's Box*, 741.
54. Ibid., 740.

55. Robert Gerwath, *November 1918: The German Revolution* (Oxford: Oxford University Press, 2020), 57.
56. Ernst Jünger, *Storm of Steel*, trans. Michael Hofmann (London: Penguin Books, 2004), 229.
57. Wysling, ed., *Letters of Heinrich and Thomas Mann*, 124.
58. Mann, *Diaries*, 11.
59. Wysling, ed., *Letters of Heinrich and Thomas Mann*, 125.
60. Hamilton, *Brothers Mann*, 192.
61. Wysling, ed., *Letters of Heinrich and Thomas Mann*, 128.
62. Quoted in Donald Prater, *Thomas Mann: A Life* (Oxford: Oxford University Press, 1995), 111.
63. Mann, *Sketch of My Life*, 51.
64. Mann, *Letters to Paul Amann*, 97.
65. Hermann Kurzke, *Thomas Mann: Life as a Work of Art; A Biography*, trans. Leslie Wilson (Princeton, NJ: Princeton University, 2002), 294.
66. Wegener, ed., *Letters to Paul Amann*, 100.
67. Gerwath, *November 1918*, 60.
68. Leonhard, *Pandora's Box*, 755.
69. Ibid., 763.
70. Laird Easton, ed., *Journey to the Abyss: The Diaries of Count Harry Kessler, 1888-1918* (New York: Alfred A. Knopf, 2011), 856.
71. Mann, *Diaries*, 4.
72. Ibid., 6.
73. Quoted in Ernst Bertram, *Nietzsche: Attempt at a Mythology*, trans. Robert E. Norton (Urbana: University of Illinois Press, 2009), xv.
74. Walter Kaufmann, *Nietzsche: Philosopher, Psychologist, Antichrist* (Princeton, NJ: Princeton University Press, 1950), 15.
75. Bertram, *Nietzsche*, 71-72.
76. Steven E. Aschheim, *The Nietzsche Legacy in Germany, 1890-1990* (Berkeley: University of California Press, 1992), 152.
77. Bertram, *Nietzsche*, 14.
78. Mann, *Diaries*, 4.
79. Ibid., 7.
80. Golo Mann, *Reminiscences and Reflections*, 22.
81. Mann, *Diaries*, 10.
82. Ibid., 12.
83. Quoted in Manfred Görtemaker, *Thomas Mann und die Politik* (Frankfurt am Main: S. Fischer Verlag, 2005), 42.

84. Peter de Mendelsohn, *Der Zauberer: Das Leben des deutschen Schriftstellers Thomas Mann*, vol. 3, *1918 bis 1933* (Frankfurt am Main: S. Fischer Verlag, 1975), Kindle edition.

85. Mann, *Diaries*, 16.

86. Ibid., 11.

87. David Clay Large, *Where Ghosts Walked: Munich's Road to the Third Reich* (New York: W. W. Norton, 1997), 73.

88. Robert Gerwarth, *November 1918: The German Revolution* (Oxford: Oxford University Press, 2020), 92.

89. Ibid., 71.

90. Mann, *Diaries*, 14.

91. Large, *Where Ghosts Walked*, 77.

92. Gerwarth, *November 1918*, 94.

93. Quoted in Michael Brenner, *In Hitler's Munich: Jews, the Revolution, and the Rise of Nazism* (Princeton, NJ: Princeton University Press, 2022), 28.

94. Quoted in Albert Earle Gurganus, *Kurt Eisner: A Modern Life* (Rochester, NY: Camden House, 2018), 379.

95. Mann, *Diaries*, 17.

96. Ibid.

97. Ibid., 18.

98. Quoted in Gerwarth, *November 1918*, 89.

99. Mann, *Diaries*, 23.

100. Kurzke, *Thomas Mann*, 252–53.

101. Mann, *Diaries*, 23.

102. Robert Gerwarth, *The Vanquished: Why the First World War Failed to End* (New York: Farrar, Straus & Giroux, 2016), 4–5.

103. Ibid., 7.

104. Gerwarth, *November 1918*, 130.

105. Eric D. Weitz, *Weimar Germany: Promise and Tragedy* (Princeton, NJ: Princeton University Press, 2007), 23.

106. Vicki Baum, *Grand Hotel*, trans. Basil Creighton and Margot Bettauer Dembo (New York: New York Review of Books, 2016), 9.

107. Joseph Roth, *The Spider's Web*, trans. John Hoare (London: Granta Books, 2004), 4.

108. Erich Maria Remarque, *All Quiet on the Western Front*, trans. Brian Murdoch (New York: Alfred A. Knopf, 2018), 248.

109. Detlev J. K. Peukert, *The Weimar Republic: The Crisis of Classical Modernity*, trans. Richard Deveson (New York: Hill and Wang, 1989), 5–6.

110. Karin Verena Gunnemann, *Heinrich Mann's Novels and Essays: The Artist as Political Educator* (Rochester, NY: Camden House, 2003), 67.

111. Heinrich Mann, "The Meaning and Idea of the Revolution," in *The Weimar Republic Sourcebook*, ed. Anton Kaes, Martin Jay, and Edward Dimendberg (Berkeley: University of California Press, 1994), 38–40.

112. Ibid., 39.

113. Mann, *Diaries*, 25.

114. Ibid., 26.

115. Ibid., 16, 17.

116. Ibid., 26.

117. Sue Prideaux, *I am Dynamite! A Life of Nietzsche* (New York: Tim Duggan Books, 2018), 373.

118. Mann, *Diaries*, 27.

FIVE. DOUBTS AND CONSIDERATIONS

1. Thomas Mann, *Diaries, 1918–1939*, trans. Richard Winston and Clara Winston (London: Robin Clark, 1984), 9–14.

2. Ibid., 40–41.

3. Ibid., 38.

4. Ibid., 48–49.

5. Robert Gerwarth, *November 1918: The German Revolution* (Oxford: Oxford University Press, 2020), 175.

6. Michael Brenner, *In Hitler's Munich: Jews, the Revolution, and the Rise of Nazism*, trans. Jeremiah Riemer (Princeton, NJ: Princeton University Press, 2022), 105.

7. Mann, *Diaries*, 19.

8. David Clay Large, *Where Ghosts Walked: Munich's Road to the Third Reich* (New York: W. W. Norton, 1997), 88.

9. Brenner, *In Hitler's Munich*, 122.

10. Volker Weidermann, *Dreamers: When the Writers Took Power, Germany, 1918*, trans. Ruth Martin (London: Pushkin Press, 2018), 105.

11. Mann, *Diaries*, 34.

12. Victor Klemperer, *Munich 1919: Diary of a Revolution*, trans. Jessica Spengler (Malden, MA: Polity Press, 2017), 55.

13. Quoted in Large, *Where Ghosts Walked*, 104.

14. Ibid., 105.

15. Richard J. Evans, *Coming of the Third Reich* (New York: Penguin Books, 2005), 158.

16. Large, *Where Ghosts Walked*, 105.
17. Ibid., 105–6.
18. Klemperer, *Diary of a Revolution*, 77.
19. Ernst Toller, *I Was a German: The Autobiography of Ernst Toller*, trans. Edward Crankshaw (New York: William Morrow, 1934), 169.
20. Klemperer, *Diary of a Revolution*, 80.
21. Gerwarth, *November 1918*, 151.
22. Ibid., 156.
23. Large, *Where Ghosts Walked*, 118.
24. Toller, *I Was a German*, 200.
25. Gerwarth, *November 1918*, 181.
26. Mann, *Diaries*, 54.
27. Large, *Where Ghosts Walked*, 120–22.
28. Weidermann, *Dreamers*, 225.
29. Quoted in ibid., 255.
30. Gerwarth, *November 1918*, 181–82.
31. Quoted in Toller, *I Was a German*, 252.
32. Quoted in Brenner, *In Hitler's Munich*, 160.
33. Ibid.
34. Thomas Mann, *Letters of Thomas Mann, 1889–1955*, ed. Richard Winston and Clara Winston (New York: Alfred A. Knopf, 1971), 95.
35. Dirk Heisserer, *Im Zaubergarten: Thomas Mann in Bayern* (Munich: C. H. Beck, 2005), 168.
36. Quoted in Hans Bürgin and Hans-Otto Mayer, *Thomas Mann: A Chronicle of His Life*, trans. Eugene Dobson (Tuscaloosa: University of Alabama Press, 1969), 49.
37. Thomas Mann, *The Magic Mountain*, trans. John E. Woods (New York: Alfred A. Knopf, 1995), 627.
38. Mann, *Diaries*, 84.
39. For an in-depth discussion of this question, see Hans Rudolf Vaget, "The Making of *The Magic Mountain*," *Thomas Mann's The Magic Mountain: A Casebook*, ed. Hans Rudolf Vaget (Oxford: Oxford University Press, 2008).
40. James F. White, *The Yale Zaubeberg-Manuscript: Rejected Sheets Once Part of Thomas Mann's Novel* (Munich: Francke Verlag, 1980), xii.
41. Mann, *Magic Mountain*, 1.
42. Edwin Frank, *Stranger Than Fiction: Lives of the Twentieth Century Novel* (New York: Farrar, Straus & Giroux, 2024), 149.

43. *Thomas Mann's The Magic Mountain: A Casebook*, ed. Vaget, 15.

44. Arthur Herman, *The Idea of Decline in Western History* (New York: Free Press, 1997), 236.

45. Mann, *Diaries*, 61.

46. Peter de Mendelssohn, *Der Zauberer: Das Leben des deutschen Schriftstellers Thomas Mann*, vol. 2 (Frankfurt am Main: S. Fischer Verlag, 1975), Kindle edition (my translation).

47. Herman Hesse, *Demian: The Story of Emil Sinclair's Youth*, trans. Damion Searls (New York: Penguin Classics, 2013), 49.

48. Ibid., 133.

49. Mann, *Diaries*, 58.

50. Ibid., 47.

51. Todd Kontje, "The German Tradition of the Bildungsroman," in *A History of the Bildungsroman*, ed. Sarah Graham (Cambridge: Cambridge University Press, 2019), 24.

52. Ibid., 26.

53. See Todd Kontje, *Private Lives in the Public Sphere: The German Bildungsroman as Metafiction* (University Park: Pennsylvania State University Press, 1992).

54. Quoted in Kontje, "The German Tradition of the Bildungsroman," 26.

55. Mann, *Diaries*, 101.

56. Ibid., 45.

57. Ibid., 48.

58. Ibid., 66.

59. As described by George L. Mosse in *The Image of Man: The Creation of Modern Masculinity* (Oxford: Oxford University Press, 1996), 144.

60. Mann, *Diaries*, 62.

61. Ibid., 103.

62. Quoted in Frederic Spotts, *Cursed Legacy: The Tragic Life of Klaus Mann* (New Haven: Yale University Press, 2016), 16.

63. Mann, *Diaries*, 96–98.

64. Mann's answers, and his relationship to Freud, is elucidated in Leslie Y. Rabkin's "A 'Relationship as Complicated as It Deserves': Thomas Mann and Psychoanalysis," *Imagination, Cognition, and Personality* 15, no. 1 (1995): 3–16.

65. Sigmund Freud, "An Autobiographical Study," in *The Sigmund Freud Reader*, ed. Peter Gay (New York: W. W. Norton, 1989), 38.

66. Philipp Blom, *The Vertigo Years: Europe, 1900–1914* (New York: Basic Books, 2008), 59.

67. Quoted in Rabkin, "A 'Relationship as Complicated as It Deserves,'" 3–16.

68. Friedrich Nietzsche, *The Joyous Science*, trans. R. Kevin Hill (New York: Penguin Classics, 2018), 13.

69. Mann, *Magic Mountain*, 9.

70. Thomas Mann, *Der Zauberberg* (Frankfurt am Main: S. Fischer Verlag, 2017), 19–20.

71. I owe this insight to Kent Tonsgaard's essay "Mon Mann læste Freud?—En analyse af psykoanalysens repræsentation i Trolddomsbjerget," *Lamella* 3, no. 4 (2018): 98–119.

72. Mann, *Magic Mountain*, 16: "He was no longer in control."

73. Ibid., 127.

74. Adam Phillips, *Becoming Freud: The Making of a Psychoanalyst* (New Haven: Yale University Press, 2014), 4.

75. Mann, *Magic Mountain*, 125.

76. Ibid., 644.

77. Ibid., 648.

78. Ibid.

79. Ibid., 672.

80. Hermann Kurzke, *Thomas Mann: Life as a Work of Art; A Biography*, trans. Leslie Wilson (Princeton, NJ: Princeton University, 2002), 311.

81. Mann, *Diaries*, 86.

82. Mann, *Magic Mountain*, 215.

83. Large, *Where Ghosts Walked*, 135.

84. Quoted in Sefton Delmer, *Weimar Germany: Democracy on Trial* (New York: American Heritage Press, 1972), 57.

85. Quoted in Daniel Schönpflug, *A World on Edge: The End of the Great War and the Dawn of a New Age*, trans. Jefferson Chase (London: Macmillan, 2018), 221–22.

86. Brenner, *In Hitler's Munich*, 163.

87. Large, *Where Ghosts Walked*, 140.

88. Ibid., 141.

89. Ibid., 133.

90. Quoted in Large, *Where Ghosts Walked*, 141.

91. Quoted in Brenner, *In Hitler's Munich*, 176.

92. Ibid., 180.

93. Volker Ullrich, *Hitler: Ascent, 1889-1939*, trans. Jefferson Chase (London: Bodley Head, 2016), 90.

94. Quoted in ibid., 91.

95. Large, *Where Ghosts Walked*, 131.

96. Joseph Roth, *The Spider's Web*, trans. John Hoare (London: Granta Books, 2004), 53-54.

97. Quoted in Brenner, *In Hitler's Munich*, 188.

98. Anthony Heilbut, *Thomas Mann: Eros and Literature* (London: Papermac, 1997), 327.

99. Quoted in Weidermann, *Dreamers*, 126.

100. Thomas Mann, *Briefe, 1889-1936*, ed. Erika Mann (Frankfurt am Main: S. Fischer Verlag, 1961), 173.

101. Mann, *Diaries*, 90.

102. Quoted in Schönpflug, *World on Edge*, 247.

103. Mann, *Diaries*, 116.

104. Mann, *Briefe*, 190.

105. Mann, *Diaries*, 118.

106. Clayton Koelb, ed., *Thomas Mann's "Goethe and Tolstoy": Notes and Sources*, trans. Alcyone Scott and Clayton Koelb (Tuscaloosa: University of Alabama Press, 1984), 227.

107. Ibid., 223-50.

108. Ibid., 231.

109. Ibid., 238.

110. Mann, *Magic Mountain*, 96.

111. Koelb, ed., *Thomas Mann's "Goethe and Tolstoy,"* 250.

SIX. CHANGES

1. Quoted in Nigel Hamilton, *The Brothers Mann: The Lives of Heinrich and Thomas Mann, 1871-1950 and 1875-1955* (London: Secker & Warburg, 1978), 202.

2. Hans Wysling, ed., *Letters of Heinrich and Thomas Mann, 1900-1949*, trans. Don Reneau (Berkeley: University of California Press, 1998), 128.

3. Thomas Mann, *Letters of Thomas Mann, 1889-1955*, ed. Richard Winston and Clara Winston (New York: Alfred A. Knopf, 1971), 117.

4. Ibid.

5. Katia Mann, *Unwritten Memories*, ed. Elisabeth Plessen and Michael Mann, trans. Hunter and Hildegaard Hannum (New York: Alfred A. Knopf, 1975), 72.

6. Quoted in Hans Bürgin and Hans-Otto Mayer, *Thomas Mann: A Chronicle of His Life*, trans. Eugene Dobson (Tuscaloosa: University of Alabama Press, 1969), 55.

7. Judith Marcus, *Georg Lukács and Thomas Mann: A Study in the Sociology of Literature* (Amherst: University of Massachusetts Press, 1987), 145–46.

8. Quoted in ibid., 156.

9. Ibid., 145.

10. Ibid., 157–59.

11. Ibid., 142–43.

12. Katia Mann, *Unwritten Memories*, 73.

13. Peter de Mendelsohn, *Der Zauberer: Das Leben des deutschen Schriftstellers Thomas Mann*, vol. 2 (Frankfurt am Main: S. Fischer Verlag, 1975), Kindle edition.

14. Quoted in Marcus, *Georg Lukács and Thomas Mann*, 7.

15. See Adam Zagajewski, *A Defense of Ardor: Essays*, trans. Claire Cavanagh (New York: Farrar, Straus & Giroux, 2004), 18–19.

16. Friedrich Nietzsche, *Beyond Good and Evil*, trans. R. J. Hollingdale (London: Penguin Books, 2003), 53.

17. Thomas Mann, *The Magic Mountain*, trans. John E. Woods (New York: Alfred A. Knopf, 1995), 453.

18. Ibid., 448.

19. Ibid., 396.

20. Ibid., 395.

21. Mark Lilla, *The Shipwrecked Mind: On Modern Reaction* (New York: New York Review of Books, 2016), xiii.

22. Lilla's remark appears in a footnote to the introduction of *The Shipwrecked Mind*, xv.

23. Jean-Michel Palmier, *Weimar in Exile: The Antifascist Emigration in Europe and America*, trans. David Fernbach (New York: Verso Books, 2006), 50.

24. Mann, *Magic Mountain*, 379–80.

25. Ibid., 400.

26. Ibid., 341.

27. Børge Kristiansen, *Thomas Mann—Digtning og tankeverden* (Copenhagen: Forlaget Rosenkilde og Bahnhof, 2013), 413.

28. Thomas Mann, *Reflections of a Nonpolitical Man*, trans. Walter D. Morris (New York: New York Review Books, 2021), 14.

29. Ibid., 188.
30. Shulamit Volkov, *Walther Rathenau: Weimar's Fallen Statesman* (New Haven: Yale University Press, 2012), vii.
31. Fritz Stern, *Einstein's German World* (Princeton, NJ: Princeton University Press, 2016), 167.
32. Quoted in Volker Ullrich, *Hitler: Ascent, 1889-1936*, trans. Jefferson Chase (London: Bodley Head, 2016), 100.
33. Stefan Zweig, *The World of Yesterday* (Lincoln: University of Nebraska Press, 1964), 336.
34. Eric D. Weitz, *Weimar Germany: Promise and Tragedy* (Princeton, NJ: Princeton University Press, 2007), 100.
35. Anton Kaes, Martin Jay, and Edward Dimendberg, eds., *The Weimar Republic Sourcebook* (Berkeley: University of California Press, 1994), 101.
36. Quoted in T. J. Reed, *Thomas Mann: The Uses of Tradition* (Oxford: Oxford University Press, 1974), 290.
37. Ibid., 291.
38. Peter Gay, *Weimar Culture: The Outsider as Insider* (New York: W. W. Norton: 2001), 23.
39. Koelb, ed., *Thomas Mann's "Goethe and Tolstoy,"* 237.
40. Ibid., 235.
41. Mann, *Magic Mountain*, 536-37.
42. Walt Whitman, *Poetry and Prose*, ed. Justin Kaplan (New York: Library of America, 1996), 400-401.
43. Thomas Mann, "Hans Reisiger's Edition of Walt Whitman: A Letter," *Modernism/modernity* 14, no. 1 (January 2007): 107.
44. Klaus Mann, *The Turning Point: Thirty-five Years in This Century* (New York: Markus Wiener Publishing, 1984), 66.
45. Tobias Boes, *Thomas Mann's War: Literature, Politics, and the World Republic of Letters* (Ithaca, NY: Cornell University Press, 2019), 37.
46. Mann, *Reflections*, 513.
47. Ibid., 522.
48. Ibid., 519.
49. Ibid., 524.
50. Ibid., 531-32.
51. Ibid., 538.
52. Ibid., 544.
53. Ibid., 546.

54. Quoted in James N. Bade, "The Magic Mountain of Weimar Politics: The Impact of the Assassination of Walther Rathenau on Thomas Mann's *Der Zauberberg*," *Monatshefte* 106, no. 1 (Spring 2014): 37–53.

55. *Letters of Thomas Mann*, 120.

56. Wysling, ed., *Letters of Thomas and Heinrich Mann*, 130.

57. Quoted in Ullrich, *Hitler*, 132.

58. Golo Mann, *Reminiscences and Reflections: A Youth in Germany*, trans. Krishna Winston (New York: W. W. Norton, 1990), 103.

59. Richard J. Evans, *The Coming of the Third Reich* (New York: Penguin Books, 2005), 107.

60. Weitz, *Weimar Germany*, 135.

61. See Friedrich Kroner's "Overwrought Nerves," in Kaes, Jay, and Dimendberg, eds., *Weimar Republic Sourcebook*, 62–63.

62. Quoted in Bürgin and Mayer, *Thomas Mann*, 58.

63. Boes, *Thomas Mann's War*, 57.

64. Ibid., 40.

65. Quoted in ibid., 43.

66. Mann, *Magic Mountain*, 463. The term *playing king* first occurs on p. 383.

67. Ibid., 465.

68. Ibid., 467.

69. Ibid., 466.

70. Ibid., 468.

71. Ibid., 471.

72. Ibid., 474.

73. Ibid., 475.

74. Ibid., 481.

75. Ibid., 485.

76. Friedrich Nietzsche, *The Birth of Tragedy*, trans. Shaun Whiteside (New York: Penguin Books, 1993), 21.

77. Ibid., 22.

78. Mann, *Magic Mountain*, 486.

79. Ibid.

80. Ibid., 271.

81. Ibid., 487.

82. Ibid., 334.

83. Ibid., 487.

84. Ibid., 489.

85. Ibid., 276.
86. Quoted in W. H. Buford, *The German Tradition of Self-Cultivation* (Cambridge: Cambridge University Press, 1975), 88.
87. Thomas Mann, "Geist und Wesen der Deutschen Republik," in *Essays*, vol. 2, *Für das Neue Deutschland, 1919-1925* (Frankfurt am Main: S. Fischer Verlag, 2001), 217-24.
88. Ullrich, *Hitler*, 133.
89. Zweig, *World of Yesterday*, 384.
90. Quoted in Hamilton, *Brothers Mann*, 232.
91. Thomas Mann, "German Letter," *The Dial* 75 (October 1923).

SEVEN. FULLNESS OF HARMONY

1. Quoted in David Clay Large, *Where Ghosts Walked: Munich's Road to the Third Reich* (New York: W. W. Norton, 1997), 159.
2. Quoted in Volker Ullrich, *Hitler: Ascent, 1889-1939*, trans. Jefferson Chase (London: Bodley Head, 2016), 148.
3. Quoted in ibid., 149.
4. Quoted in ibid., 151.
5. Richard J. Evans, *The Coming of the Third Reich* (New York: Penguin Books, 2005), 110.
6. Klaus Mann, *The Turning Point: Thirty-five Years in This Century* (New York: Markus Wiener Publishing, 1984), 81.
7. Thomas Mann, *Doctor Faustus*, trans. John E. Woods (New York: Alfred A. Knopf, 1997), 384.
8. Thomas Mann, *Past Masters and Other Essays*, trans. H. T. Lowe-Porter (New York: Alfred A. Knopf, 1933), 220.
9. Theodor Adorno, *Minima Moralia: Reflections from a Damaged Life*, trans. E. F. N. Jephcott (New York: Verso, 2005), 192.
10. Large, *Where Ghosts Walked*, 201.
11. Stefan Zweig, *The World of Yesterday: Memoirs of a European*, trans. Anthea Bell (London: Pushkin Press, 2009), 386.
12. Thomas Mann, *Letters of Thomas Mann, 1889-1955*, ed. Richard Winston and Clara Winston (New York: Alfred A. Knopf, 1971), 127.
13. Hans Wysling, ed., *Letters of Heinrich and Thomas Mann, 1900-1949*, trans. Don Reneau (Berkeley: University of California Press, 1998), 130.
14. The letter is dated April 11, 1925, and is included in *Letters of Thomas Mann*, 140.

15. Thomas Mann, *The Magic Mountain*, trans. John E. Woods (New York: Alfred A. Knopf, 1995), 541.
16. Ibid., 565.
17. Ibid., 611–12.
18. Max Weber, *Charisma and Disenchantment: The Vocation Lectures*, trans. Damion Searls, ed. Paul Reitter and Chad Wellmon (New York: New York Review Books, 2020), 84–85.
19. Mann, *Magic Mountain*, 574.
20. Ibid., 556.
21. Ibid., 594.
22. Ibid., 587.
23. Ian Bostridge, *Schubert's Winter Journey: Anatomy of an Obsession* (New York: Alfred A. Knopf, 2015), 114–15.
24. Ibid., 109.
25. Mann, *Magic Mountain*, 643.
26. Alex Ross, *Wagnerism: Art and Politics in the Shadow of Music* (New York: Alfred A. Knopf, 2021), 526.
27. Hans Rudolf Vaget, ed., *Thomas Mann's "The Magic Mountain": A Casebook* (Oxford: Oxford University Press, 2008), 136.
28. Quoted in Ross, *Wagnerism*, 312.
29. Klaus Mann, *Turning Point*, 96.
30. Quoted in Tilmann Lahme, *Die Manns: Geschichte einer Familie* (Frankfurt am Main: S. Fischer Verlag, 2015), 19.
31. Quoted in John C. Thirlwall, *In Another Language: A Record of the Thirty-Year Relationship between Thomas Mann and His American Translator Helen Tracy Lowe-Porter* (New York: Alfred A. Knopf, 1966), 4–5.
32. Quoted in Hans Bürgin and Hans-Otto Mayer, *Thomas Mann: A Chronicle of His Life*, trans. Eugene Dobson (Tuscaloosa: University of Alabama Press, 1969), 63.
33. Quoted in Donald Prater, *Thomas Mann: A Life* (Oxford: Oxford University Press, 1995), 148.
34. Wysling, ed., *Letters of Thomas Mann*, 127.
35. Mann, *Magic Mountain*, 673.
36. Ibid., 676.
37. Ibid., 680–81.
38. Ibid., 690–96.
39. Ibid., 699.
40. Ibid., 475.

41. *Letters of Thomas Mann*, 144.
42. Ibid., 145.
43. Karolina Watroba, *Mann's Magic Mountain: World Literature and Closer Reading* (Oxford: Oxford University Press, 2022), 42.
44. Prater, *Thomas Mann*, 151.
45. Walter Benjamin, *The Correspondence of Walter Benjamin, 1910–1940*, trans. Manfred R. Jacobson and Evelyn M. Jacobson (Chicago: University of Chicago Press, 1994), 265.
46. Robert Musil, *Diaries, 1899–1941*, trans. Mark Jay Mirsky (New York: Basic Books, 1997), 377.
47. Hugh Ridley, *The Problematic Bourgeois: Twentieth-Century Criticism on Thomas Mann's "Buddenbrooks" and "The Magic Mountain"* (Columbia, SC: Camden House, 1994), 11.
48. Wysling, ed., *Letters of Thomas Mann*, 175.
49. Ibid., 139.
50. Ibid., 140.
51. Quoted in Ridley, *Problematic Bourgeois*, 36.
52. Quoted in ibid., 46.
53. Watroba, *Mann's "Magic Mountain,"* 22.
54. Quoted in Thirlwall, *In Another Language*, 9.
55. Quoted in Boes, *Thomas Mann's War*, 66.
56. *New York Times*, May 8, 1927, 41.
57. Boes, *Thomas Mann's War*, 62–63.
58. Charles Neider, ed., *The Stature of Thomas Mann* (New York: New Directions, 1947), 46.
59. Watroba, *Mann's "Magic Mountain,"* 42.
60. Wysling, ed., *Letters of Heinrich and Thomas Mann*, 175.
61. Stanley Corngold, *The Mind in Exile: Thomas Mann in Princeton* (Princeton, NJ: Princeton University Press, 2022), xiii.
62. Quoted in Benjamin Moser, *Sontag: Her Life and Work* (New York: Ecco, 2019), 69.
63. Milan Kundera, *The Art of the Novel*, trans. Linda Asher (London: Faber and Faber, 1990), 128.

EPILOGUE

1. Tobias Boes, *Thomas Mann's War: Literature, Politics, and the World Republic of Letters* (Ithaca, NY: Cornell University Press, 2019), 36.

ACKNOWLEDGMENTS

My greatest debt is to my wonderful and patient editor Jennifer Banks, without whose close, judicious reading this book would be infinitely poorer. Thanks also to Eva Skewes for confidently stewarding the manuscript through its various early stages and to Andrew Frisardi for his invaluable copyediting. I'd also like to extend my thanks to the entire staff at Yale University Press for all the incredible work they do.

I owe an enormous debt to the invaluable work of many critics and scholars of Thomas Mann, but in particular to the work of Tobias Boes, Børge Kristiansen, Hermann Kurzke, T. J. Reed, Rodney Symington, Hans Rudolf Vaget, and Hermann J. Weigand.

A number of institutions and organizations were incredibly helpful at various times throughout the years. I'm very grateful to the staff of the Schatzalp Hotel in Davos for patiently putting up with my constant presence for seven weeks in the winter of 2018 and for ensuring that my stay was both a comfortable and a memorable one. Reading *The Magic Mountain* in the environment that inspired it is one of the greatest literary experiences of my life. Shortly after my sojourn in Davos I visited Villa Aurora and Thomas Mann House in Los Angeles. I'm grateful to the entire staff for welcoming me and for taking an interest in the book. Thanks especially to Nikolai Blaumer and Benno Herz for inviting me to contribute to their beautiful volume, *Thomas*

ACKNOWLEDGMENTS

Mann's Los Angeles: Stories from Exile, 1940-1952. Thanks also to the Dokumentationsbibliothek Davos and the Beinecke Rare Book and Manuscript Library at Yale University. For inviting me to the Kandersteg seminar in 2025, I'm very grateful to NYU's Remarque Institute and to Merve Emre, Stefanos Geroulanos, Samantha Paul, and Zvi Ben-Dor Benite.

For their invitation to read from the manuscript at the 2021 Literary Studies Alumni Reading, I'm grateful to Albert Mobilio, Elizabeth Kendall, and Stephanie Belk at Eugene Lang College at the New School. Kai Sina and Tobias Boes's generous invitation to contribute to a special issue of *Literatur für Leser* helped me sharpen some of my thoughts about *The Magic Mountain*. At Princeton University, Stanley Corngold and Peter Makhlouf very kindly invited me to a thrilling seminar discussion of Mann's novella "Mario and the Magician." I owe a thanks also to the editors of *The Yale Review* for inviting me to contribute an essay on Thomas Mann's contributions to *TYR*.

Many people provided much needed encouragement over the years. I'm immensely grateful to James Wood, Celeste Marcus, Leon Wieseltier, Kati Marton, Casey Schwartz, Jack Hanson, Helen Rouner, Stephen Lehmann, Lizzie Jennings, Daniel Mendelsohn, Matt Sitman, Boris Dralyuk, and Flemming Rose. Thanks also to my old professors at the New School for their continued interest in my writing, particularly Noah Isenberg and Juan E. De Castro.

For reading individual chapters and early drafts of the manuscript, I'm grateful to George Packer, Jacob Høi Jensen, and Nevada Ryan. The manuscript's earliest reader, my father, Bjørn, has been a champion and supporter of the project from its very beginning, and I wouldn't have written it without his constant encouragement.

At a very crucial moment, Christina Cacouris walked into my life and inspired me to complete the manuscript at last.

ACKNOWLEDGMENTS

Last but not least, my warmest thanks to my entire family, in Denmark and in the United States, for their love, support, and patience.

CREDITS

Excerpt(s) from THE MAGIC MOUNTAIN by Thomas Mann, translated by John E. Woods, translation copyright © 1995 by Penguin Random House LLC. Used by permission of Alfred A. Knopf, an imprint of Knopf Doubleday Publishing Group, a division of Random House LLC. All rights reserved.

Excerpt(s) from LETTERS OF THOMAS MANN by Thomas Mann, selected and translated by Richard and Clara Winston, copyright © 1970, copyright renewed 1998 by Penguin Random House LLC. Used by permission of Alfred A. Knopf, an imprint of Knopf Doubleday Publishing Group, a division of Penguin Random House LLC. All rights reserved.

Excerpts from GESAMMELTE WERKE by Thomas Mann, edited by Hans von Bürgin and Peter de Mendelssohn (S. Fischer Verlag: Frankfurt am Main, 1990). Courtesy of S. Fischer Verlag GmbH, Frankfurt am Main.

Excerpts from REFLECTIONS OF A NONPOLITICAL MAN by Thomas Mann, translated by Walter D. Morris, copyright 2021 by New York Review Books Classics. Used by permission of New York Review Books Classics and Walter D. Morris Jr. All Rights Reserved.

INDEX

Adorno, Theodor, 173
aestheticism, 150–51
Ahlbeck, 154, 182
Allgemeine Zeitung, 173
Almanach der Psychoanalyse, 132
Amann, Paul, 83, 85, 87, 92, 101, 102, 106
Angell, Joseph Warner, 189
Anglo-German Friendship Committee, 73
anti-Semitism, 62–63, 117–18, 137–38, 152, 183
Apollonian, 94, 165
Arco auf Valley, Anton Graf von, 118
Arosa, 38, 60
artistic sensibility, 24–25
Aschheim, Steven E., 104
Auer, Erhard, 107, 118
Austro-Hungarian Empire, 65, 66, 106

Bab, Julius, 186
Bach, Johann Sebastian, 60
Bad Griesbach, 139
Bad Kissingen, 88
Bad Tölz, 64, 76, 79, 85, 101, 123
Baerwald, Leo, 118
Bahr, Hermann: "The Irretrievable Self," 131
Baltikum Brigade, 136

Bamburg, 119
Bansin, 182
Barbusse, Henri: *Under Fire*, 84
Baum, Vicki: *Grand Hotel*, 111
Bauschan, 104
Bavaria, 106, 116–18, 120, 138, 170, 174; Bavarian Soviet Republic, 119; Beer Hall Putsch, 170–72, 174; People's State of Bavaria, 108, 109. *See also* Munich
Bayerische Kurier, 117
Beer Hall Putsch, 170–72, 174
Belgium, 78, 82
Benjamin, Walter, 186; "The Storyteller," 52–53
Benn, Gottfried, 83, 103
Bergamin, Klaus, 9
Berlin, 120, 137
Berliner Illustrirte Zeitung, 160
Berliner Tageblatt, 42, 106
Bertram, Ernst, 51–52, 53, 90, 101, 140; correspondence with Mann, 38, 87, 95, 145, 147, 153, 154, 182; *Nietzsche: Attempt at a Mythology*, 52, 103–4
Bie, Oskar, 33
Bielschowsky, Albert, 141
bildungsroman, 41, 128–29, 159
Bircher-Brenner private clinic, 15

INDEX

Biryukov, Pavel, 141
Bloch, Ivan, 73
Blom, Philipp, 69
Blue Angel, The, 40–41
Blue Review, The, 38
Blüher, Hans: *Role of Eroticism in Masculine Society, The*, 130
Boehm, Gottfried, 135
Boes, Tobias, 21, 156, 161, 188
Bolzano, 174
Bonner Zeitung, 139
Böök, Frederik, 189–90
Bostridge, Ian, 178
Boy-Ed, Ida, 26, 141, 159
Brandes, Georg, 161; *Main Currents of Nineteenth Century Literature* (1872–90), 49; *Romantic School in Germany, The*, 49
Brantl, Maximilian, 51, 87, 88
Braunfels, Walter, 108
Brecht, Berthold, 169
Brehmer, Hermann, 12–13
Bremen, 109
Britain, 66, 73
Broch, Hermann: *Sleepwalkers, The*, 36
Bronnen, Arnolt, 187
Brontë sisters, 15
Browning, Elizabeth Barrett, 15
Brussels, 101
Bulgaria, 106
Byron, Lord, 15

Carel, Havi, 24
Chekhov, Anton, 15, 40
Chotek, Sophie, 64
Clark, Christopher, 73
Clavadel, 181
Corngold, Stanley, 190

Curhaus, 13
Curtius, Ernst Robert, 161

Das Forum, 82, 86
Das Gewissen, 159
Davos, 8, 11–13, 30, 189; Berghotel Schatzalp, 8–9; Villa am Stein, 18; Waldhotel, 8; Waldsanitorium, 8, 16, 18, 30
Davoser Blätter, 16
Dawes, Charles, 172
Dawes Plan, 172
death, sympathy with, 19, 43–47, 48–50, 52–53, 96, 185; Aschenbach, Gustav von, 49; Buddenbrook, Thomas, 48–49; Castorp, Hans, 44–46, 47–48, 54, 55–60
Defregger, Franz, 101
Dehmel, Richard, 71, 79
democracy, 5, 6, 41, 95, 187; Heinrich Mann's love of, 5, 40–42, 88, 89; Thomas Mann's defense of, 153–55, 157, 159, 168, 173
Deutsch-Sozialer Verein, 62
Dial, The, 161, 169
Diederichs, Eugen, 126
Die Neue Rundschau, 33, 127, 174
Die Tat, 126
Die Weissen Blätter, 86, 88, 90
Dionysian, 37, 94
Dohm, Hedwig, 30
Dostoevsky, Fyodor, 141
Dowden, Stephen D., 35
Drexler, Anton, 138
Dürer, Albrecht, 52

Ebenhausen health resort, 17
Ebert, Friedrich, 110, 120, 136, 156

INDEX

Ehrenberg, Paul, 130
Ehrhardt, Hermann, 136, 137
Einwohnerwehren, 123
Eisner, Kurt, 107–8, 109, 112, 116–19
Eliot, T. S.: *Waste Land, The,* 161
Elling, Eskil, 96
Ellison, George, 82
Epp, Franz von Ritter, 120–21
Erpenbeck, Jenny, 6–7
Erzberger, Matthias, 110, 139–40
Essener Volkszeitung, 101
Evans, Richard J., 160, 172–73
Ewers, Ludwig, 41

Falkenhayn, Erich von, 81
Feldafing, 124, 125, 162
Ferdinand, Archduke Franz, 64
Feuchtwanger, Lion, 169
First World War, 5, 72–73, 78, 81–82, 87, 99, 102–3; commencement of, 64–66, 75, 184; end of, 105, 106–7, 110–11; enthusiasm for, 66–71; Schlieffen Plan, 78; shortages in, 90–91
Fischer, Samuel, 26, 85, 105, 155, 156, 174, 181, 185
Foch, Ferdinand, 110
Förster-Nietzsche Elisabeth, 103, 114, 126
France, 66
Frank, Bruno, 51, 87, 102, 105
Frank, Edwin, 126
Frank, Hans, 118
Frankfurter Zeitung, 106, 155, 167
Freikorps, 120, 121–22, 136
Freud, Sigmund, 133; *Three Essays on the Theory of Sexuality,* 131, 133
Freyer, Hans, 126

Fulda, Ludwig, 71
Fussell, Paul, 69

Galsworthy, John, 181
Garborg, Arne, 61
Gareis, Karl, 139
Gay, Peter, 154
Geißendörfer, Hans W., 6, 9
Gerhard, Adele, 93, 141
German Workers' Party (DAP). *See* Nazi Party
Germany, 73, 93–94, 106; ideology, German, 80–81; after World War I, 110–12, 116–23, 135; during First World War, 66–71, 90–91, 102–3, 106. *See also* Bavaria; Munich; Weimar Republic
Gertz, Nolen, 36
Gerwarth, Robert, 111, 120
Gibo, Arthur, 22
Gide, André, 161, 182–83, 186, 190; *Corydon,* 182; *Incidences,* 182
Glöckner, Ernst, 90
Görbersdorf, 12
Goethe, 40, 141; *Faust,* 142; *Wilhelm Meister's Apprenticeship,* 128, 142, 168
Gogol, Nikolai: "How the Two Ivans Quarrelled," 115–16
Goltz, General von der, 136
Göring, Hermann, 170, 171
Graf, Oskar Maria, 108
gramophone, 124–25, 178
Gumbel, Emil Julius, 152

Hague Conventions, 73
Hallgarten, Richard, 129
Hamburg, 109

INDEX

Hamsun, Knut: *Growth of the Soil, The*, 140
Harden, Maximilian, 31
Hardwick, Elizabeth, 1
Hauptmann, Gerhart, 71, 153, 156, 174–75, 182, 187; *Till Eulenspiegel*, 182
Hayman, Ronald, 29
Hedwig, Franz, 187
Heilbut, Anthony, 139
Heimdahl, Haus, 182
Held, Heinrich, 174
Helfferich, Karl, 152
Heligoland, 109
Heller, Erich, 83
Herrenessen, 51
Herzog, Wilhelm, 32, 82–83, 88, 108
Hess, Rudolf, 118
Hesse, Hermann, 83, 103, 127; *Demian*, 127–28
Heym, Georg, 70
Himmler, Heinrich, 135
Hindenburg, Paul von, Field Marshal, 105, 185
Hitler, Adolf, 63, 67, 79, 152, 160, 174, 191; Beer Hall Putsch, 170–72; *Mein Kampf*, 67; oratorical skills, 138
Hoffmann, Heinrich, 121
Hoffmann, Johannes, 119, 120, 137
Hofmann, Ludwig von, 32–33; *Spring, The*, 33
Hofmannstahl, Hugo von, 161
Holsboer, Willem Jan, 12, 13
Holsboer-Jones, Margaret, 12, 13
humanism, 6, 154, 155, 158, 167, 168; pessimistic, 173–74, 193–94
Hungary, 119
Hurt, General, 101

Huxley, Mrs. Aldous, 1
hyperinflation, 160, 172

inflation, 160

Jackson, Charles R., 189; *Fall of Valor, The*, 189; *Lost Weekend, The*, 189
Jacobsen, Jens Peter, 15
Jaffe, Heinrich, 105
Jaspers, Karl, 103
Jessen, Friedrich, 31
Johst, Hanns, 187
Jünger, Ernst, 99; *Storm of Steel*, 67–68
Jünger, Friedrich Georg, 187

Kafka, Franz, 67
Kahr, Gustav von, 137, 138, 170, 171–72, 174
Kampfbund, 117–18
Kapp, Wolfgang, 136, 138
Kapp Putsch, 135–37, 139
Kassner, Rudolf, 113
Kaufmann, Walter, 103
Keats, John, 15
Kessler, Harry, 82, 103
Keyserling, Hermann Graf, 139
Kiel, 109
Killinger, Manfred von, 121, 140
Kirsch, Adam, 25
Klemperer, Victor, 118, 119, 120, 160
Kloster, 182
Knopf, Alfred A., 181, 188–89
Knopf, Blanche, 181
Kontje, Todd, 128
Kracht, Christian: *Imperium*, 6
Kristiansen, Børge, 35–36, 150
Kühn, Sophie von, 49
Kultur, 71, 80, 94

INDEX

Kun, Béla, 119, 145
Kundera, Milan, 190
Kurz, Isolde, 123
Kurzke, Hermann, 83, 110

Lagarde, Paul de, 93
Lagerlöf, Selma: *Gösta Berling's Saga*, 40
Lake Tegernsee, 101
Landauer, Gustav, 119, 122
Lang, Josef Bernhard, 127–28
Large, David Clay, 119
Lawrence, D. H., 38–39
Lehmann, Julius Friedrich, 63
leitmotifs, 54, 55, 163
Leonhard, Jörn, 68, 82
Lepenies, Wolf, 42, 81
Levin, Harry, 190
Leviné, Eugen, 122
Liebermann, Max, 188
Liebknecht, Karl, 120
Liegekur, 13
Leipziger Neueste Nachrichten, 118
Lilla, Mark, 149
Lindner, Alois, 118
Lossow, Otto von, 170, 171–72
love, 133, 166
Lowe, Elias Avery, 182
Lowe-Porter, Helen Tracy, 2, 4, 181–82, 187–88
Lübeck, 20, 21, 140, 141
Lublinski, Samuel, 19
Ludendorff, General, 99, 102, 105, 136, 137, 171
Ludwig, Gustav, 115
Ludwig III, 108
Luft, David S., 129
Lukács, Georg, 145–47; "Bolshevism as a Moral Problem," 146; "Tactics and Ethics," 146; *Theory of the Novel, The*, 145
Lüttwitz, Walther von, 136
Luxembourg, Rosa, 120

Magic Mountain, The, 1, 2, 3–5, 6–9, 31, 103, 114, 124–25, 142; "Analysis," 133; "At the Tienappels," 36–37; Behrens, Hofrat, 14, 44, 45, 55; as bildungsroman, 128–29; Brand, Elly, 134; Bunge, Pastor, 128, 146, 147; Castorp, Hans, 3–4, 33–37, 43–46, 47–48, 50, 51, 54, 55–60, 71–72, 74, 128, 132, 134–35, 149–50, 162–67, 176, 177–80, 184, 193–94; "Changes," 143; Chauchat, Clavdia, 43–44, 49, 55–56, 57–58, 59–60, 175; "Encyclopedia," 74; forbidden love in, 56–57, 130; "Fullness of Harmony," 178–80; "Hippe," 130; Hippe, Pribislav, 56; Krokowski, Dr. Edhin, 132–35; Naphta, Leo, 72, 147–50, 183–84; Peeperkorn, Mynheer, 175–78; publication of, 185–86; public readings of, 32–33, 65, 101, 182; reception of, 6, 185–90; Settembrini, Ludovico, 46–48, 54, 57, 72, 73–74, 97–98, 128, 147, 183–84; "Snow," 162–67, 174, 178, 185; "A Stroll on the Shore," 51; as time-novel, 50–51, 125–26; translations of, 6, 187–88; "Walpurgis Night," 57, 59–60, 140; Wiedemann, 62; writing of, 4, 7, 37–38, 79, 85–86, 114, 115–16, 125–26, 140–41, 174–75, 183; Ziemssen, Joachim, 3, 43, 50, 54, 72, 74, 132, 134–35
Mahler, Alma, 136

INDEX

"Manifesto of the 93," 70–71
Mann, Carla, 20, 22, 162
Mann, Elisabeth, 52, 101, 181
Mann, Erika, 61, 129, 181
Mann, Golo, 74–75, 91, 92, 104, 118, 160, 181
Mann, Heinrich, 20, 26, 42, 84, 112–13, 114, 119, 122, 155, 162, 169; "Abdication," 28–29; correspondence with Thomas, 17, 19–20, 22, 26–27, 28–29, 38, 43, 75, 76, 144, 160, 174–75; democracy, love of, 5, 40–42, 88, 89; *Der Untertan*, 41, 76–77, 112; health of, 15, 88, 144; *Hunt for Love, The*, 26–27, 95; *Little Town, The*, 41; *Power and People*, 112; *Professor Unrat*, 40; relationship with Thomas, 5, 26–28, 77–78, 82, 87–90, 95, 99–100, 144–45; "Spirit and Action," 41; war, opposition to, 76, 77–78, 79, 88–89; "Zola," 5, 86, 88, 89–90, 99–100
Mann, Julia, 20, 162
Mann, Júlia da Silva Bruhns, 20, 21, 22, 27, 88, 100, 162
Mann, Katia Pringsheim, 2, 29–30, 53, 91, 96–97, 104, 105, 108, 118, 144, 146–47; family holidays, 76, 140, 154, 174, 182; health of, 8, 16–17, 30, 31, 38, 60, 115, 181; marriage of, 28, 29, 130–31; meeting with Lukács, 145
Mann, Klaus, 22, 60, 61, 64–65, 84–85, 91, 92, 118, 129, 130–31, 156, 173, 181
Mann, Michael, 181
Mann, Mimi Kanova, 77, 144
Mann, Monika, 53, 60, 181
Mann, Thomas, 7, 20, 22–23, 53, 91–92, 107, 108–9, 118, 121, 122, 123–24, 160–62; correspondence with Bertram, 38, 87, 90, 95, 145, 147, 153, 154, 182; correspondence with Heinrich, 17, 19–20, 22, 26–27, 28–29, 38, 43, 75, 76, 144, 160, 174–75; Davos. journey to, 10–11, 16–18, 30–31; family holidays, 64–65, 76, 101–2, 140, 141, 154, 174–75, 182; family life, 60–61; health of, 15, 115, 130–31; illness, interest in, 23–24; marriage of, 28, 29; meeting with Lukács, 145–47; meeting with Susan Sontag, 1–3; occult, interest in, 135; political sympathies, 5–6, 42, 43, 96, 110, 139, 152–53; reading performances, 32–33, 65, 87, 101; relationship with Heinrich, 5, 26–28, 77–78, 82, 87–90, 95, 99–100, 144–45; sexuality of, 28–29, 129–31; war, attitude toward, 75, 76, 79, 82–84. *See also* Mann, Thomas—works
Mann, Thomas—works, 20; address to Gerhart Hauptmann, 156–59, 167; *Bashan and I*, 188; *Buddenbrooks*, 3, 4, 5, 19, 20, 23, 24, 27–28, 38, 48–49, 181, 190; *Confessions of Felix Krull*, 86; *Death in Venice*, 5, 17, 20, 23, 37, 38–39, 42–43, 49, 83–84, 131; *Doctor Faustus*, 3, 23, 66, 173; Dürer, essay on, 52; essay in *Allgemeine*, 173; *Fiorenza*, 20, 101; "German Letter," 169; "Goethe and Tolstoy," 141–43, 145, 150, 153, 154; "Intellect and Culture," 20; "The Joker," 23; *Joseph* novels, 3, 131; "Lübeck as a Way of Life and Thought," 21; *Maya*, 20; "A Miserable Man," 20; "Railway

Accident," 10; Rathenau speech, 167–68; *Reflections of a Nonpolitical Man*, 5, 86, 87, 92–97, 105–6, 113–14, 150, 151, 159, 192; *Royal Highness*, 20, 38; *Song of the Child: An Idyll, The*, 101, 113; "Thoughts in Wartime," 79–81, 82–83, 84; *Tonio Kröger*, 19, 20, 25, 38; *Tristan*, 15–16, 19. See also *Magic Mountain, The*

Mann, Thomas Johann Heinrich, 20–21
Mann, Viktor, 20, 22, 66, 78, 162
Marcus, Judith, 146
Martens, Armin, 28
Martens, Kurt, 24, 42, 113, 161
März, 42
masculinity, 130–31
Mayr, Karl, 138
Meinecke, Friedrich, 109
Mencken, H. L., 181
Meyer, Katherine von, 188
Milosz, Czeslaw, 151
Mitterbad, 15
Moltke, Helmuth von, 81
Moritz, Karl Phillip: *Anton Reiser*, 128
Motz, 85
Mühsam, Erich, 79, 84, 88, 119
Müller, Wilhelm, 178–79
Münchner Blätter für Dichtung und Graphik, 106
Münchner Neueste Nachrichten, 33, 113, 117, 122
Munich, 10, 21, 61–63, 75, 115, 117, 137, 168–69; Bürgerbräukeller, 170–71; Café Fahrig, 67; Café Stefanie, 61; Galerie Caspari, 32; Hofbräuhaus am Platzl, 79, 138; Karlsplatz, 67; Leopoldstrasse, 77; Löwenbraukeller, 171; Luitpold Gymnasium, 121; Mäthaserbräu beer hall, 108; München Herrenklub, 113; Odeonsplatz, 67, 172; Poschingerstrasse, 38, 60–61; revolution in, 107–9; Theresenwiese, 107, 119; Tonhalle, 108; Torggelstube, 78–79; White Terror, 118–23; Zirkus Krone, 160

music, 47, 53, 54
Musil, Robert, 83, 161, 186; *Man without Qualities, The*, 65

nationalism, 62–63, 93–94
Nationalist Association, 136
National Socialist German Workers' Party (NSDAP). See Nazi Party
Naval Brigade, 136
Nazi Party, 118, 121, 123, 138, 168–69; national attempts to control, 170
Nehamas, Alexander, 34–35
Neue Freie Presse, 185
neurasthenia, 15
New York Times, 188
Nietzsche, Friedrich, 18, 52, 69, 74, 80, 94, 103–4, 148, 180; *Anti-Christ, The*, 104; *Beyond Good and Evil*, 97; *Birth of Tragedy, The*, 25, 47, 52, 164–65; *Case of Wagner, The*, 47; *On the Genealogy of Morals*, 24; *Joyous Science, The*, 132; *Thus Spake Zarathustra*, 80; *Will to Power, The*, 36, 80
Nietzsche Society, 103
nihilism, 36, 40
Niko, 2
Nobel Prize, 4, 189–90
Nordau, Max: *Degeneration*, 69–70
Noske, Gustav, 122, 136

INDEX

Novalis, 49–50, 158, 159; *Hymns to Night*, 49
Novels of the World (book series), 161

occult, the, 134–35
Organization Consul, 137, 139, 152
Orwell, George, 7
Osel, Heinrich, 118
Ostjuden, 62
Ottoman Empire, 106

Palmier, Jean-Michel, 149
Pan-German League, 62–63
Parr, John, 82
Pascal, Roy, 70
patriotism, German, 66–67
PEN Club, 181
Peukert, Detlev J. K., 112
Pfitzner, Hans, 105, 108, 185
Planck, Max, 71
Pöhner, Ernst, 137, 138, 140
Prideaux, Sue, 114
Princip, Gavrilo, 64
Pringsheim, Alfred, 51, 87
Pringsheim, Hedwig, 17, 31
Pringsheim, Heinz, 66
Protocols of the Elders of Zion, 117
psychoanalysis, 131–32
Publisher's Weekly, 188

Rathenau, Walther, 71, 83, 151–52, 167
Reed, T. J., 37, 154
Reich-Ranicki, Marcel, 19
Reinhardt, Max, 181
Reisiger, Hans, 155
Remarque, Erich Maria: *All Quiet on the Western Front*, 84, 91, 111
Richter, George Martin, 123, 124

Ricoeur, Paul, 51
Riemer, Friedrich Wilhelm, 25
Rilke, Rainer Maria, 83, 113, 122, 123
Rohde, Erwin, 74
Röhm, Ernst, 121, 171
Rolland, Romain: *Above the Battle*, 95
Romanticism, German, 21, 180, 185. See also death, sympathy with
Röntgen, Wilhelm, 71
Rosenberg, Alfred, 117, 118
Ross, Alex, 54, 55, 180
Roth, Joseph: *Radetzky March, The*, 64; *Spider's Web, The*, 111, 139
Ruhr region, 160, 172
Russia, 66, 99

Safranski, Rüdiger, 94
Sandmayr, Marie, 137
sanitoriums, 12–14, 15–17. See also Waldsanitorium
Scheffauer, Herman George, 188
Scheler, Max, 83
Schickele, René, 90
Schiller, Charlotte von, 40
Schiller, Friedrich, 15, 141; *Bride of Messina, The*, 81
Schnitzler, Arthur, 6, 161
Scholem, Gershom, 186
Schopenhauer, Arthur, 53; *World as Will and Representation, The*, 19, 48
Schrenck-Notzing, Albert von, 135
Schubert, Franz: "Der Lindenbaum," 178–80, 184, 186
Sebottendorf, Rudolf von, 117
Secker, Martin, 181
Seeckt, Hans von, 136
Serbia, 66
sexuality, 28–29, 129–31

INDEX

Shaw, George Bernard, 161, 181
Simmel, Georg, 83
Simplicissimus, 28, 41
Sinclair, Emil, 127–28
Sinkó, Ervin, 146
Sombart, Werner, 70
Sontag, Susan, 1–3, 190; *Illness as Metaphor*, 14
Spartacus League, 120
Spengler, Alexander, 12, 14; *Deutsche Klinik*, 12
Spengler, Oswald, 158; *Decline of the West, The*, 126–27, 173
Speyer-Ulmann, Agnes, 82
Stellungskrieg, 81
Stern, Fritz, 62, 152
Stifter, Adalbert, 102
Stresemann, Gustav von, 170, 172
Sturmabteilung (SA) troops, 170–71
supernatural, 134–35
Suttner, Bertha von: *Lay Down Your Arms!*, 73

Thayer, Scofield, 161
Thule Society, 117
Tieck, Ludwig: *Franz Sternbald's Wanderings*, 128
time, 13, 18–19, 50–51, 125–27, 183
Timmendorf, 140, 141
Tokarczuk, Olga: *Empusium*, 6
Toller, Ernst, 67, 91, 119, 121, 122
Tolstoy, Leo, 141, 142
"To the Civilized World," 70–71
Treaty of Brest-Litovsk, 99
Treitschke, Heinrich von, 93
Trilling, Lionel: "Art and Neurosis," 25
Troeltsch, Ernst, 139

tuberculosis, 12–15; treatments for, 12–14
Turban, Karl, 13–14
Turgenev, Ivan, 141

United States, 99, 102
Untergangsstimmung, 126

Vaget, Hans Rudolf, 6, 85, 180
Verhey, Jeffrey, 66
Verlag, Insel, 41
Virchow, Christian, 16–17
Völkische Beobachter, 170
von Baden, Max, 99, 106, 109
von Faulhaber, Michael, 118
von Seisser, Hans, 171–72

Wagner, Richard, 47, 54, 180; *Tannhäuser*, 18; *Tristan and Isolde*, 53
Waldsanitorium, 8, 16, 18, 30
Walter, Bruno, 122, 169
Walter, Elsa, 118
Wassermann, Jakob, 186
Watroba, Karolina, 187
Weber, Hermann, 12
Weber, Max, 83; "Politics as a Vocation," 176
Wedekind, Frank, 89
Wedekind, Pamela, 182
Weigand, Hermann J., 7; *Thomas Mann's Novel "Der Zauberberg": A Study*, 50, 189
Weimar Republic, 5, 149, 151, 157–58, 159–60, 172, 191; beginning of, 110–12; Kapp Putsch, 135–37, 139
Weisser Hirsch sanatorium, 15
Wells, H. G., 111, 161, 181

INDEX

Wenningstedt, 141
Werner, Otto, 159
West, decline of, 69–70, 80, 126, 142
Whitman, Walt, 154, 155, 158, 159
Wilder, Billy, 189
Wilhelm II, 65, 109
Wilson, Woodrow, 106-7
Wirth, Chancellor, 152
Witkop, Phillip, 123
Wolff, Kurt, 89–90

Wood, James, 54–55
World War I. *See* First World War

X-ray examinations, 55, 135

Zagajewski, Adam, 8, 147
Zeit im Bild, 76–77
Zeitroman, 51
Zivilisation, 46, 80, 94
Zola, Émile, 5, 42, 89; *Earth, The*, 89
Zweig, Stefan, 64, 83, 152, 161, 169, 174; *World of Yesterday, The*, 68